Where EGOs Dare

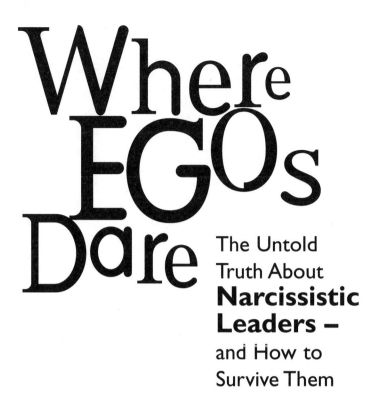

Where EGOs Dare

The Untold Truth About **Narcissistic Leaders –** and How to Survive Them

Dean B McFarlin & Paul D Sweeney

KOGAN
PAGE

First published in 2000
First published in paperback in 2002

Kogan Page Limited
120 Pentonville Road
London N1 9JN,
UK

Kogan Page US
22 Broad Street
Milford CT 06460
USA

© Dean B McFarlin and Paul D Sweeney, 2000

The right of Dean B McFarlin and Paul D Sweeney to be identified as the authors of this work has been asserted by them in accordance with the Copyright, Designs and Patents Act 1988.

British Library Cataloguing in Publication Data

A CIP record for this book is available from the British Library.
ISBN 0 7494 3773 1

Typeset by Saxon Graphics Ltd, Derby
Printed and bound in Great Britain by Creative Print & Design Group (Wales), Ebbw Vale

Contents

To Laurie, Andrew, Elizabeth and Nathaniel . . .
for all your inspiration and support.

Dean

To Victor, a natural leader, and to Yu Ping
and Jin Zhen, leaders to be.

Paul

Part 1

Introduction

Introduction

Leadership. The word conjures up images of dynamic action, inspiring visions and corporate success. Everybody these days idolizes good leaders. How else can we explain the thousands of books that promise to reveal the 'secrets' of leadership? Unfortunately, many employees feel their leaders do anything but lead. In fact, all too often they say that bosses spend their time pursuing their own selfish agendas, usually at someone else's expense. Despite these pervasive experiences, however, few books focus on this hidden underbelly of leadership.

Ours does. And we know that some might consider the subject matter 'too negative' and limited to 'a few crackpots' who have made headlines. We disagree. Our message is fundamentally optimistic. We provide the tools and tactics to fight back against the worst excesses of leaders – to turn negatives into positives. At the risk of using a cliché, this kind of knowledge can empower employees! Plus, the backbone of this book is academic research. Our advice is solidly grounded in the latest research findings. Yes, we do tell some horror stories about corporate leaders. These examples are anonymous and come from a variety of research sources, including our own narrative surveys distributed to hundreds of employees.

The result is a fascinating – and sometimes shocking – inside look at scores of leaders wreaking havoc up and down the corporate ladder across a variety of organizations. At its core, this book isn't about distant CEOs in the world's biggest firms, but about the kind of bosses that many of us are stuck with right now.

In fact, let's give credit where credit is due. Over the past 15 years, we've met thousands of employees in our roles as researchers, consultants and teachers. In a very real sense, this book was inspired by them. One of the common threads that tie together our interactions with employees is that most of us have experienced bad leadership at some point in our careers. That basic observation and our motivation to give something back are what gave birth to this book.

PROFILING NARCISSISTIC LEADERS

Of course, 'bad leadership' can take many different forms and have a variety of underlying causes. But we aren't interested in producing a catalogue of various types of bad bosses. That inevitably results in a superficial product full of catchy labels but little else of substance. Instead, we chose to focus on a particular type of leader who:

- has tremendous destructive power, both in terms of employee motivation and, ultimately, corporate performance;
- is surprisingly common throughout the ranks of many corporations;
- is extremely challenging for employees to cope with, much less defeat.

The narcissistic leader fits this profile. Naturally, there are plenty of lousy bosses who are not narcissistic. So why focus just on narcissists? We believe that narcissistic bosses possess a specific set of traits – as well as certain skills – that often make them far more dangerous than a run-of-the-mill bad boss. One of the things that we found especially fascinating when employees discussed bad leaders was how frequently they concluded that obsessive egotism and vanity fuelled the worst abuses of leadership. In fact, most employees we've talked to have had personal experience of a narcissistic leader whose warped self-absorption created problems for the employees or their colleagues.

Features to Look for

Now that we've given you a brief overview of the book, we want to draw your attention to two special sections that you'll find in each chapter. The sections entitled 'Me, myself and I' provide detailed and hard-hitting examples of narcissistic leaders that match the central theme of each chapter. To protect sensitive sources, all information that might identify people, places, or companies in these sections has been removed. Much of the material in these sections comes from our own research.

Finally, at the end of each chapter is a section entitled 'Chapter takeaways'. As the name suggests, the purpose of this section is to highlight the main points that we want you to take from each chapter. We think you'll find this feature especially useful for the action recommendations provided in Chapters 3–12.

Our Intended Audience

Before we begin our exploration of narcissistic leadership, we want to say a few things about our intended audience. Of course, authors always say that their books will have wide appeal. So we will too! But seriously, everyone who works for a living, be they managers or employees, can use this book. It will help those working for a narcissistic leader to re-establish a sense of control over their jobs. For those fortunate enough not to have worked for a narcissistic leader, this book is a cautionary tale. Hopefully, we can raise employees' sensitivities about narcissism and how to detect it if they do cross paths with a narcissistic leader. After all, forewarned is forearmed!

Human resource managers and organizational development professionals can also use this book to help shape corporate policies, training procedures and cultures in ways that limit, if not prevent, the risk posed by narcissistic leaders. Educators teaching courses in leadership, management and organizational behaviour will also find our book useful. Simply put, narcissism represents the seamy side of leadership. Putting a relentlessly positive spin on leaders won't change that reality, and does students a disservice when they hit the workforce. Excessive narcissism turns leaders into corporate vampires. Fighting back requires the organizational equivalent of a wooden stake. That's where this book comes in.

Chapter 1

Why we're concerned about narcissistic leaders

ME, MYSELF AND I

Ugly lessons: Challenging 'the fairest one of all'

Five minutes before my speech began, the marketing VP told me, 'Forget about your talk. Just say exactly what is on this list.' I started to protest since the list was basically a rundown of the VP's accomplishments and had nothing to do with what I planned to say. But with a snap of his fingers, the guy cut me off, saying, 'Do it – your fucking job can be made to disappear like that.' The funny thing was that I didn't even report to him.

Unit manager, manufacturing company

I typically meet with the company president and other senior managers several times a year to discuss various issues. The first time I was in one of these meetings, I told the president that some customers had said that we needed to provide better after-sale service. This man literally jumped out of his chair screaming, 'That's bullshit! You're trying to embarrass me! You're trying to embarrass me!' After that, I never said anything remotely critical in his presence.

Regional sales director, telecommunications firm

WELCOME TO THE CORPORATE REFLECTING POOL

These shocking incidents were reported by employees who participated in our research on narcissistic leadership. They capture the
essence of what it's like to work for a narcissistic leader. And we've seen
it over and over again. We can't tell you how many times employees
have said they've been mortified, humiliated, or outraged (sometimes
all at once!) by the actions of narcissistic leaders. Another common
reaction employees have is a kind of reeling, stunned surprise – like
being punched repeatedly by a prize-fighter.

Narcissistic leaders often strike in unexpected ways with a brutal and
overwhelming ferocity. They are users who play 'for keeps', especially
when their own often carefully crafted images of power and success are
threatened. This perspective effectively sanctions any behaviour –
lying, cheating, bullying, manipulating, credit-stealing, grandstanding,
throwing temper tantrums (if not objects!), and so on. Over time, such
behaviour saps employee morale, draining them of their will to fight
back. Needless to say, employee performance often suffers as a result.

And 'warped' is the operative word for the narcissistic perspective.
There's certainly nothing wrong with being ambitious, especially when it
is backed up with real talent. But narcissistic leaders possess a pathological egotism. They are completely consumed by a desire to be seen as
successful and will do whatever it takes to ensure that nothing tarnishes
their carefully crafted and polished images; plus, they have no concern
about who gets hurt in the process. If threats, temper tantrums or other
outrageous behaviours are necessary, so be it. This degree of self-
absorbed thinking combined with the ruthless pursuit of a selfish agenda
is usually the result of a deeply flawed self-concept. Narcissistic leaders
are fundamentally insecure individuals who crave adoration. They
compensate by projecting an inflated sense of self-worth and competence to those around them. Unchecked, narcissistic leaders can suck the
motivation out of subordinates and destroy the organizations that
they're supposed to serve. These individuals are the focus of this book.

In Chapter 2 we'll discuss the often delusional roots of narcissism in
more detail. For now, imagine being so self-absorbed that you care
about your own image to the exclusion of everything else. This
describes exactly the mythical figure of Narcissus – a boy who literally
fell in love with his own reflection in a pool. To the narcissistic leader,
the corporation is one big reflecting pool that only exists for gazing and

self-aggrandizement. But the Narcissus of myth
a vain effort to possess his own reflection.
employees faced with narcissistic leaders aren'
tear narcissistic leaders away from the reflectin
images usually provokes a furious attack.

That's why helping employees survive – i
sistic leaders is the main goal of this book. This ᴄʜᴀᴘ
few steps toward that objective by outlining the nature of the threat
posed by narcissistic leaders. You might be tempted to dismiss narcissistic leaders as rare and unusual creatures who, as a consequence,
aren't likely to be much of a personal threat. But a careful analysis of
existing studies, management trends and our own research suggests
otherwise:

- **Narcissistic leaders are far more prevalent than most of us would
  like to believe.** As you'll see throughout this book, the academic and
  business literatures are replete with examples of narcissistic leaders
  in corporations. In addition, most of the managerial and professional
  employees we've encountered have had contact with narcissistic
  leaders at some point in their careers.
- **Narcissistic leaders often last longer and go further than you'd
  expect.** Despite their many flaws and drawbacks, narcissistic leaders
  often have good political skills and insights – attributes that can
  prolong, if not enhance, their longevity in corporations. In many
  cases, the selfish nature of their agendas can go undetected for a
  remarkably long time by key players in the corporation. This is
  something we'll explore more in Chapter 2.
- **If anything, we tend to underestimate the havoc that narcissistic
  leaders wreak.** Their arrogance and apparent overconfidence can
  lead to incredibly bad personnel decisions (eg surrounding themselves with fawning incompetents) and business moves (eg dramatically overpaying to acquire companies that only they can 'save').
  What tends to get overlooked, however, is the portion of their
  negative legacy that is far more insidious (and also more difficult to
  reverse). This includes demotivated employees who are cynical,
  distrustful and risk-averse. In fact, if enough employees are affected,
  the culture of corporation can rot from within to the point where the
  firm's survival is threatened.

ST OF TIMES: WHY THE TABLE IS SET FOR NARCISSISTIC LEADERSHIP

t perhaps the most important reason why we need to be concerned about narcissistic leaders has to do with the context in which businesses – especially in the US – tend to operate. For example, while these are 'good times' in much of the business world (certainly in the United States and Europe), workloads have also risen considerably and many companies are running 'lean'. When combined with an already high level of cynicism and detachment, the long and the short of it is that employees are often in poor shape to offer much resistance to narcissistic bosses. In addition, the US business media often chase corporate leaders around like star-struck teenagers, embellishing their accomplishments and their fame. This kind of fawning attention is hard for narcissists to resist. We'll examine these and related issues next.

The Media and the Leadership Bandwagon

Few people would disagree with the idea that good leadership is important. But the 'l-word' is so hot these days that there's barely enough room left on the bandwagon. There's certainly no room left on the shelves! In the US, some 30,000 articles and books on leadership have been written in the last several decades.[1] The management sections of US bookstores are stocked with hundreds of leadership titles, many with a common theme – that the rise and fall of corporations depends on 'the leaders'. Other segments of the business media, especially in the United States, have also helped fuel this fire. Glossy business magazines tell gossipy tales of corporate leaders turning companies around as if the employees doing the real work didn't exist. Each new issue seems to bring longer profiles, with juicier personal titbits, and more staged action shots of the leaders 'leading'. For example, publications like *Business Week* are constantly putting out lists of 'top managers' and 'managers to watch', giving us plenty of new 'stars' to think about.[2] Published lists also tighten the perceived link between leaders and corporate success, as Table 1.1 illustrates. There you'll find 10 of the individuals named by *Business Week* in 1998 as 'top managers of the year'. As you can see, the snippets describing each manager's accomplishments invariably suggest that the leader is personally responsible for firm performance. If you're in any doubt about the slavish attention devoted to image and career-climbing in the US, take a look at the accompanying 'Me, Myself and I' box on personal public relations.

Table 1.1 The top 10: *Business Week*'s managers of the year

Manager	Position/Firm	Leader's 'Impact' on Company Performance
Charles M Cawley	President/MBNA	'pushed net income up 30%'
Michael Dell	CEO/Dell Computer	'continues to redefine the PC industry'
Donald V Fites	CEO/Caterpillar	'reaping the benefits of restructuring'
William W George	CEO/Medtronic	'has pumped Medtronic into higher gear'
Harvey Golub	CEO/American Express	'carried out a fierce counterattack on Visa'
James F Halpin	CEO/CompUSA	'engineered a masterful turnaround'
Jeanne P Jackson	President/Banana Republic	'has worked magic at long-struggling firm'
Lois D Juliber	President/Colgate-Palmolive	'C-P has been sparkling since she took over'
Nobuhiko Kawamoto	President/Honda	'has Honda barreling down the fast lane'
Ellen R Marram	President/Tropicana	'she boasts three years of profit hikes'

Adapted from: *Business Week*, 12 January 1998, The top 25 managers of the year, pp 54–68

ME, MYSELF AND I

Help with the hype: Promoting a narcissistic agenda

'Leadership is all hype.'
Peter Drucker[3]

And hype, as long as it's about themselves, is what narcissists arguably love most. Wannabe leaders are certainly scooping up books, training seminars and consultants in record numbers. We wonder what percentage of the estimated $25 billion annual tab for this stuff is being purchased by narcissists. What's fascinating is the extent to which the leadership development industry arguably plays to a narcissistic agenda.

For instance, executive coaches will teach CEOs how to present a vision in a way that will 'dazzle' audiences. Leadership books by or about CEOs are another popular – and cheaper – option that have a narcissistic tint to them. Many of these books have a 'how to' quality that's expressed through some kind of self-focused theme (eg 'I did things my way' or 'Good leaders like me can fix anything').

On a broader level, it has become downright fashionable to openly engage in self-promotion designed to advance your career. As one senior executive recruiter put it: 'People are too busy politicking and positioning these days. Whatever happened to making a difference? Show me what you've done that puts you in the top 10% of what you do and I can get you an interview'.[4]

Of course, self-promotion is nothing new. Nor is it all bad. There's nothing wrong with being recognized for your accomplishments. The problem occurs when the pursuit of self-promotion becomes obsessive and eclipses the real work. One wonders about this when managers talk about needing to develop and execute a 'personal public relations campaign' to get ahead. And there are plenty of expensive career development consultants around to give executives just that kind of help.

For instance, managers are often advised that personal PR is a critical part of their career plan. Some 'experts' argue that crafting a PR strategy starts with managers figuring out what they want most (say, promotion to president). Next, managers should develop messages that might advance their agendas, decide how they should be sent, and identify who needs to receive them. This kind of advice often produces a 'showbiz' mentality, especially among managers with narcissistic tendencies. In short, the process of self-promotion becomes the real work. But if personal public relations make you queasy and uncomfortable, take heart – it probably means that you're not a narcissist!

In essence, US executives have become the new centrefolds of our time. Another problem is that this centrefold mentality, while perhaps strongest in the US, is arguably becoming more common in boardrooms around the world. There is increasing evidence that an 'American' style of leadership is spreading, along with the narcissistic tendencies that it encourages.

Our Own Attitudes About Leadership

But the roles played by the media and the consulting industry raise another question. Are they driving this narcissistic phenomenon or merely reflecting – and perhaps exacerbating – underlying attitudes about leadership in the US? Clearly, people in the United States are well known for holding 'personal fulfilment', 'getting ahead' and 'being number one' in high esteem. These 'winner-take-all' values arguably encourage narcissism. Today, leaders in US companies are walking symbols of personal achievement and as such provide 'heroic' role models for everyone else, especially given the current level of US economic prowess. In fact, corporate leaders have been romanticized in the United States to the point where they easily give pop stars, sports figures and movie idols a run for their money. CEOs occupied 7 of the top 10 spots in a recent poll of 'most important' people in the United States (Bill Gates, CEO of Microsoft, was second on the list, just one step behind another Bill – William Jefferson Clinton).

In short, the media and consulting industry may simply mirror US assumptions about leadership. Many of us assume that corporate success is the direct result of effective leaders. And we have no problem identifying corporate leaders who we feel are outstanding. CEOs like Bill Gates (Microsoft), Herb Kelleher (Southwest Airlines), Michael Eisner (Disney) and John Welch (General Electric) undoubtedly come to mind for many of us. And it's those attitudes that, at least in part, have contributed to excesses in the areas of compensation and leader selection. In turn, those excesses undoubtedly reinforce and attract managers with narcissistic tendencies in the first place.

Golden Glory: Executive Compensation and Narcissism

Perhaps nowhere are US assumptions about leadership better reflected than in the compensation packages of US CEOs. It certainly seems as if money is a great way to 'keep score' in the power and image race. And compensation levels for US executives are climbing at dizzying rates. It's not uncommon for CEOs to rake in tens of millions of dollars – in good years and bad. That's often several hundred times what the average employee in the company takes home. Employees lucky enough to pull down a 4 per cent rise can look up at senior executives galloping along with double-digit pay increases and a stack of stock options.

In fact, the average CEO at a large, publicly traded company in the US took home almost $11 million in 1998. That figure represents a nearly 40 per cent increase over 1997 and a 440 per cent jump since 1990, when CEO pay averaged a paltry $2 million (the Dow Jones Industrial Average rose 260 per cent in the same period). By comparison, blue-collar and white-collar employees in the US had to settle for 1998 rises that averaged 3 per cent and 4 per cent respectively. But had US workers earning, say, $25,000 in 1994 seen their pay soar as fast as their corporate leaders', they would have pocketed almost $140,000 in 1999.

At the very top of the CEO pay pyramid, words like 'obscene' and 'grotesque' come to mind. In 1998, the 10 highest paid CEOs in the US all made more than $50 million. King of the hill was Disney CEO Michael Eisner, who pocketed over $575 million (that's right, over half a billion, which, if you're curious, works out to around $1.6 million daily). Regardless of what you might say about Eisner's decade-long reign at Disney, 1998 was hardly a great year – the firm's earnings sagged and its stock lagged behind the rest of the market. And that's exactly the point. Many studies suggest that all too often the link between pay and performance for CEOs gives new meaning to the word 'loose'. Even Berkshire Hathaway CEO Warren Buffet described option-laden executive pay packages as 'wildly capricious in their distribution of rewards, inefficient as motivators, and inordinately expensive for shareholders'.[5]

Clearly, stock options are part of this runaway compensation train. And a rising stock market lifts all boats, including those steered by lousy CEOs at mediocre firms. Of course, even when stock prices fall, many CEOs have enough clout to get their options repriced. That also speaks to why stock options have become such an issue. Boards of directors increasingly feel the need to hire 'superstar' CEOs – and swallow the narcissistic demands they often bring with them – rather than take chances on internal or lesser-known talent. As a consequence, self-fulfilling prophecies are set up such that only a handful of 'name' people are seen as having what it takes. And if you have a 'valuable' commodity, then you'll pay dearly to keep it as well as get it in the first place! The irony is that with baby boomers hitting their late 40s, the actual pool of managers experienced enough to contend for top executive positions has never been bigger.[6]

Think again if you believe that this compensation orgy only fuels narcissistic dreams in US companies. There's plenty of evidence that the internationalization of business has put pressure on foreign firms, especially those in Europe, to pay by US rules. For instance, European companies often have to part with millions to hold onto US employees when they acquire US firms. France's Alcatel recently plunked down

$350 million to buy California-based Assured Access Technology – $60 million of which was aimed at keeping a few 'key employees' from leaving what was perceived to be a 'low-paying foreign employer'. Similarly, Deutsche Bank coughed up $187 million to keep the five top managers at Bankers Trust after it bought the company.

In some cases, US pay levels have become the standard European firms use to hire international management talent of any kind. Case in point: the $143 million British drug giant SmithKline Beecham paid to snag as its new CEO Jan Leschly, a Dane who spent years in the US. British firms hiring US executives may offer base pay levels 30 per cent higher than in the UK and incentive bonuses 100 per cent higher. One consequence of these trends is higher salary demands at home. When Daimler-Benz bought Chrysler in 1998, CEO Jurgen Schrempp significantly raised compensation levels for German executives. Schrempp had little choice after learning that Chrysler CEO Robert Eaton earned more than the entire German management team put together and that it would cost Daimler almost $400 million to pay off the stock options owned by Chrysler's 30 most senior executives. All of this suggests that US-style compensation packages will increasingly show up in other countries, despite their often more restrictive laws and heavier income tax burdens.[7]

Looking for that 'Certain Something'

Companies also help fuel narcissistic impulses by communicating that managers are a 'special breed' who have to be identified and nurtured. Leadership development programmes aimed at identifying 'key' traits have become increasingly popular in the past several years. AT&T and British Airways are just a few of the firms that have spent considerable sums to develop 'profiles' of the 'ideal' corporate leader. Germany's Siemens at one point had developed a system to assess potential executive talent against nearly two dozen desired traits and skills in six general areas (including intuition – what Siemens refered to as 'a sixth sense').

But many leadership development efforts have a dubious track record. They often lack validity and fail to recognize that the recipe for effective leadership can vary dramatically across situations. For instance, in 1988 Asea Brown Boveri (ABB) relied on an in-house screening programme to select some 300 senior executives. But by 1994 nearly 50 per cent had left the firm. During that six-year period, former CEO Percy Barnevik changed ABB's culture in response to new international challenges. As a result, ABB executives needed a different set of skills to be effective).[8]

Stepping Back from the Mirror: Leadership in Reality

Of course, there is a relationship between effective leadership and firm performance. But that relationship is more complex, less direct and smaller than you'd expect.[9] Individual and firm performance is an interactive function of many factors, including:

- the needs, skills, and attributes of leaders and subordinates;
- the firm's external environment (eg competitive pressures);
- the firm's internal environment (eg corporate culture, how work is organized, firm strategies and formal policies).

In a nutshell, effective leadership really starts with an accurate diagnosis of these factors. The leader then must design and execute an interpersonal influence process that matches the demands of the context. By 'influence' we refer to the behaviours that a leader uses in an effort to get other people to do what he or she wants them to do.[10] Figure 1.1 summarizes this view of leadership in graphic form.

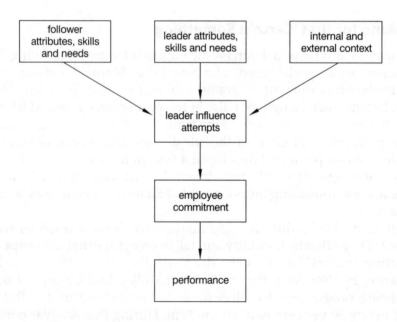

Figure 1.1 Designing effective leadership

In any event, one consequence of this perspective is that 'what works' can vary considerably. Just look at the incredible variation in personal styles among 'successful' CEOs. For instance, CEOs like Edward Crutchfield (First Union Corp.) or Herb Kelleher (Southwest Airlines) are known for their folksy charm. At the other end of the spectrum is General Electric CEO John Welch, someone well known for his decisive style.[11]

Of course, as you'll see, narcissistic leaders are unable to match their behavioural styles to fit the real needs of a particular context. They tend to be inflexible because they can't step back from their own need for adoration. And, as we've suggested, narcissists are attracted to management roles because of the control, power, money and glory they appear to offer. Once a narcissist is ensconced in a management job, the consequences can be severe. When leaders are interested chiefly in self-aggrandizement, subordinates are unlikely to be motivated to perform at their best over the long haul. And, unfortunately, even in lower levels of management, narcissistic bosses can create cynical and demotivated employees.

OUR PLAN OF ATTACK

So where do we go from here? At this point, a variety of questions have probably popped into your head. Who exactly are these narcissistic bosses? What specific characteristics do they have? How can they 'get away with it' for so long? How can they be flushed out? We will address all of these questions in this book. Ultimately, our main goal is to give employees – and organizations – a repertoire of options for responding. But first things first. Effectively dealing with narcissistic leaders has to begin with a basic understanding of the threat and an ability to recognize narcissistic characteristics. That's our starting point.

Know Your Enemy: Understanding the Narcissistic Leader

Dealing with narcissistic leaders also requires a deep understanding of what kind of people they are, what drives them and what managerial clues will help in the identification process. That's the goal of Chapter 2. We use the term 'enemy' deliberately here. One theme we'll be hammering at over and over again in Chapter 2 and throughout this book is that people often underestimate the single-minded ruthlessness of the narcissistic leader. So if you choose to oppose a narcissistic leader, viewing that person as an enemy is really the only appropriate perspective. It is how you will be viewed by the narcissist.

Chapter 2 will tackle these issues directly by creating a personal profile of the narcissistic leader. Fortunately, there's plenty of good research that can be drawn on to build this profile and we rely on it extensively. We'll sketch out the personality characteristics that narcissistic leaders possess and how they developed. But we'll spend most of our effort in Chapter 2 focusing on the behavioural implications of these personality traits. As it turns out, putting narcissistic personalities in corporate leadership positions results in a pathological management style. This style has six basic behavioural attributes that Chapter 2 will describe in detail.

Chapter 2 will also explain that what makes narcissistic leaders especially dangerous is that their true nature is often surprisingly difficult to detect. In part, this is a result of their conflicting personae and not-to-be-underestimated skills. For instance, narcissistic leaders often dream about being the objects of everyone's admiration, yet feel entitled to manipulate people to secure it. And from a skills perspective, they are often quite good at pulling it off. Likewise, some narcissistic leaders can project a participative image to their superiors while at the same time treating their subordinates with a contempt usually reserved for prison inmates. Especially troubling are the narcissistic leaders who are charismatic enough to mesmerize and inspire subordinates, but whose 'vision' is driven by nothing more than self-absorbed fantasies and perceived infallibility.

Combating Narcissistic Leaders: Guidelines for Employees

Chapters 3–8 focus on how to respond to the narcissistic leader. Each of the chapters in this group takes one of the six behavioural tendencies associated with narcissistic leadership and suggests specific ways to respond. These suggestions are an amalgamation from various sources, including published research and our own consulting experiences, as well as the cumulative wisdom of employees who completed our narrative surveys on narcissistic leadership. Taken together, Chapters 3–8 offer a very applied, hands-on set of guidelines that employees can use to combat each of the major behavioural tendencies that they are likely to encounter with narcissistic leaders.

As you'll see, employees have a variety of options to choose from in most cases, including coping and avoidance strategies, indirect opposing behaviours, and direct confrontation. For example, we discuss various coping strategies designed to lower the employee's profile on the narcissistic leader's 'radar screen'. These strategies include a variety of avoidance behaviours and a heightened awareness of the 'triggers' that can provoke some of the worst that narcissistic bosses have to offer. We also discuss ways to more directly counterattack narcissistic bosses. These involve strategies for protecting employees against credit-stealing and limelight-hogging as well as riskier options like forming coalitions against the narcissist, bypassing the chain of command and exposing the narcissist's self-focused agenda.

We also spell out the risks associated with each type of strategy and the circumstances under which they are most likely to pay off. In fact, to make an intelligent strategic choice, employees must be able to:

- recognize narcissistic behaviour when they see it;
- understand the various options for responding to narcissistic leadership;
- assess the situational and personal factors that might make certain options more or less effective.

An Ounce of Prevention: Reining in the Threat of Narcissism

Of course, the best strategy for dealing with narcissists is to stop them from gaining a foothold in the first place. To do this, organizations need to recognize how they aid and abet narcissism. Chapters 9 and 10 explain how corporations encourage narcissism and what adjustments might help reduce the emergence of narcissistic leaders. In particular, Chapter 9 shows how organizational change efforts and the management fads that often go with them can make it easier for narcissistic leaders to get a foothold in corporations and pursue their visions of grandeur. For instance, narcissistic bosses can cleverly use the latest management buzzwords and hottest consulting firms to convince subordinates that the hostile and abusive environment they create is 'necessary' to 'fulfil the vision'.

Chapter 10 follows up on this theme by explaining how certain corporate cultures act as fertile incubators for narcissistic leaders. Some companies draw narcissists because of a 'win at all costs' atmosphere in which 'winning' is mainly defined in terms of how much power and money individual managers can accumulate. Plus, many corporations have made it easier for narcissists by killing off any semblance of loyalty to employees. Today, corporations often feel that they must embrace ruthless efficiency or risk being swept aside in a hyper-competitive marketplace. These new corporate values are easily exploited by narcissistic leaders. They can experiment and tinker in order to advance their personal agendas – all in the name of 'corporate transformation'. The rapidity of real changes and the volatility of the business environment also provide cover for narcissistic bosses, be they at the top of the management hierarchy or lower in the ranks. In senior management positions, narcissists can pass off their excesses and self-focused agenda as simply being what's needed to confront 'the competition'. Narcissists in middle management ranks can also have a field day. As companies struggle to change, adapt and 'reinvent' themselves, it's easy to miss the shenanigans being perpetrated by narcissists in middle management ranks.

Finally, Chapter 11 describes how managers can re-energize demotivated subordinates once a narcissistic leader is out of the picture or even with one still in place. Most organizations have plenty of good and decent managers down through the ranks. These people must step forward and reverse the downward spiral of crippling cynicism and fear that is the most frequent legacy of narcissistic leaders.

Clearly, this type of reversal won't be easy. But there are answers and we provide them in Chapter 11. For instance, a manager may have to demonstrate a willingness to counterattack the residue of narcissism that might have seeped into the corporate culture – something that employees often feel helpless to do themselves. If a narcissistic leader is still on the scene, managers might follow a more reactive strategy in which they try to act as a buffer and isolate employees from the excesses of narcissistic leadership. This could involve building alliances within the organization aimed at making the manager and his or her subordinates a more difficult target for the narcissistic boss.

Cain and Abel: Distinguishing Between Healthy and Unhealthy Levels of Narcissism

In Chapter 12, we come full circle by pointing out that narcissism isn't always a bad thing. In fact, some of the best leaders we've ever come across arguably have some narcissistic tendencies. Moderate levels of narcissism can actually be quite positive – for both the leader and the corporation – if channelled properly. One of the goals of this chapter is to provide examples of leaders who are 'positive narcissists'. These are leaders who enjoy the limelight and 'performing' for subordinates. But while they excel at showmanship, they also have a purpose in mind that speaks to some larger good. Herb Kelleher, the effusive and charismatic showman who runs Southwest Airlines, is one such example. Richard Branson, the renowned 'adventure capitalist' who leads the Virgin Group is arguably another.

Overall, narcissism is best viewed as a characteristic that can vary in severity and intensity. A racing car is a good metaphor for what we mean here. Speed wins races, but only to a point. Above a certain speed threshold, drivers invariably lose control. Likewise, a certain level of narcissism can prove to be an asset for managers as well as for the corporations they lead. But once the line is crossed – as blurry as it sometimes is – narcissism becomes a force that drains the life out of subordinates and the corporations that they work for.

CHAPTER TAKE-AWAYS

▪ Narcissistic leaders are pathologically obsessed with their own images. They crave fame, glory and adoration. Unchecked, they can suck the motivation out of subordinates and destroy the organizations that they're supposed to serve. They can be brutal users who resort to any tactics (eg bullying and lying) to get what they want.

▪ Narcissistic leaders: a) are far more prevalent than most of us would like to believe; b) last longer and go further than you'd expect; and c) tend to be underestimated in terms of the damage that they cause.

▪ A variety of factors contribute to the current unhealthy level of narcissism in business leaders: a) the embrace of US 'winner take all' values; b) the attitude that only leaders matter when it comes to saving companies; c) the current success of the US economy; d) the promotion of executives as objects of fame, gossip and celebrity by the business media; and e) the often obscene level of pay and perquisites showered on corporate leaders.

▪ The actual relationship between effective leadership and firm performance is complex and often smaller than you'd expect. Effective leadership starts with an accurate diagnosis of the context. Leaders must match their behavioural strategies to the needs of the context in which they lead. Narcissistic leaders tend to be inflexible because they can't step back from their own need for adoration.

Part 2

Surviving the narcissistic leader

Chapter 2

Identifying the narcissistic leader

ME, MYSELF AND I

Cracked with the mirror

I was a department head at my last place and probably would have stayed there had I not crossed paths with Larry. He blew in from the outside and was made director of the facility I was in. I reported to him and let me tell you, it was sheer hell. The only thing Larry gave a damn about was making himself look good. That meant everybody else had to look bad. After a couple of months, this guy was overturning or second-guessing all my decisions.

Early on, I'd always consult with Larry in advance on big decisions. I hated meeting with him. . . he always acted like he was above it all, preening and pompous. The guy never did his homework on anything – details only got in the way. He'd lean back in his big leather chair and ask me a lot of vague, stupid questions. All Larry really wanted was for me to ask him what in the hell he was talking about. That would give him an opening so he could lecture me about how brilliantly he handled this, that, or the other thing in his previous job. But in the beginning at least, he'd end up going along with my recommendations. Several times I walked out thinking we were in agreement on the way to go.

I'd make plans, tell people what we were going to do, and so on. Then at the last minute, Larry would pull the rug out from under me, announcing his intent to go in a completely different direction. Another favourite scam was to let me implement my decisions, but invent some way to hammer me on execution. One time he approved my cost estimates for a new project. I actually came in way under budget. Later I heard he met with the financial people to bitch about my 'outrageous' and 'out of control' expenditures! Even on small issues, there was interference. Once I shuffled responsibilities for a couple of my subordinates. Somehow Larry found out and ordered me to reverse the changes. No explanation.

All of this stuff pissed me off big time. The choice was to do nothing and look like a complete fool or stand up and call my boss a goddam snake to anyone who would listen. Telling Larry about my concerns with his style only made matters worse. The one time I tried it, his only response was to growl, 'Start looking for another fucking job. I'm not gonna let you bring me down!' I just couldn't believe he said that to me.

When I did some digging I found out that Larry was 'a climber' who jumped from company to company. He'd blow smoke and charm the idiots who hired him — while making sure to stomp on any subordinates who might get in his way. Anybody with competence was in trouble, especially if they challenged him or were achieving something on their own.

I avoided Larry as much as I could, but the harassment and micro-managing crap continued. At one point, he heard about some suggestions I gave to another manager for improving customer service. I caught hell for that. To Larry, making a few lousy suggestions was a direct personal attack. He sent me this blistering memo saying I was 'insubordinate' and deliberately trying to embarrass him.

This kind of bullshit wore me down. It was a sick situation. Every day I went to work with a big knot in my stomach. I quit as soon as I found another decent job. Later I heard that Larry was running around telling people that I was his first 'tough call' where he had to 'kick ass and fire someone!' That was classic. . . a perfect example of how he would twist things around to his advantage. It was actually a double win for him. He was able to drive me out and make himself look good at the same time.

Department manager, research firm

Glory is fleeting, but obscurity lasts forever.

Napoleon Bonaparte

BEGINNING THE IDENTIFICATION PROCESS

We've opened this chapter with an example that captures many elements of narcissistic leadership. Like Napoleon, what drove Larry as a narcissistic leader was the pursuit of a grand vision for personal success and glory. But you also get a hint of the paranoia and insecurity that lie behind the positive images that the narcissistic leader projects. That insecurity is often what drives the kind of brutal and mean-spirited tactics that would have made Machiavelli proud. The result is predictable. Employees who find themselves in the line of sight between narcissists and their house of mirrors pay the price. Ultimately, their companies do too.

There are ways to combat narcissistic leadership. But it isn't easy. And recognizing what you're really dealing with is the first step. In this chapter we'll explore the six major behavioural characteristics commonly associated with narcissistic leadership in corporate settings. Taken together, these behaviours provide a consistent and reliable way to identify narcissistic leadership. Later chapters will tackle each behaviour in turn, with the goal of providing specific ways to cope and fight back.

But we don't want to gloss over the fact that these behaviours are merely symptoms of more fundamental issues. The roots of narcissism run deep into the personality of the leader. An understanding of that psychology should improve your ability to spot narcissistic leaders. It will also underscore how dangerous it is to underestimate them. We'll briefly examine the narcissistic personality next.

INSIDE THE HOUSE OF MIRRORS: THE NARCISSISTIC PERSONALITY

Most scholars view narcissistic behaviours as manifestations of a personality characterized by anxieties about self-worth. A major goal of the narcissistic personality is to suppress those anxieties and craft an edifice on which self-worth can be hung. Experts believe that the narcissistic personality often evolves out of childhood difficulties. The exact developmental sequences are subject to debate, but there appear to be several pathways that lead to narcissism. One common denominator seems to be negative comparisons or conflict-ridden relations with parents that were experienced early in life. These result in serious insecurities which in turn produce dysfunctional coping mechanisms – attitudes and behaviours that, at the extreme, provide the basis for what clinicians refer to as the narcissistic personality disorder.[1]

We certainly don't want to get bogged down in an extended psychological discussion about the causes of narcissism. But it may be useful to describe one specific developmental pathway to underscore how central narcissism can become to a person's sense of self. It's that obsessive focus that drives the worst excesses of narcissistic leaders.

For instance, parents who are affectionate when children perform up to an idealized image (eg charming or brilliant), but who are hostile when they fail to perform well may be sowing the seeds of narcissism. As the children mature, they begin to realize that their parents' love was conditional. The result is anger, hostility and self-doubt. Grandiose fantasies for power, glory, success and adoration often develop to protect the self from the depression that would come from facing that self-doubt and insecurity head on.[2]

What this leads to in adulthood is a desire to put on attractive performances in pursuit of a glorious vision, with the audience being parents or some other authority figure (superiors, mentors, etc). At the same time, there's a strong need to dominate peers and more junior individuals. That provides an outlet for the pent-up hostility, rage and anger against parents that cannot be expressed directly. When successful, dominance also produces self-esteem and reinforces the narcissist's pursuit of personal fantasies. In other words, dominance creates a process that feeds delusional self-images – especially when exploitation, manipulation and authoritarian bullying are needed to ensure a dominant position in the first place. Put simply, the feelings of vanity, superiority, exhibitionism and entitlement that go with narcissists' delusions of grandeur become more 'real' – and more dangerous to the people around them.[3]

We've summarized these basic points about the path to narcissism in Figure 2.1.

BELLING THE CAT: THE BEHAVIOURAL PROFILE OF NARCISSISTIC LEADERS

We turn our attention in the remainder of this chapter to narcissistic behaviour. Of course, narcissistic behaviour – like insufferable bragging

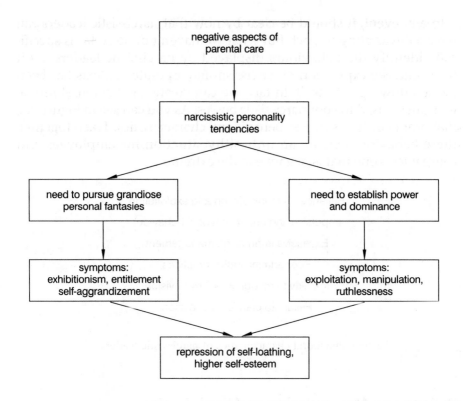

Figure 2.1 The narcissistic pathway: Following the mirrored road

or treating people with contempt – can occur in just about any part of everyday life.[4]

But narcissism also drives many people to seek out leadership positions in the first place, for reasons we've suggested. That's likely to be especially true today since, as we argued in Chapter 1, these are 'fat times' for corporate leaders. The ranks of corporate management undoubtedly consist of a higher percentage of narcissists than we'd find in the broader population. Of course, pinning down the exact percentage of managers who are narcissists is impossible. But some tantalizing hints exist. One study found that about 15 per cent of managers who participate in 360-degree feedback programmes turned out to be 'legends in their own minds' according to their subordinates. We doubt whether narcissistic leaders with any real power would allow themselves to be evaluated by their subordinates to begin with![5]

In any event, it should be clear by now that narcissistic leaders can have a devastating impact. But what we haven't done so far is specifically identify the behaviours displayed by narcissistic leaders. As it turns out, the expression of narcissism in corporate contexts has been pinned down pretty well. In fact, we can create a behavioural profile that can be used to spot narcissistic bosses. As you can see in Figure 2.2, that profile includes six key behavioural characteristics. Taken together, these behaviours create an unhealthy situation for employees and companies – one that is negative in the extreme.

Reliance on manipulation and exploitation

Impulsive and unconventional behaviour

Excessive impression management

Poor administrative practices

Inability to recognize a flawed vision

Failure to plan for succession

Figure 2.2 The six behavioural characteristics of narcissistic leaders

Reliance on Manipulation and Exploitation

Narcissistic bosses crave attention and admiration, but have no genuine concern for people or relationships. The needs and feelings of others are just not on the radar screen. Hurting or using others is fine when it services their agenda for glory or helps settle grudges (which are often long-standing and petty). This can also involve the abuse of company policies or resources to strike back at 'enemies'. In short, narcissists tend to be highly Machiavellian. They often feel perfectly entitled to use manipulation and exploitation. Lying, misleading, 'divide and conquer' strategies, domination ploys and bullying are all part of their repertoire when necessary.

Of course, these behaviours can be packaged and implemented in a variety of ways. Sometimes the exploitation is blunt and straightforward, like getting hit with a rock. For instance, one division president would routinely return staff proposals and suggestions with the words 'STUPID IDEA' stamped in bold letters on the front cover. That both reinforced his sense of power and gave him a way to shoot down threatening ideas.[6]

In other cases, however, a more sophisticated strategy might be involved. For example, one nursing director continuously and unpredictably reassigned subordinates and rewrote their job descriptions – all part of an effort to market herself as an 'empowering leader' and successful 'change agent' to the senior executives in her health care organization. Privately she would lambaste the performance of her nursing staff when they inevitably failed to keep up with her constant 'shake the box' strategy. This combination of job manipulation and verbal abuse kept the nursing staff weak, demoralized and off balance. Staff turnover was high and outsiders viewed her as a power-hungry climber.[7]

Of course, manipulation and exploitation are intensely resented by subordinates. Not surprisingly, work that depends heavily on subordinate initiative or effective team functioning suffers enormously. Staff turnover is likely to be extraordinarily high, especially if subordinates have decent options. Over time, suspiciousness about the leader's true motives will slowly leak out, fuelling more rumours and innuendo, all of which distracts and undercuts the organization. If left unchecked, the narcissist's manipulative tendencies can eventually demoralize large segments of a workforce and even jeopardize a firm's ability to compete.[8]

ME, MYSELF AND I

Manipulation 101

At first, the new plant manager was a breath of fresh air. . . he sat down with people and talked to them about their concerns and he gained a lot of people's trust and enthusiasm. This went on for eight or nine months. And then it was like somebody turned a switch. We soon found that when he was interviewing everyone, he was actually getting the scoop on everyone. Anybody who'd spoken out about not agreeing with how something was run, he tucked it away. And then he began the systematic elimination of all the people he didn't want. He was actually fairly open about what he was doing – it was a paring of individuals he didn't like. He laughed at the fact that people had swallowed what he had told them, saying things like, 'I can't believe people are so naïve as to have bought that line.' I don't think I'll ever forget the devastation that followed in terms of using people's trust and then betraying it. It was horrible.

Manufacturing employee[9]

Impulsive and Unconventional Behaviour

Narcissistic bosses will throw 'tantrums' where they scream, swear, berate, or threaten subordinates. Usually these behaviours occur when the narcissist is unexpectedly challenged by events or subordinates. We use the word 'challenged' loosely here since even the most trivial of slights can set off narcissistic bosses. Since all that matters is their image, their power and their personal success, anything that is perceived to get in the way will be attacked viciously and without quarter. Until they experience it directly, many subordinates underestimate narcissistic bosses' capacity to be irrational, brutal and ruthless.

That's because most of us don't understand the narcissistic mind-set. Just beneath the surface of the narcissistic leader's smiling public face is a constant fear of humiliation. That fear is accompanied by embitterment and suppressed rage, often due to slights that go back to childhood, as we've discussed. Any perceived insult can act to trigger a paroxysm of rage. This exaggerated response typically has a self-righteous quality to it in which the target person, usually a subordinate, is tagged as a bumbling incompetent or inferior. A fierce and often sadistic attack serves to shift blame on to subordinates while at the same time serving as an exhibition-istic forum for the narcissist's grand schemes (ie 'What I'm doing is incredibly important. And you're screwing it up!'). The especially disturbing thing about this is that the narcissist typically feels exhilaration when 'raging'. The tirade serves a dual purpose: it releases pent-up emotions and reinforces feelings of dominance .[10]

ME, MYSELF AND I

Your job description: Fetching pizza and cleaning dog butt

One day when I was leaving to meet my mother for lunch, my boss asked me to get him a slice of pizza. I offered to get him a slice from where I was going, but he said he'd rather have it from this place all the way across town. So I told him that I was sorry, but that wasn't where I was going. And I figured that was that. But when I got back to work, the guy started screaming at me for not getting him his lunch – he said I had to consider who signed my pay cheque and that my job was to do whatever he told me to do. I just remember him screaming, 'If I tell you to wipe my dog's butt, that's what you'll do! This went on for over half an hour, and by the end of it, I was crying. The next day in the hallway, he walked up to me, sniffled and said, 'Need a tissue?' I left the company not long after that.

Project manager[11]

Excessive Impression Management

One of the reasons that narcissists often do surprisingly well is that they can be good actors with certain audiences. Many of their most destructive and negative behaviours are aimed at subordinates and are carefully hidden from everyone else. And it would be wise not to underestimate the extent to which impression management tactics can successfully insulate managers from being held accountable for their abuses. Plus, we also tend to underestimate the frequency with which impression management motives may be driving even the most innocuous of behaviours. Even apparently selfless acts may actually reflect selfish motives (eg helping managers in other departments solely to generate 'positive press' that will make it harder for people to believe that you mistreat your subordinates).[12]

Of course, impression management is a huge issue for narcissistic leaders who, by definition, are preoccupied with crafting their images. Common strategies would include:

- exaggerating accomplishments and responsibilities;
- credit-stealing or failing to note the contributions of others;
- speaking to fulfil the stereotypes, values and beliefs of the immediate audience ('tell them what they want to hear');
- stressing the 'unique' aspects of whatever it is they're supposedly doing;
- presenting selfish goals in a more appealing package (eg as an attractive and inspiring vision);
- withholding negative information and overemphasizing the positive (including the use of language to skirt negative issues carefully or preclude worrisome questions – like telling a few positive stories to distract attention away from harder, less favourable data).

Obviously, not everyone who uses these tactics is a narcissistic leader. The problem occurs when impression management becomes a way of life. Another danger is that impression management efforts work all too well – on the narcissistic leader. Over time, the leader's fantasies and glorious self-descriptions are reinforced, especially if audience feedback is positive. In short, narcissistic leaders actually start to believe their own lies.

Narcissistic leaders often seem most concerned with how they are viewed by superiors, peers and outsider groups. But narcissists are also keen to manage subordinate impressions, as long as it doesn't overshadow their own self-aggrandizing agenda. In other words, subordinates are convenient scapegoats and idea generators for the narcissist's publicity machine. When push comes to shove, narcissists will not accept responsibility for failure, but will blame subordinates. Likewise, they tend to be shameless self-promoters whose credit-stealing behaviour and self-important airs typically cause alienation among subordinates.[13]

ME, MYSELF AND I
The walking infomercial

My boss is a walking infomercial for herself. You can't have a conversation with the woman – anytime, anywhere – without her bringing up how hard she works, her financial well-being, her latest media interview and her close relations with the company president. She also makes us do practice sessions for her upcoming executive meetings. We role-play other senior managers so she can put on a better performance. Of course we all have better things to do with our time. It's a complete waste.

HR manager, consumer products company

Poor Administrative Practices

Narcissistic leaders make lousy managers – on both an operational and strategic basis. Their decision-making is dysfunctional because they rarely analyse things in depth. No real effort is made to examine how well company resources or liabilities match up against competitive opportunities and threats. The self-delusional arrogance of the narcissist is that there's really no need to study something that you already 'control'. It's as if the world is too insignificant to mount a serious threat against the leader's brilliance – therefore it can be ignored.

When projects are undertaken, they tend to be overblown, poorly planned and, in many cases, doomed to fail – often because enormous resources are committed without adequate preparation. In many cases, narcissistic leaders think that they can successfully juggle a dozen 'initiatives' at once. The search for success from 'big' projects, ideas and products, which will increase their fame, is what's important. From an operational standpoint, this means that the leader is often 'parachuting' into and out of projects of interest, dropping in momentarily to issue edicts, change directions, or control the agenda, often without the necessary knowledge or skills.

As a consequence, narcissists are rarely interested in the details of executing anything and tend to delegate responsibility for doing the 'real work' to others. Put another way, as soon as a project or idea reaches the implementation phase, there's a strong desire to move on to the next highly visible activity, leaving subordinates behind to sweat over the details.

Of course, this extreme delegation only lasts if things are going well. When problems occur (ie, their images are threatened or pet projects start coming unravelled), narcissists swing to the other extreme and become intolerable micro-managers, often second-guessing subordinates and overturning their decisions based on 'intuition' or 'gut feel'. This vacillation between loose delegation and micro-management is not a winning combination.

ME, MYSELF AND I

How narcissists run a meeting

The medical director I used to work for had a great routine when he ran staff meetings. He'd almost always avoid expressing a clear opinion about potential ideas, policies, or decisions that were being discussed. Later, if the idea or policy failed, he'd tell his staff, 'Didn't you all notice that I never said anything to encourage this? Are you all that blind and stupid? I knew this would fail from the start! Why didn't you?' Of course, when some policy or decision worked, he'd later tell us that 'silence is golden' and that it meant he 'agreed with the idea from the beginning' and that after some 'fine-tuning' was able to 'sell it up the line'. This alternating between defensiveness and credit-stealing drove us nuts.

Department head, medical college

Inability to Recognize a Flawed Vision

Narcissistic bosses project an exaggerated and misplaced level of self-confidence in their skills and abilities. They have incredibly poor self-insight and cannot accept the possibility that the 'vision' they paint for subordinates is either impossible to achieve or fundamentally flawed. In other words, they believe that they are infallible and invulnerable. There's no need to listen to anyone when only you can make informed judgements.

This is especially destructive because the 'vision' is really a cloak for a personal agenda. The vision is not the product of careful competitive analysis or strategic planning in the firm's best interest, but a reflection of the idealized role that narcissists wish to play in their own fantasy world. Narcissists' self-absorption and illusion of invulnerability simply render them incapable of accepting advice. They can brook no dissent and see only what they want to see.

As a result, when things start to unravel, there is no process or forum in which to provide criticism, much less develop contingency plans. And since they tend to surround themselves with only weak and subservient subordinates – something we'll tackle next – there may literally be no one willing to present the bad news. But if the narcissistic leader is confronted with evidence that the empire is collapsing, he or she will: a) deny the problems exist; b) 'shoot the messenger' ('you're an enemy, a naysayer'); and/or c) become extraordinarily defensive and deny any responsibility.

This sorry scenario is connected to some of the behavioural tendencies we've already mentioned. Especially important are the excessive impression management tendencies and poor decision-making practices of the narcissistic leader. Since the vision is really a reflection of the narcissist's personal needs, there's a tendency to miscalculate both market opportunities and the resources required to pursue them. Plus, the personal nature of the leader's vision makes it extremely unlikely that important changes in the competitive environment will be detected – changes that would require redirecting or scrapping the vision.[14]

ME, MYSELF AND I

Blindly losing business

My boss insisted on going along on visits to major clients, especially when there was money on the table and he could play the hero by sealing the deal. This guy was so arrogant, self-absorbed and demanding that on more than one occasion, clients told us not to come back. One client even took me aside and in no uncertain terms told me that if we wanted to do business we should 'never bring that bastard here again!' The worst thing was that he was clueless about how he came across and was convinced that he had what it took to reach the top of the company. The rest of us were just fools who got in the way. We lost a lot of business because of him.

Sales manager, equipment distribution firm

Failure to Plan for Succession

There's a natural tendency for subordinates to want to impress and please their leaders. After all, that's how you nail down those superb performance evaluations and get ahead yourself, isn't it? But seriously, 'pleasing the boss' will have an intensely personal ring to it if you work for a narcissist. We've said that narcissistic bosses want the limelight. They also want to keep it for themselves. As long as subordinates help keep the narcissistic leader on top – without becoming threatening – they may survive. Usually, this requires plenty of fawning praise and acquiescence from the subordinate, not to mention the ability to take abuse. As nauseating as this may sound, a surprisingly high number of people buy in. Just as narcissists are drawn to leadership positions, some people are attracted to the role of sycophant or 'enabler'. For instance, subordinates who are highly dependent may be enamoured with someone who will do their thinking for them and who appears to be everything they are not (eg confident, skilled, decisive, etc). Abusive behaviours can be rationalized as the price to be paid when working for 'brilliance'.

But what happens when the narcissistic leader has competent and independent-minded people to deal with? That's the real long-term threat – a competent subordinate who could develop into a rival for fame and power. As a result, narcissists make no real effort to develop subordinates or groom successors. In fact, what they really want is to keep those closest to them subservient and weak. The ideal lieutenant is someone who: a) is an adoring lap-dog who will do what he or she is told; and b) has skills that are seen to be clearly inferior to the narcissist's. More competent subordinates, especially those who ask questions or have ideas, are either ignored or driven off. Once again, this is dysfunctional for both subordinate development and the corporation as a whole.[15]

ME, MYSELF AND I

The one-two punch: Hire the worst, steal from the best

Our engineering manager considered all subordinates as potential rivals so he surrounded himself with incompetent boot-lickers when he had the chance to hire someone new. He also made the rest of us put his name on all patent applications and reviewed all our presentation materials so we gave him the 'proper credit'. He never did anything to encourage or develop any of us. Our only value was to make him look like a star to his boss. I think deep down he knew he wasn't any good and grooming someone to replace him risked exposing that. On days when his boss was in, he'd come to work extra early so he could park his car directly outside his boss' window. I got out of his department as fast as I could.

Engineer, environmental services firm

Pulling things together

Our goal in this chapter was to help you identify narcissistic leadership. We've explored the narcissistic personality and described key behavioural 'symptoms'. In fact, we've laid out a 'narcissistic profile' that consists of six behavioural characteristics. Over the next several chapters, we'll explore how subordinates and organizations can cope with, if not defeat, narcissistic leaders. But we also want to sound a note of caution. Narcissism is not an either-or proposition. As we'll explain later, a modest degree of narcissism can be healthy, if not critical, for the company. What we're concerned about is pathological narcissism.

CHAPTER TAKE-AWAYS

- Narcissistic behaviours reflect a personality characterized by anxieties about self-worth.
- The origins of the narcissistic personality begin early in childhood, often being the result of conflict-marked relations with parents. Grandiose fantasies for success and adoration often develop to protect the person from self-doubt and insecurity. A need to dominate also provides an outlet for pent-up anger, produces self-esteem and reinforces the narcissist's pursuit of personal fantasies.
- Narcissistic leaders tend to exhibit six key behavioural characteristics. Taken together, the presence of these characteristics indicates a pathological level of narcissism that can prove extremely destructive to employees and also corporations.
- Narcissistic leaders consistently rely on manipulation and exploitation when pursuing their personal agendas.
- Narcissistic leaders will explode into rage when perceived threats or insults occur, no matter how slight or trivial. This impulsive and unconventional behaviour often surprises and shocks subordinates.
- Narcissistic leaders tend to be obsessed with their images and engage in excessive impression management.
- Narcissistic leaders use poor administrative practices – their decision-making processes are usually flawed and they tend to swing back and forth between extreme delegation (when things are in the idea stage or are going well) and micro-management (with pet projects or when problems arise).
- Narcissistic leaders are incapable of recognizing their flawed visions for what they really are – deluded schemes for achieving personal glory.
- Narcissistic leaders fail to plan for succession because developing competent and more sophisticated subordinates is tantamount to creating rivals. Given the latent insecurities that are at the core of the narcissistic personality, rivals are unacceptable. Narcissists prefer inferior 'disciples' who present no threat.

Chapter 3

Responding to manipulation and exploitation

ME, MYSELF AND I

Pawns on the narcissist's chessboard

My regional sales manager believed that he was the only reason that any good things happened in his sales territory. He'd start off performance appraisals by saying, 'I am your boss, never forget it! Anything you achieve is because of me being here.' The only people he promoted were reps that publicly praised his role in their success. Those that refused – including many of our sales stars – were consistently passed over. The best ones usually left to work for competitors.

Sales representative, pharmaceutical firm

I used to work for the owner of several high-quality restaurants (all four stars). His parents were the founders of the original restaurant. He was consumed about building and expanding now that he was running the show. It was like he was trying to get beyond his parents' shadow or something. He was very image-conscious and charming to customers, but treated employees like they were his servants. I remember one slow evening when the owner saw an employee standing around looking bored. The employee was given a steak knife and told to go out behind the dumpster at the back of the parking lot. He was then forced to use the knife to pull weeds out from between cracks in the concrete for several hours. Once, two other employees and I were told to drive out to the owner's estate. When we got there we were informed that our job was to remove a dead tree that had become tangled in some power lines. The owner then told me to climb up on a front-end loader and untangle the branches by hand! I said, 'You're kidding!' He yelled, 'Get up there, ya little pussy! I can't believe you're so fucking afraid of a fucking tree!' I thought I was going to be electrocuted. Another time, an employee was out at the owner's property raking up leaves and collecting dead branches. He piled the stuff up and was told to burn it. In the process, his clothes accidentally caught fire. He wound up with severe burns that were visible on his face, arms and neck. The owner refused to pay his medical bills.

Former waiter, four-star restaurant

THE ENDS HAVE IT

Experts have described the impact of narcissistic leadership behaviours as: 'quite frightening. They describe individuals who are capable of being extremely charming and manipulative and extremely cruel to others. Such individuals appear to be willing to use their charm to engage in cruel and punitive behaviour whenever it is in their self-interest to do so. Further, narcissists appear to experience little self-doubt or psychological disturbance as a result of their behaviour'.[1]

In many ways, it's this combination of charm and ruthlessness that powers narcissists' agendas and enables them to go farther than we'd like to think. It also explains why many of us consistently tend to underestimate narcissistic leaders.

That's certainly a theme that we've hit over and over in this book – that narcissistic leaders are willing to do anything to fulfil their self-absorbed fantasies. In this chapter we focus on those narcissistic behaviours that, more than anything else, exemplify the credo 'the ends justify the means'. Common expressions of these Machiavellian tendencies include activities deliberately designed to manipulate or exploit subordinates for personal advantage (eg lying and disinformation campaigns). For narcissists, manipulation and exploitation 'work', regardless of the circumstances.[2]

Of course, corporate circumstances can act to exacerbate – or inhibit – narcissistic behaviour. But we'll consider that side of the equation later in this book. Likewise, a variety of narcissistic behaviours that could arguably be described as 'manipulative' or 'exploitative' we save for later chapters. For instance, narcissistic leaders often try to seduce subordinates into following their flawed visions. We consider narcissistic vision in Chapter 7. Narcissistic leaders also engage in excessive image and impression management. That's a subject we deal with specifically in Chapter 5.

Our concern here is to identify specific behaviours most likely to make subordinates feel that they are marionettes who are being moved around, sometimes quite skilfully, at the hands of their narcissistic puppeteer. After all, the Latin word *manipulus* – the origin of 'manipulate' – literally means 'a handful'. And there's nothing better for narcissistic leaders than feeling that they have subordinates right in the palms of their hands. That's one reason why cutting those marionette strings is so difficult – narcissists enjoy the sense of dominance that manipulation provides. Plus, they've usually had years of practice at it and can often be surprisingly subtle. In other words, you may not always realize what is really happening to you. Even Pinocchio had to be told that he wasn't a real boy, that he was made of wood.

The recognition problem is a key reason why it's so difficult to keep narcissistic manipulation and exploitation from spiralling out of control. Obviously, the more extreme and blatant the behaviour, the easier it is to 'know it when you see it', like the kind of narcissistic tirades we examine in Chapter 4. But 'successful' manipulation means getting what you want without being tagged as a self-interested no-good. And accurately diagnosing intent with subtle forms of manipulation is a tricky business. Identifying an individual's motivation is inherently difficult and indirect in any case. So, before we go any further, this is a good point to remind you that pathological narcissism consists of a cluster of behavioural tendencies, which we'll explore in detail over the next six chapters. Understanding those behaviours will provide some triangulation and help you assess whether you are being manipulated and exploited by a narcissistic leader as opposed to a run-of-the-mill bad boss. Once that assessment is made, we hope the advice that we offer in this chapter for responding to manipulation and exploitation can be put to good use.

TACTICS USED TO MANIPULATE AND EXPLOIT

The tactics we'll review in this section can be used by narcissistic leaders for offensive (eg to get what they want) or defensive (eg to deflect threats, destroy enemies, etc) purposes – and sometimes both.

Scapegoating

When things go wrong for narcissistic leaders, the consequences can be pretty serious. If they are somehow blamed for a problem or failure, narcissists' fragile self-images – and the dreams of conquest that prop them up – can collapse. As a result, scapegoating becomes an irresistible way of transferring blame on to others or the environment. This often takes the form of direct attacks on the 'responsible' parties (eg 'I was let down by incompetent subordinates' or 'My superiors didn't give me the time and resources to pull that restructuring off'). But scapegoating is hardly exclusive to narcissistic leaders. One reason that scapegoating is so common is that it works reasonably well to insulate executives – narcissists included – from débâcles. In fact, research suggests that executives often successfully deflect blame for serious performance problems by pointing fingers at more junior colleagues, who may find themselves looking for work as a result.[3]

Withholding Information

On the other hand, information can be manipulated for either offensive or defensive purposes. By definition, managerial positions come with a degree of information control. Having access to unique information combined with the ability to control its distribution is a source of power that is frequently abused by narcissists. Plus, certain units may have tremendous control over information because of their importance, uniqueness, or function within the firm.[4] As a result, narcissists may try to worm their way into those locations within the company hierarchy that offer a level of power and influence based, at least in part, on their control over information.

For example, we'd imagine that narcissists looking in from the outside might salivate at the prospect of running a unit like Disney Corporation's strategic planning department. The department sets company direction and watchdogs Disney's business units. The head of the department reports to the CEO. In essence, all roads to the top lead through strategic planning, with the executives running business units having to deal with the department first before reaching the CEO. Critics claim that unit executives are also deliberately kept in the dark about each other as well as the competitive changes that the strategic planning department is thinking about. Some have argued that this information vacuum forces unit executives to compete against each other when they want to pitch their own schemes to strategic planning. This fuzzy environment – where the information flow is scant – may help explain some of the turnover experienced by Disney's unit leaders in the past few years. Control over information may be a big reason why strategic planning is a force to be reckoned with at Disney.[5]

Of course, at the hands of a narcissist, the ability to keep information secret is an important weapon that can be used to:

- undercut challengers (eg not sharing marketing information with rival unit managers);
- make yourself look good (eg suppressing the fact that your 'success' was really the result of idea theft and others' hard work);
- keep uppity subordinates in line (eg withholding information that could help them do their jobs or keeping quiet about opportunities available in the firm).

And the reverse is also true. Turning the information tap wide open can have appeal. By burying opponents with reports, inquiries and new projects, narcissists can successfully distract attention, mislead people and generally keep enemies off balance while they pursue their real goals.

One reason why manipulating information is such a ripe area for abuse is that it is both devastating and tough to detect. Perhaps the most common form of information abuse by managers is to let information dribble out like water from a leaky tap. Subordinates get just enough useful information to perform adequately, but are otherwise kept weak and dependent. And that's very appealing to narcissistic leaders. Plus, keeping subordinates from gaining a firm grasp on the complete picture has another benefit – it makes the narcissistic leader seem more dominant, 'necessary' and expert.

ME, MYSELF AND I
Leading liars

The biggest lie in business life today is that the boss wants honest feedback
. . . the grapevine is full of stories about people who told some unpleasant
truth and got fired for it.

Steven Berglas, Harvard clinical psychologist
specializing in executive behaviour

Obviously, this business truism is especially apt if the boss is a narcissist.
Telling a narcissist some 'unpleasant truth' is likely to earn the messenger
some even more unpleasant consequences. Better to lie and tell narcissists
only what they want to hear – that they're wonderful, infallible, brilliant,
etc, etc.

But for narcissists, lying is also a powerful tool for advancing and
protecting themselves. And it doesn't matter who gets hurt in the process
as long as their own stature, and successful image are preserved. Lying
can be used for a variety of selfish purposes, including destroying challengers, undercutting rivals, manipulating events and exploiting subordinates. In fact, narcissistic leaders can be incredibly brazen about their use
of lying.

Stephen Berglas has heard plenty of that in his consulting practice.
Once, Berglas was hired to help a unit president stop sexually harassing
his female subordinates. The chairman of the parent firm had hired
Berglas because he believed the president was a brilliant, rising star who
needed to be educated about restraining his impulses. Indeed, the president's out-of-control behaviour had finally resulted in a lawsuit being
filed against the firm. That lawsuit was soon going to trial. But at their first
meeting, the president made it clear, with apparently breezy disdain, that
he knew what to do and was in complete control of the situation: 'Look, I
don't need your help. I'm going to trial on these sexual harassment
charges, and I'm going to lie. What's more, my two top executives have
agreed to lie for me. Hell, I could tell all my workers that I'm intending to
lie under oath, and it wouldn't make a damn bit of difference. Cash, stock
in the company, they're what matter today. What makes you think
integrity matters?'

This shocking and arrogant admission is consistent with the narcissist's
view of the world. Lying is simply another way to get what you want. But
lying at the top has an insidious effect on the

company over time, eating away at the corporate culture and trickling down to infect employees. Berglas himself put it this way: 'If your employees know you to be corrupt, their attitude toward work will be shaped by what you do, your mission or values statement be damned. When people at the top of an institution behave in a self-centred, narcissistic way, their "screw the rules" attitude is likely to be emulated by all they come in contact with.'[6]

Lying and Distorting

As this 'Me, Myself and I' box suggests, withholding information isn't the only option for narcissists. Lying and distorting are also possibilities. Now don't misunderstand us. We're not saying that managers should always tell subordinates the complete truth in all situations. Sometimes there are good reasons for presenting a picture that is somehow shaded or nuanced (eg to protect people's feelings or to avoid provoking unnecessary conflict). The trouble occurs when the motivation behind such 'parsing' – to use a word popularized by Bill Clinton's language skills – is driven by the selfish needs of narcissistic leaders. But we wonder how many managers actually make clean distinctions between 'good' lying and self-interested yarn spinning. What surveys suggest is that while US business leaders tend to describe lying as 'wrong' in general, a majority also say that lying 'isn't always bad' and that they 'sometimes tell lies'.[7]

In any case, a pure, unadulterated lie is certainly one way that narcissists can manipulate events for personal gain (eg spreading false information to undercut a rival for a coveted promotion). Distortions, on the other hand, might involve 'half-truths' – accurate, but incomplete information. For example, as a narcissist you might tell a superior that you've done a fantastic job of turning around your underperforming unit because sales are up 25 per cent. What you fail to mention is that you've effectively lost ground because, in your push to get product out the door, the cost of obtaining those sales has jumped 50 per cent. And all too often, higher-ups do precious little checking into those kinds of details, preferring instead to believe the narcissist's rosy spin. In the meantime, the narcissist will often be plotting to seize his or her next promotion or to hook up with a new company, the idea being to get out before the full extent of the damage caused becomes known.

Alternatively, distortions may combine lies with a few nuggets of truth. For instance, let's say that you are a narcissistic boss in charge of marketing for your firm. You're a bit nervous at the moment since one of your subordinates is waiting to hear whether you will support her new market research project. Of course, you can't let her project get off the ground. So, you truthfully tell the subordinate that her project will not be approved. When pressed for an explanation, you follow up with a lie, saying that the reasons were budgetary and that the CEO (whose job you desperately covet) felt that the project was too expensive. Your real reasons, however, include needing the money for your own pet projects and preventing the subordinate from making a big splash that would take attention away from you. The beauty of it all is that the subordinate would be hard pressed to detect the complete truth. Let's say she is suspicious and angry, and decides to do an end run to the CEO to check up on your stated reasons for shooting down the project. Such a manoeuvre is politically risky in many corporations and invites a backlash. Plus, being the clever narcissist that you are, you've already laid the groundwork to forestall an end run by planting seeds with the CEO about the 'expensive' nature of the subordinate's project. In essence, you 'guide' the CEO to reach a false conclusion. That way, when reached by your subordinate, your superior will end up parroting the public position you took in quashing the project in the first place.

Emotional and Psychological Games

In fact, narcissists are often quite good at playing off from people's needs, desires and personalities. They excel at emotional warfare. For instance, in the example above, the narcissist might be counting on the subordinate's professionalism and pride to bubble up when the project is rejected. In other words, the narcissist might know that the subordinate's project is reasonable and well justified. Shooting the project down will be a shocking slap in the face. That could spark a level of outrage and a desire to 'get to the bottom of things' that will actually help the narcissist discredit her. If she raises questions or makes an end run to higher authorities, she can be painted as one or more of the following:

 'selfish';
 'immature';
 a 'hot-head' or 'loose cannon' who won't follow the chain of command;
 someone who has failed to 'act in the best interests of the company';
 a 'troublemaker' out to satisfy a 'personal vendetta'.

You get the point. And ironically, many of these same unflattering portraits are quite accurate as descriptions of narcissistic leaders!

Then there's the time-honoured ploy of playing up to people's unmet needs, perhaps as part of a 'divide and conquer' strategy for keeping subordinates weak and at each other's throats. Speaking of weakness, subordinates with poor self-esteem are perfect from a narcissist's perspective. Subordinates with weak self-systems are especially likely to look to what appears to be a strong, confident figure – the narcissistic leader – for guidance and protection. Such a relationship is dysfunctional given the kind of subservience and fawning hero-worship that often goes with it. But that kind of a relationship is simply fodder for narcissistic manipulation. If subordinates become enablers of a narcissist's agenda and have suspended their own critical judgement, they will be exploited. As one expert put it, it's as if subordinates are 'sucked into being a co-dependent with an alcoholic'. The narcissist knows that subordinates will crave opportunities to demonstrate loyalty to managers whom they identify with and admire. As a consequence, subordinates will be targeted for frequent personal appeals that directly try to influence their loyalties and feelings for the narcissist ('remember, you're doing this as a personal favour for me'). In fact, narcissistic leaders may 'dip into the well' so deeply and so often that they eventually get into trouble, especially if what they want subordinates to do is excessive or extreme (eg fudging financial data to make the narcissist look good). Even subordinates who are initially blinded by the narcissist's aura may finally start to wonder if he or she is being manipulative or insincere.[8]

Manipulating Rewards

Narcissists can also have a field day playing games with rewards. These include: 1) pay rises, bonuses, promotions, status symbols, and so on (things we commonly associate with the performance appraisal process); 2) resources such as equipment, materials and project budgets; and 3) assignment to coveted job duties or highly visible projects. Firms give managers surprisingly wide latitude to make reward distributions. There may be few, if any, procedures that would preclude a narcissist from giving favourable schedules, jobs, promotions and status symbols (eg a bigger office) to lackeys and sycophants. And the higher up the narcissist is, the more likely he or she will find that rank has its privileges in that regard, with senior positions having more discretion with rewards. Narcissists can also use rewards to trade favours and garner resources from peers. In fact, certain management positions – like product manager – typically come with a large set of peer relationships. Studies show that 'horse trading' among peers really does help managers get what they want.[9] And that can be trouble if the trading partner is a narcissist.

Manipulating Punishments

Of course, narcissists can also manipulate the system to demote, fire, reprimand, or just plain make life miserable for subordinates who otherwise don't deserve it. You can bet that if a narcissistic leader is involved, the only real 'crime' the subordinate is guilty of is: a) failing to completely support the narcissist's agenda; b) being perceived as a threat who might outshine or upstage the narcissist; or 3) doing something that embarrassed the narcissist (eg raising questions in a public forum).

Ostensibly, there are more systems, procedures and controls in place that govern the use of punishments in corporations. So the narcissist has to be a bit more careful. But only a bit. That's certainly the case when it comes to nailing someone with a bad performance appraisal. The methods used in most firms to evaluate performance are notoriously subjective and unreliable, and often lack validity. That gives the narcissist plenty of opportunity to slant the evaluation process to slap at real or imagined enemies. Narcissists may also have direct control over determining how performance appraisal actually works in the first place – which increases their ability to influence it for nefarious purposes. For instance, narcissistic leaders might create deliberately vague performance standards so they can reward allies and punish opponents as they see fit. Or they might choose to rely on qualitative measures of 'performance' and ignore more objective performance criteria. Then there's the option of setting performance targets so high that no one can reach them – a sure-fire way to bring subordinates back down to earth. Finally, in the US, most employees work under an employment-at-will arrangement. In effect, that means that most can be fired for any reason at any time.[10]

ME, MYSELF AND I

Born to manipulate

My boss is the president of the company. It's family owned and his brother is the CEO. So he has this big chip on his shoulder. He's told me many times that he was 'born to run the company', yet he's very threatened of me. He constantly tests me to see if I'm after his job. For two years, I've literally had these closed-door meetings with him just about every other day. The meetings last about an hour and start with him asking me whether I really want to keep working for the company or some variation on that theme. What he always wants to hear from me is, 'I support you' and 'I don't want to be president.' A couple of times he said he heard that I was spreading rumours about him to employees and otherwise talking behind his back. Once he even accused me of 'sabotaging the books' to make him look bad because I 'wanted his job'. His accusations are always vague and general because he never has any proof.

He's also resorted to a variety of underhanded tricks. He arranged for our corporate attorney to take me to lunch, during which time I was told that as an executive, I could 'be fired for any reason'. The attorney also told me that my job description 'included supporting the president no matter what he says'. Last year he took away my bonus and added it to his own. When I asked him about it, he said that although my bonus was justified based on 'profits, seniority, and performance', it was still his 'personal discretion' not to give it to me. I know he's trying to drive me out and it's working. I'm tired by it all and fed up.

Vice-president of finance, container manufacturing firm

COUNTERING MANIPULATION AND EXPLOITATION

It's amazing to hear employees talk about the manipulation and exploitation that they experience at the hands of their narcissistic bosses. Even more stunning, however, is that many employees do little about it. Of course, if employees don't realize they are being manipulated (not an uncommon occurrence!), then they can't be expected to respond. But even when there is awareness, employee passivity is understandable if not excusable. After all, studies suggest that a real fear of repercussions and the perception that nothing will change are the two top reasons why employees are reluctant to fight back and speak up against this kind of management abuse.[11]

The First Step: Diagnose Your Situation (and Yourself)

And repercussions are part of the diagnostic equation that you should look at before deciding what, if any, action to take. But there's much more to it than that. We suggest asking yourself these questions to help you decide how to respond to narcissistic manipulation and exploitation:

- Am I really dealing with a narcissist or is this a salvageable situation?
- How much pain and suffering am I experiencing? Can I stand it? For how long?
- Does the manipulation or exploitation I'm experiencing threaten my career or my reputation?
- How many other people (peers, superiors) view the narcissist the way I do? To what extent are they aware of his or her behaviour? How much support, either explicit or implicit, might they be willing to offer?
- Does the corporate culture encourage narcissism? Are there grievance or whistle-blowing procedures in place in case I need them?
- Is my boss's behaviour illegal, unethical, or immoral?
- Is the unit's or company's performance – or even survival – being put at risk?
- How do I handle conflict and the stress that goes with it? Can I endure any likely counterattacks and repercussions?
- Am I willing to leave if this blows up in my face? What are my employment options at this point?

Actually, these diagnostic questions are a useful starting point for thinking about how to respond to all aspects of narcissistic leadership. Although we won't be repeating these questions in subsequent chapters, we will be amplifying certain diagnostic themes that are particularly relevant to a chapter's topic. For instance, in Chapter 4 we suggest that you examine your level of self-worth, especially if you have endured repeated episodes of narcissistic rage. Your own self-image could be making you a bigger target for narcissistic temper tantrums than would otherwise be the case. In any case, you can refer back to the questions raised here to jump-start your thinking about the action-planning process.

Avoidance

That brings us to some specific options for responding to narcissistic manipulation and exploitation. For example, your diagnosis might point toward avoiding the narcissistic boss whenever possible as a way of minimizing manipulation and lowering your profile. Perhaps you think that you can endure whatever the narcissist throws your way, either because you're 'up to it' or because you have decent employment options. Alternatively, you might embrace avoidance because you expect little in the way of support from colleagues if you take stronger action. But avoidance is really a short-term tactic. Over time, avoidance wears people down and creates cynicism. Plus, it does nothing to slow down the narcissist and could arguably be viewed as implicit encouragement. In short, avoidance is a defensive coping strategy, nothing more.

Creating a Paper Trail and Protecting it

Regardless of your response strategy, we'd recommend keeping a detailed 'incident log' and file with supporting documents. That way you have some ammunition in case of counterattacks or if you reach a point where you have to support your allegations directly. Marshalling evidence is especially important with manipulation, something that by definition is harder to prove than other narcissistic behaviours (like the explosions of narcissistic rage we talk about in Chapter 4, where there are often plenty of witnesses). First, keep hard copies of all notes, memos and e-mails that you send to or receive from the narcissistic leader. Also keep meticulous dated notes about instances of manipulation or exploitation that you experience. Include what you did in response (eg complained to the narcissist) and how the leader reacted (eg your complaints were ignored or dismissed, or you were lambasted – better known as 'shooting the messenger').

Where you store your documents is also an issue. Some experts will go so far as to say that you should not keep your log or other documentation in your office. While this sounds a bit paranoid, it's important to recognize whom you are dealing with. For instance, we are personally aware of situations where employees have had their offices searched by unknown parties, with files of incriminating evidence against narcissistic higher-ups rifled if not removed. In fact, we would go one step further and extend our warning to all manner of computers. Company desktops and laptops can be seized and searched. Erased files on hard drives or diskettes can be restored. When you hop on the Internet for virtual counselling (because your boss is driving you nuts) or to share stories about your narcissistic leader (try disgruntled.com, one of our favourites!), your computer typically keeps a record of every Web site you visit and every file you download. That's like giving your narcissistic boss a digital rope to hang you with! Finally, sending, receiving, or storing sensitive messages using company e-mail systems is also a recipe for trouble. Many employers reserve the right to monitor and read all e-mail traffic. . . so Big Brother may be watching after all.[12]

Nevertheless, documentation can make the difference when you're in either a defensive or offensive mode with a narcissist. As we've said before (and will say again), documentation strikes at one of the narcissistic leader's soft spots – a tendency not to sweat over the details. Narcissists tend to think they're above it all and so detailed work often has little appeal. In many cases, they're ill prepared to deal with well-documented challenges and may respond by lashing out irrationally. That's something we'll examine more closely in the next chapter. Overall, documentation is an important part of your response to the narcissist. Documentation could come in handy even if you've decided to hunker down and try avoidance. First, there's no guarantee that avoidance will work, so you need to be prepared to defend yourself in any event. Second, if things get worse you may have to drop avoidance and take a more proactive approach, in which case having the paper trail may prove critical.

Building coalitions

If you believe that stronger action is warranted and think that you can take the heat, remember the old adage about 'strength in numbers'. Whatever the specific action is, you'll probably have more success enacting it as a group. That's certainly true when dealing with a narcissistic leader – someone used to playing dirty and who usually starts with more power to boot. Of course, soliciting the support of colleagues is easier said than done. There's usually a fair amount of self-interested fear to overcome. When you approach people, no doubt you'll hear a chorus of soothing words and be offered plenty of shoulders to cry on. But beyond empathy and sympathy you may get precious little else! Even if people say that they'll support you, getting them to actually follow through is another matter. We've certainly seen our share of situations where people who were supposedly 'on board' suddenly vanished when it came time to speak up at meetings, attest to narcissistic abuses, or sign affidavits. But that doesn't mean giving up on forming coalitions. It just means that you need to be careful whom you select (ideally people who've gone through what you have and have some moral backbone). You also must be persuasive and prepared to hold people's feet to the fire. For a detailed example of how coalitions can be used to blunt narcissistic leadership, take a look at Chapter 4. There we examine how a coalition strategy can effectively counter narcissistic rages. In fact, responding as a group to narcissistic leadership is a viable strategy for countering all types of narcissistic behaviour.

Fighting Fire With Fire

Regardless of whether you're responding to a narcissist individually or as part of a group, you can choose to fight fire with fire, including the manipulation of information. But let's start by dousing the complaints we sometimes get about what we're going to suggest here. Yes, in the abstract and taken out of context, what we'll be advocating in this section can be labelled 'negative', or 'sneaky'. And we certainly wouldn't recommend these options for general use – relying on them will paint you as a political animal or worse. But if you've done a proper job of analysing your boss and have concluded that narcissism is an issue, then the options in this section are appropriate.

Getting the word out

The grapevine is always a powerful tool for spreading negative information about a narcissistic boss. We're not advocating that you lie or make stuff up (embellishing things is another matter) – with a narcissist, truth is stranger than fiction! Rather, we're suggesting that you use every opportunity to tell your peers, colleagues and subordinates about:

▨ examples of manipulation and exploitation that you're aware of;
▨ why the narcissist might be engaged in such behaviour;
▨ the damage it is causing to individual morale, your unit and the firm.

The idea here is to chip away at the carefully crafted image that the narcissist is trying to project. Of course, you need to be cautious about whom you choose to share this information with (if word gets back to the narcissist, you may find yourself being chased down the hallway!) and how you position yourself. Obviously, you can be blunter with like-minded sympathizers. With people you're less sure about, however, it is safer to focus on your concern for the firm or other 'big picture' issues. The last thing you want is to be tarred and feathered as a vindictive grenade-thrower. We talk more in our 'end run' section below and in Chapter 4 about these and related positioning details.

Another option for reaching audiences where your connections are weak or unclear is to identify third parties who might be willing to listen to your message and carry it forward. The need to make an audience aware can be stated in ways that fall short of a direct request (eg 'I think that our leadership situation is something that the people up at division headquarters need to know about for their own good, but I'm just not in a position to be the messenger'). A word of caution: if you choose to conduct this kind of informational war, restrict yourself to face-to-face communications. At this point, avoid using memos, e-mail and voice-mail. But keep documenting things on the side just in case: later you may have to take the campaign to another level or use written outlets to defend yourself. Finally, keep the flow of information coming. Study the narcissist and look for inconsistencies between words and behaviours.

In fact, there may be opportunities for you to use the information-gathering apparatus in your firm to expose manipulation. Here's an example of what we mean – and it's one of our favourite stories. The leader in this case was a narcissistic VP at a large energy company. Known for her intense desire to get ahead, the VP lobbied successfully to get control of an ongoing reengineering process for several business units. One particular unit was suspicious and worried about its jobs – with good reason since the VP had already decided to disband the unit and fire its employees. One of the unit's managers called the VP to ask for a progress report on the reengineering plan. The basic response was, 'This is complex and we're working on it around the clock. . . be patient.' Several weeks went by and once again enquiries were made. Again, the answer was the same, 'We're still working on it.' The manager in question didn't buy it and decided to see if the narcissistic leader could be tripped up, with the help of the company intranet. The firm's computer network had a 'schedule surfing' feature that allowed employees with access to pull up the daily schedule for every manager in the corporation. Pulling up the evasive VP's schedule revealed this damning entry: 'Out of office all day. Installing car phone in my Lexus.' After that point, any semblance of co-operation with the VP disappeared and was replaced with outright resistance, with the rallying point being the 'car phone story'. This example also underscores how inattentive – both to details and to employee sensitivities – narcissistic leaders can sometimes be.

Sabotage

Of course, there are many forms of 'resistance'. But trying to 'gum up the works', especially in subtle ways, may be an effective way of responding to narcissistic manipulation and exploitation. You might, for instance, delay as much as possible when responding to the narcissist's requests, deliberately miss deadlines, do the minimum amount of work, or leave key information out of reports. Especially useful would be to feed narcissists incomplete or misleading information that might prove embarrassing or raise questions when they make important presentations up the line. The basic idea is to lower performance and operational effectiveness, ideally without laying yourself wide open as the culpable party.

But if things have become nasty and there is now open warfare with the narcissistic leader, then a more open, albeit riskier, version of this strategy might be viable. In this case, you might want to 'take things public' (eg to peers, or people above the narcissist). This might include telling people that, as a direct result of the crushing and demoralizing effects of your narcissistic leader, either your performance is sagging and you're not working up to your potential, or you can't stand it any more and have no choice but to engage in withdrawal behaviours (eg you're going to stop attending meetings). It would be helpful in this situation to have other members of your unit supporting you and making a similar case. If you're saying these things by yourself, you could easily be branded as a whiner or complainer.

Sandbagging

Sandbagging tactics can also be used to distract narcissists. You could take a deliberately subservient line with narcissistic leaders, broadcasting your failings and limited skills. The conclusion you want them to draw is that you are a weak adversary and no threat. This message may go down easily since narcissists want to feel dominant anyway and are looking for excuses to feel superior. Your goal is to lull them into a false sense of security so that they let down their guard or exert less effort to keep you under control. Once their attention is elsewhere, you would have a freer hand to gum up the works as we've described. In any event, research shows that sandbagging tactics are most likely to occur when the stakes are high and the outcome is uncertain. This certainly describes what it's like to deal with a narcissistic leader! Nevertheless, sandbagging tactics are risky. They're likely to be more effective when used as a one-shot effort to undercut a specific performance event (eg a major presentation) than as a long-term strategy. But more research needs to be done to clarify when sand-bagging can best be used to deal with narcissistic leaders.[13]

End-running the narcissist

Despite our earlier warnings to the contrary, you may find yourself in a place where going around the narcissist is one of your few remaining options. Consider this situation. A female manager finds herself working for a boss whose top subordinates tend to turn over quickly. And things are not going well. The boss refuses to be specific about why he doesn't like certain aspects of her performance and behaviour. In fact, after one meeting where she thought her performance was excellent, the boss threatens to prohibit her from having any contact with other important managers. Figuring that she is about to be fired anyway, the manager decides that seeking out the opinions of more senior executives entails little additional risk. In doing so, she makes a smart decision – she doesn't go in complaining about her boss or begging for help. Instead, she positions herself as someone looking for advice about how she could better serve the company and its executives. The results of this foray are enlightening. One executive tells her that she should already have been promoted and another passes along contacts that eventually allow the manager to land a fulfilling job elsewhere.[14]

Although it has a happy ending, this example underscores the care that must be taken when end-running your boss, especially if he or she is a narcissist. Let's face it, the chain of command is still held in high esteem in most corporations. Plus, the people you're running to are likely to be the same people that put your boss in power in the first place. In other words, they're unlikely to easily embrace a message that effectively says, 'You made a mistake – your guy is a bozo and you need to either sit on him or dump him.' So in many firms, an end run inherently tags you as someone who is insubordinate, disloyal and not to be trusted.

As a consequence, your end run may be ignored or, worse yet, you may be thrown back down into the lion's den. One manager who went over his boss's head was chagrined to be told that a line-by-line tran-script of his conversation was given to his boss, who promptly made every second from that moment on a living hell. Another manager we are familiar with decided to go around her narcissistic boss to the CEO after being fed up with the constant manipulation and game-playing she was exposed to, including: a) not being copied on key memos;

b) being made the object of personal and malicious gossip spread by her boss; and c) finding herself hung out to dry for 'spending too much money' on a project even though her boss had approved the amount that was actually spent.

She figured that she was playing the game right. Her performance was excellent – she had done more to shape the unit up in six months than her boss had done in six years. That was a plus since experts point out that outstanding performers are most likely to be listened to. In addition, instead of directly complaining about her boss, she tried to sell herself as coming forward with a broad plan to restructure the unit, arguing that job descriptions and personnel needed to be shuffled if the company really wanted the unit to 'be a star'. Referring to her boss, the CEO had only one question: 'OK, but do you think Mary is up to the challenge? Can she lead the type of organization that you're describing?' After receiving an 'unfortunately, I don't think so' response, the CEO had this to say to her: 'Let me give you a piece of advice. . . and it's a piece of advice that I would give to anybody. Never come in here and try to get your boss fired. It won't work.'

Despite her protests to the contrary, the CEO cut off the conversation right then and there. Within a week the manager got a call from the human resources department saying that she was to report for mandatory sessions with the company's organizational psychologist 'to learn how to get along with people'. At that point, the manager realized that she had lost and began looking for another job in earnest.

In hindsight, there are probably a few things that this manager could have done differently. Perhaps she could have been a bit more indirect and queried the CEO as to whether he was satisfied with where things stood in her unit. That might have prompted the CEO to ask questions that would have allowed the manager to use her responses to more gently direct the conversation closer to the real issues. She might also have told her boss that she was going to see the CEO to have a discussion about the future of the unit. While that would have been tipping off the narcissist to her intentions, it might also have mitigated against being labelled 'sneaky' or 'untrustworthy' by higher-ups.

In any case, the moral here is that executing an end run means that you have to be prepared to get out – either to transfer within the firm or to find yourself work elsewhere. Again, we're not saying that there is no place for sidestepping your boss. But weigh the costs and benefits carefully. Of course, the long-term answer to making end runs less risky is to open up the corporate culture and take a bite out of the hierarchy. But that's an issue for another chapter.

Other whistle-blowing moves

If an end run leads nowhere, other options might include filing grievances with the human resources department (in larger firms), writing
memos to higher-ups, or even seeking legal redress (which may be
your only option in smaller, privately held firms). Here's where all
your hard documenting work will pay off when you present your
case! But these are long, difficult options that leave the employee
exposed to retribution. Nevertheless, under the right circumstances,
they can be viable. In fact, we'll address these options in a bit more
detail in the next chapter.

For now, we'll briefly mention a few 'half-way' moves that you might
want to consider under the general heading of whistle-blowing. These
include suggesting to human resources, the legal department, or the
firm's controller that it might be worth 'looking into' certain issues associated with the narcissistic leader. But should you do this 'suggesting'
(or 'complaining'!) anonymously? Sometimes there's really no way to
hide anyway. For example, if you are the sole subordinate, you can bet
that you'll be the primary suspect when an unsigned memo suggests
that your boss's activities need to be put under a microscope. And identifying yourself in the process generally entails more personal risk. On
the other hand, truly anonymous allegations are simply dismissed in
many companies. However, that's changing to some extent. In recent
years, some firms have started to take unsigned or anonymous
'concerns' more seriously. A few companies, such as Eastman Kodak
and Browning-Ferris Industries, have even set up sophisticated e-mail
systems or telephone hotlines run by third parties to openly solicit
anonymous feedback.[15]

Turn your resignation into a morality play

If all else fails and you decide to quit, consider seizing the moral high
ground. Request exit interviews with top leaders and otherwise tell as
many people as you can about the narcissist's manipulation and
exploitation. Of course, you want to avoid being viewed as someone
who is just taking a personal slap at the narcissistic leader on the way
out the door. So it makes sense to pitch your argument more broadly
and argue that what's really at stake is the future of the unit or the firm.
You might state you have nothing to gain by bringing these points into
the open after the fact – you were simply in an intolerable situation and
had to get out. But there's a lesson that the firm can learn from your
situation if it is willing to listen and take a closer look at what's going on.

Obviously, it would help your argument if you did in fact quit on your own and could demonstrate that you were a competent, if not outstanding performer. It would be better still to be able to say that you've already got another job lined up (here you're playing to the corporate stereotype which says that only the good employees leave) and that other people 'with options' may be following in your footsteps if nothing is done. Other company leaders may sit up and take notice if you – and perhaps other good people that work for the narcissist – start leaving.

But keep your expectations reasonable when exercising this option. Yes, it would be nice if by quitting and putting your reasons on the table, the firm snaps out of its stupor and takes action against the narcissist. But in companies that embrace narcissism or are otherwise highly politicized, it may not matter how good a case you make. There is often a 'circling the wagons' effect that occurs in which the departing employee is vilified (eg labelled as a selfish yahoo lured away by money). Although this becomes a harder act to pull off if several employees are leaving at once, we are aware of organizations where the 'blame the victim' strategy still works pretty well. As we discuss in Chapter 4, narcissistic leaders often have a variety of accomplices who hypocritically attack departing employees out of a fear of losing their own perquisites, power and empires.

Overall, it's probably best to take the position that speaking up on your way out the door serves you, first and foremost. It can be a very healthy way of getting things off your chest and achieving some cathartic release, even if nothing happens and the narcissistic leader ploughs blissfully on. And psychologically, having your say about a narcissistic leader – even if you don't get your way – may make you feel like some small measure of justice was done.[16]

CHAPTER TAKE-AWAYS

Common tactics used by narcissistic leaders to manipulate and exploit include: a) scapegoating; b) withholding information; c) lying and distorting; d) playing emotional and psychological games; e) manipulating rewards; and f) manipulating punishments.

Countering narcissistic manipulation and exploitation starts with a diagnostic process. Ask yourself a serious of questions to: a) assess the seriousness of the situation (eg am I really dealing with a narcissist? how much suffering am I experiencing? what are the career implications?); and b) evaluate the viability of various options (eg do others view the narcissist the way I do? are they willing to come forward? are there grievance or whistle-blowing procedures in place?).

Avoidance can be a viable coping strategy, but only in the short run (eg if you can endure the narcissist for the next few months until you land another job). Over the long haul, avoidance is self-defeating. It's stressful, and creates bitterness and cynicism.

Regardless of how you respond, create and maintain a paper trail. Keep copies of all relevant documents you've sent or received. Maintain a log that describes all incidents in meticulous detail, including any responses made by you or the narcissistic leader. Also take care to protect your documentation. Avoid storing materials in your office or on company computer systems – these can be examined or even seized by the narcissist.

If you take proactive action against manipulation and exploitation, try building a coalition of supporters first. A united front always has a better chance of success than a solo act. But beware: building coalitions is time-consuming and difficult. Overcoming the self-interested fears of potential coalition partners will be a challenge.

Use the grapevine to pass along information about the narcissist's manipulative behaviours. Scrutinize the narcissist's behaviour carefully and gather 'intelligence' about inconsistencies and scams that can be shared with others.

Use subtle forms of sabotage to lower performance and operating efficiency (eg delay work, miss deadlines, perform to minimum standards, exclude key information from reports, etc). This may increase scrutiny of the narcissist and his or her leadership.

Use sandbagging tactics to lull the narcissist into a false sense of security (eg acting docile and proclaiming your weaknesses around the narcissist) while you 'gum up the works'. But be aware of the risks associated with sandbagging and sabotage.

- Consider end runs to higher-ups or filing formal complaints as options of last resort. Both have major weaknesses. But they can work, especially if you: a) can demonstrate that you are a good performer; and b) position yourself as a problem-solver interested in making the company work better as opposed to someone 'out to get the boss'.
- If all else fails, seize the moral high ground on your way out. Demand exit interviews with top managers and tell anyone who will listen about what has happened. Position your message as trying to help the company and the employees that remain. Doing so will be cathartic and allow you to leave with a clear conscience.

Chapter 4

Responding to impulsive and unconventional behaviour

ME, MYSELF AND I

Raging bulls, part 1

This one manager at my level was always trying to get ahead. Every few months, we'd have planning meetings. People joked about how he would always meet with the president privately right after these meetings to kiss his ass and snipe at the rest of us. After one meeting, this guy and I walked out together. As I was going into the men's room, I said, 'I guess you're on your way to the president's office.' A moment later, this guy bangs the door open and comes right after me. He's got this crazed look and his face is all flushed. He jabs his finger into my chest, shouting, 'Don't ever say anything like that to me again! Just who the fuck are you to mouth off to me? You're not going anywhere! I am!' I grabbed his wrist and pushed his hand back, but he kept leaning in on me, yelling, and clenching his fists. I thought I'd have to hit him to get out of there. Finally, I said 'You're way out of line.' That slowed him down for a second and I walked out. After that, I imagined him coming after me at work with a shotgun. It was a very negative situation and I heard stories about him threatening other people too. Several months after I left the company they promoted him to VP.

Development manager, publishing company

THE NARCISSISTIC LEADER AS RAGING LUNATIC

Back in Chapter 2 we said that narcissistic leaders tend to have periodic fits of rage. Of course, being on the receiving end of one of these impulsive meltdowns is extremely unpleasant – unless you enjoy being the target of profanity-laced tirades, if not thrown objects! Over time, these episodes grind down subordinates – who often end up walking on eggshells whenever they're around the narcissistic leader – and companies alike. In this chapter we address these behaviours more specifically. We'll provide plenty of examples of the kind of one-on-one displays of explosive rage that many of us have witnessed – or experienced – at the hands of a narcissist. As you saw in our opening 'Me, myself and I' box, these rages are often sparked by events that are trivial or inconsequential, at least to the person on the receiving end. This unpredictability creates a paralysing environment marked by uncertainty and fear.

In the first part of this chapter, we'll briefly review the origins of narcissistic rage. We'll then sketch out a common context where narcissistic rages come into play in corporations, with particularly devastating consequences: group decision-making. Most major decisions in corporations are ostensibly made within some group framework. There are executive committees, steering committees, *ad hoc* problem-solving groups and cross-functional teams, just to name a few. What happens when narcissistic rage poisons groups charged with making important decisions? What happens to the group process as a result? As you'll see, the answers aren't pretty. This will underscore the corrosive impact of narcissistic leaders' impulsive and abusive behaviours. The remainder of this chapter will discuss how to respond to the rages of narcissistic leaders, either in a group context or one on one.

The Roots of Impulsive Rage

It's important to remember that what stalks the narcissistic leader is a combination of repressed anger and constant fear of humiliation. When triggered, a fierce and ruthless attack on unsuspecting subordinates is usually the result. The severity of the attack demonstrates the stakes – at least as the narcissistic leader sees it – as well as the lack of normal self-regulatory mechanisms. Unlike most of us, the narcissist experiences no guilt, feels no broader sense of morality or justice and has no empathy for the plight of others. In other words, there is little to inhibit the narcissist's impulses and destructive tendencies.[1]

And anything that is perceived to threaten the narcissist's fragile image of omnipotence and desire for glory could act to trigger a towering rage. As a consequence, subordinates are often surprised by explosions that seem to be caused by seemingly innocuous or trivial events. But regardless of the trigger, the narcissistic leader views the source – the subordinate – as an aggressor with hostile intent. That intensifies and brings to the surface the anger and bitterness that the narcissistic leader always carries. It also justifies the extreme measures – the rages – needed to combat and defeat the 'enemy'. Plus, the release of that anger is exhilarating because it puts the narcissistic leader back where he or she wants to be, in a position of dominance.[2]

And it usually works, at least in the short run. Subordinates are often shocked by the intensity of the emotional venom that is unleashed upon them. So while the tantrum is playing out, many subordinates just sit there, stunned into a dumbfounded and mortified silence. As one manager put it, 'I'd imagine that people hauled up in front of a firing squad have similar looks on their faces.' Sometimes the impact of the narcissist's tirade is so intense that it literally causes a collapse. For example, one subordinate working in a large firm's data processing unit had a nervous breakdown on the spot when her boss delivered a humiliating lambasting in public. The poor woman was rushed to a hospital. Witnesses said that the boss's reaction was: 'I can't help it if she is overly sensitive'.[3]

But 'raging' may work in the long run too. Of course, there's been plenty of talk about how managers need to be 'warm and fuzzy' to motivate employees. Often the spin on this point in the US is that empowerment and real empathy are important in a tight labour market, because caring management helps firms hold on to valuable employees. Nevertheless, there's plenty of evidence that meanness is still rewarded, especially if managers can somehow pitch their tantrums as bottom-line-oriented rather than personal. In fact, a recent survey of 3,600 US and European managers found that abusive behaviour pays, with mean-spirited bosses earning more money than their 'nice' counterparts. This pattern tended to be weaker among the Europeans, suggesting once again that US business culture is still tops when it comes to equating 'mean and tough' with 'success'.[4] Of course, an environment that excuses, if not encourages, the psychological abuse of employees is made to order for narcissists. In fact, those are themes that we'll explore later in this book.

Narcissistic Rages and Decision-Making Groups: An Unhealthy Mix

For now, however, we want to explore how narcissistic raging degrades a group's ability to function effectively. What's always fascinated – and flabbergasted – us is how long narcissists can last given their sometimes unbelievably outrageous behaviour. In part, that's due to their not-to-be-underestimated Machiavellian tendencies and skills in other areas (eg up-the-line impression management) – issues that we address in other chapters.

But here we focus on how the narcissist's unconventional behaviour can cripple a group and, ultimately, even the firm itself. In fact, the slow destruction of the group's decision-making capability often takes place in a series of five identifiable stages. An irony, as you'll see, is that the narcissistic leader usually does face challenges and criticism from within the group. But the narcissistic leader often has powerful allies, including group members' own entrenched passivity and desire to protect themselves. Consider this scenario about narcissistic rage in an executive group – we'll be referring back to it when we walk you through the five stages later in this section:

Phil was the CEO of a manufacturing company and chaired a group of senior executives that met weekly. At one meeting, John, a VP, said he was unexpectedly presented with a chance to buy critical parts at an incredible price for his business unit. Unfortunately, he could not move quickly enough because procedure required him to submit a written proposal to the CEO before making such a large purchase. As a result, a competitor snatched up all the parts available.

Phil's response was to criticize John severely for not acting immediately to buy the parts on the company's behalf. Then Phil went on to say that there was no policy requiring prior approval. John's reply was that everyone on the management team had in fact received a memo saying that the CEO must approve major purchases. Furthermore, John explained, his reason for bringing the whole issue up was to discuss – and, he hoped, change – what he felt was an inefficient policy.

With that, Phil exploded. He stood up, flushing red with rage and screamed that John was accusing him of incompetence. Yelling at the top of his lungs, he went on to say that John had misunderstood his memo and that 'only a fool' would have failed to order the parts instantly. Phil's tantrum went on for several minutes. He lashed into the managers in the room, hissing that they couldn't be trusted to 'keep up with changing times'. Because of that, Phil declared that he would continue to insist on approving major orders before they were placed.

The stunned executives in the group struggled to reconcile what they'd just heard. A manager was hammered for not acting independently even as the policy prohibiting it was effectively reinforced by the CEO! But no one objected. Finally, another VP brought up the next agenda item as if nothing unusual had happened.

A week later, the executive group met again. The circumstances this time were even more unpleasant. Because of poor decisions by Phil, operating expenses were predicted to exceed projected income by the end of the fiscal year. In fact, a magazine article about the expected deficit had appeared that same day.

Jill, the company's financial controller, presented options for cutting expenses, including layoffs. Phil breezily waved off all the proposed cuts, saying that they were 'beneath' him and could be made by subordinates. One executive then raised the possibility of launching new products to boost revenues. Phil responded with wild enthusiasm, launching into a rambling and idealistic speech on the merits of 'new opportunities'. Trying to get things back on track, Jill pointed out that any new directions could add to the looming deficit and might require deeper cuts in various areas. With a snort, Phil said that Jill's remarks reflected 'the cowardice of a puny mind'. Jill was shocked, but didn't respond. At that point, John jumped in and pointedly said that Phil's failure to consider new costs and cuts together was putting the entire company at risk.

Once again, Phil exploded, yelling that he was surrounded by 'idiots and morons'. Phil then turned on John, saying, that if he said another word, 'I'll fire you right now for trying to undermine me'. The current crisis, Phil went on to declare, was caused by others who were 'making too many decisions'. At that point, Phil stormed from the room, angrily stating that he would have to 'reengineer this place myself'.

After Phil left, John looked around the room with explosive anger of his own. 'What the hell's the matter with all of you? Doesn't anybody here have any guts? Don't you see what's happening? The last two years under Phil have been a complete disaster! This clown's wrecking the company! We need to do something!' Bob, the VP of human resources and a 20-year veteran, spoke for most of the executive group when he said, 'Yes, we've got some big problems now, but you're going too far in accusing Phil of screwing up the company. Personalizing things and name-calling doesn't help anything.' Then it was John's turn to walk out in anger, saying, 'This isn't over yet. I'll be back with more evidence for you all to consider.'

But at subsequent meetings, John never got the chance. He watched with chagrin and horror as the rest of the group rallied around Phil and his deluded explanations for company problems. Increasingly, John realized that he was being made the 'fall guy' as a 'cynic' and 'naysayer'. Within a month he was fired.

What happened in this scenario is unbelievable – at least to those who haven't seen it first-hand – yet all too common. Despite a history of narcissistic rages from the CEO, the group not only did nothing to stop him, but also actually ended up tacitly supporting his bullying tantrums. What's interesting here is that the destruction of the group process in this case is actually fairly predictable. In fact, that process often unfolds through the five stages summarized in Figure 4.1.[5]

Stage 1: Passive reactions to initial rage
Stage 2: Upping the ante with intensified rage
Stage 3: Rallying around the narcissist
Stage 4: Appeasement and apology
Stage 5: Endgame convulsions
       Complete destruction
       Internal genocide
       Palace coup

Figure 4.1 The stages of doom: How narcissistic rage destroys the group process

Stage 1: Passive reactions to initial rage

Once in a leadership position, the narcissist periodically throws temper tantrums whenever he or she feels threatened within the group. The source of the threat (John in our scenario) is identified as 'the enemy' and becomes the main target of the narcissist's rage. But as you can see in our example, the rest of the group also comes in for some brow-beating. In essence, members of the group are being pushed to choose sides. They can either suffer similar treatment at the hands of the leader (which they are beginning to get a taste of) or side with the leader and join the attack.

Sometimes group members will openly side with the leader, but they are usually quite cautious in this early stage and often refrain from commenting or explicitly committing to a position (which is what our scenario depicts). This passivity is predictable given the leader's intense anger and the fact that the distribution of power is lopsided, with the source of any perceived threats usually being lower-ranking subordinates. Psychologically, group members often engage in what amounts to wishful thinking, hoping that the leader's outrageous behaviour is transitory, temporary, or has no serious consequences – even after witnessing repeated incidents. But this 'wait and see' or 'non-aligned' approach is seen by narcissists as a vindication of their views and a sanctioning of their behaviour. In short, silence is interpreted as agreement. And it fuels subsequent fits of rage.

Stage 2: Upping the ante with intensified rage

As periodic rages and tantrums continue, some brave soul may challenge the narcissist directly within the group context. In other words, someone may eventually say the unthinkable in front of the group, that the leader is wrong. By 'drawing a line in the sand', the challenger basically throws the gauntlet down to the group – once again they are being asked to choose sides. From the narcissist's perspective, however, a personal and direct challenge is potentially the most devastating. Left standing, it represents the destruction of the narcissist's fantasies for glory and the ultimate in public humiliation. Such a humiliation is the narcissistic leader's gravest fear, one that must be prevented.

As a result, the leader's response to a direct challenge is usually the most intense and explosive display of rage seen to date. This includes personal threats to the challenger (Phil threatened to fire John). The rest of the group also suffer, but in a more diffuse fashion ('idiots and morons'). In effect, the members of the group are being warned by the leader that they are culpable and will suffer enormously if they fall into the challenger's orbit. It's possible that the group may rise up at this point and side with the challenger. But their prior passivity already makes it more difficult to act against the leader. As a result, continued passivity and acquiescence are likely. Group members would rather endure the indirect bricks thrown their way than face the personal attacks inflicted on the challenger. Of course, this provides further support for the narcissist.

Stage 3: Rallying around the narcissist

An irony at this point is that the challenger, nonplussed by the group's passivity, may respond with anger and righteous indignation of his or her own. The narcissistic leader's rages make it easier for the challenger to display fits of temper because it has become an 'acceptable' part of the group process. As seen in our example, John took some hard slaps at the leader – for both present and past 'indiscretions' – as well as at members of the group.

However, this approach often backfires. The challenger's rages are met with disapproval, just like the leader's are. Group members may see the challenger as going too far for not sticking to the issues of the moment or for advocating 'extreme' measures against the leader. What's different about the group's disapproval this time is that it's expressed – as it was in our scenario when the VP of human resources basically tells John that he's gone over the line.

It's really at this moment that the group openly chooses sides. What's shocking is that in many cases, it's the challenger who is rejected. Of course, what's underneath all of this is not love of the leader so much as fear. In most organizations, managers have positions, pay and perquisites that they want to keep as long as they can. If that means putting their own needs ahead of the organization's, so be it. That's a political fact of life in many corporations.[6]

Simply put, it often seems less risky to support the narcissist. Plus, recall that the inherent conservatism of the group is usually evident from the beginning. That type of conservatism is present to varying degrees in most hierarchical organizations. From the start group members were looking to excuse the leader's tantrums and impulsiveness rather than face the possibility of losing their own empires.

But in siding openly with the leader and rejecting the challenger, group members now must perform some complex cognitive gymnastics. The challenger must be publicly painted as the irrational person who is out of control and needs to be 'corrected'. But what about the leader's temper tantrums? The group members may concoct a variety of justifications, including:

- The leader is so emotional because he or she 'really cares about the organization'.
- The leader's tantrums aren't that serious because they're just a matter of personal style (eg 'He's a New Yorker, you know they tend to be hot-headed, abrasive and obnoxious').
- The tantrums stem from the 'stressful situation' – the leader deserves support to help him or her 'cope'.
- The leader deserves support because there are no other alternatives and a crisis exists (or, things seem to be going well and taking on the leader would be tantamount to committing political suicide).
- Supporting the leader allows us to project a 'stable image' to clients, customers and employees.

In a nutshell, group members become nothing more than accomplices of the narcissist at this stage. The leader's vainglorious self-right-eousness is buttressed and the group ends up relying on the same irra-tional and warped arguments used by the narcissist. Not surprisingly, the net effect of all this is very deflating for the challenger. It also has a chilling effect on any remaining group members who are undecided or who have sympathies for the challenger's complaints. All open dissent is now crushed and effective group decision-making is compromised.

Stage 4: Appeasement and apology

Having clearly staked out their position, group members now have no choice but to continue to distort events to appease the narcissist. Privately, group members typically have conflicting feelings about the leader. They recognize their dependence on the leader and may even believe that he or she has positive attributes. But they are also resentful and disapprove of the leader's rages and irrational impulsiveness. Of course, these negative feelings are suppressed. Naturally, the narcissistic leader now feels more comfortable – the enemy has been vanquished (John's been fired) and only loyalists remain in the 'court'. In fact, the leader may view this as the best of times. The leader's rages may become less frequent and directed to sources outside the group when they do occur. This relative calm may also help group members feel vindicated about their decision to support the narcissist in the first place.

But the narcissistic leader will also continue to pursue personal fame and glory. When brought before the group, however, the leader's self-focused actions and inappropriate decisions will be neither challenged nor corrected. If anything, tough decisions will be put off so as not to provoke the narcissist. For the organization this means a continuing spiral downward toward disaster.

Stage 5: Endgame convulsions

Consequently, the 'halcyon days' of Stage 4 cannot last forever. Ultimately, the chickens come home to roost for both the narcissist and the members of the group. At some point, performance problems will become too severe to be ignored, at either the unit or the firm level (eg a consistent failure to exploit marketplace opportunities and effectively mobilize internal resources will attract undesired attention). As a result, the narcissist will feel threatened from all sides and will frequently lapse into towering rages. Heads may start rolling in cascading fashion down through the entire hierarchy as the narcissist looks for people to blame in every nook and cranny of the firm. Group members may escape much of this type of lashing out initially since they are seen as the last loyal servants, the palace guards. Ironically, these 'loyal followers' may be privately enjoying the entire spectacle since many of their own enemies and rivals are being swept away in the narcissist's explosions and purges. They may also relish the prospect that the narcissistic leader could fall in the process, provided they can avoid becoming victims themselves. The probable outcome of all of this? At the firm level, likely candidates include the following:

- **Complete destruction.** The firm goes under or is taken over by a competitor.
- **Internal genocide.** The narcissistic leader fires most subordinates and may slice off major units or divisions to save money or eliminate perceived enemies. Vast resources may be redirected toward new pet ventures.
- **Palace coup.** The narcissistic leader is overthrown by a new challenger or group.[7]

REACTING TO NARCISSISTIC RAGE

Now comes the hard part. What can be done when a narcissistic leader starts pounding on people with irrational tantrums and the like? There is a variety of possible answers, each with pros and cons. But as we said in Chapter 3, our focus at this point is on steps that groups and individuals can take. We'll be saving organization-level strategies, including preventive measures, for later chapters.

Forming Coalitions: Pushing the Narcissist Over the Edge

That said, the key in a group setting is not to let the narcissist go unchallenged at the start. Preventing the group process from spiralling downward means forcing matters early, before a pattern of passivity and acquiescence is firmly established. That means arresting the spiral in Stage 1 or certainly well before the end of Stage 2. Of course, that's easier said than done. It means that individuals in the group must: a) recognize narcissistic behaviour when they see it or be willing to be persuaded to that effect; and b) be willing to stick their necks out to challenge the leader after the initial outbursts occur.

We say 'individuals' deliberately here. A 'lone ranger' challenge by one person is a recipe for trouble, as we discussed above. It's all too easy in that situation for the narcissist to use divide and conquer strategies to isolate and wear down the challenger (eg painting the entire issue as a 'personality conflict' with one person etc). That's especially true if there are weak-kneed members in the group who are unlikely to lend their support to a challenge without prior prompting, coaching, or encouragement. Instead, members of the group should meet on their own to develop a strategy for confronting the narcissist at the earliest possible opportunity, hopefully after only a few tantrums or noxious impulses are observed. This assumes a quick and accurate diagnosis of the leader by at least one member of the group. It may require sifting through the group's prior experiences with the leader and trying to understand where the rage or other unconventional behaviour is coming from and whether it is part of a wider narcissistic pattern. In any case, this effort to form a united coalition requires that someone step forward and try to rally the group. As we've said, this will be no easy chore.

Ideally, the result will be a collective challenge, one in which all members of the group have an opportunity to state that the narcissist's rage and the behaviours that go with it (eg the threats and name-calling) are unacceptable and must not be repeated. For example, a spokesperson for the group could state the position of the members at the next meeting and then ask each member to express his or her disapproval. It would also be advisable to have the group's opposition stated in writing, either to provide as a follow-up or to present to the leader on the spot if an explosion of temper erupts (which is not unlikely!). Contingency plans should be made for how the group will respond if the leader reacts with intense, uncontrolled rage. If that happens, the group spokesperson might, with the blessing of the members, be prepared to respond with a statement like the following: 'Your unprofessional and unacceptable conduct makes further discussion impossible. We have agreed not to attend future meetings until you are willing to control yourself and act in a calm and reasoned manner.' The group could then get up and walk out of the meeting *en masse*.

There's little doubt that such a dramatic move would plunge many narcissists into fits of frothing anger. This might include threats of firing or even on-the-spot dismissals. Again, this underscores the importance of making a collective challenge in a public forum with plenty of witnesses. Most leaders would have a hard time explaining such impulsive and hostile behaviour, especially if it was directed toward a group with little or no apparent warning. Short of firings, exercising such an approach is likely to produce some pretty strange behaviour. For example, members of one executive team described how their narcissistic VP dissolved into a kind of cornered animal, shaking and spitting out venom in the face of a united challenge. When team members threatened to leave during one abusive episode, the VP blew up, 'forbidding' managers to leave the room and stating that such a move was 'illegal' and inconsistent with 'Robert's rules of order'.

Of course, that pathetic display made no sense since meetings had never been run using such formal procedures. At the next meeting, which was boycotted by half of the group, the VP refused to answer future questions from managers 'designed to distract me from my agenda' and threatened to fire anyone who 'continues to waste my time'. He then went on to proclaim that he would only respond to questions 'submitted in writing'. When the managers tried to take the VP at his word and operate more formally at subsequent meetings (eg by calling for votes on the leader's initiatives, putting formal motions of no confidence on the floor, and other parliamentary manoeuvres), they were rebuffed or ignored without explanation. When word of the leader's bizarre and inconsistent behaviour reached the president's office, enquiries were made that eventually resulted in the VP's dismissal.

We can't say enough about how important it is that group members steel themselves for an onslaught of rage once the narcissist has been challenged. Remember that the psychology of the narcissist is such that humiliation cannot be tolerated; it's the potential for shame and the shattering of the leader's fantasies that prompt impulsive, unconventional and irrational outbursts. But that isn't **necessarily** a bad thing in this case. In fact, we'd go so far as to say that pushing the narcissist into even more insane behaviours should be the goal of the group's challenge. If the narcissist will not desist, then by forcing matters early group members increase the odds that the leader will react with behaviour that is so outrageous that superiors or other important constituencies will be forced to take notice. When a leader's bizarre behaviour escalates to throwing objects, hitting people, firing people in fits of pique, or whatever, it's hard to ignore, especially if group members are doing their best to share that information with anyone who will listen. The point is that any actions that increase the likelihood that the leader will be seen as a narcissist or be subjected to additional scrutiny (which may further ratchet up their rages in the short run) are ultimately in the best interests of the firm. The more the group can paint the leader as irrational and out of control, the more likely that the narcissist will be stopped (ie fired, removed, or reassigned).

One rebuttal that we sometimes hear is that it isn't realistic to expect subordinates to put themselves at risk by challenging the destructive impulses of a narcissist. We have several responses to that concern. First, remember that we are advocating that group members team up to take on the narcissist. Granted, forming a coalition is considered a 'hard' tactic, one that is unlikely to produce a happy, committed response from the narcissist or anyone else! But as we've said in earlier chapters, there really is no room for reason, coaching, training, or other 'developmental' approaches when dealing with pathological narcissism. That stuff simply won't work. The good news is that coalition-oriented strategies can be successful when the target is a superior, and a committed response isn't needed from the person in question. Plus, being part of a coalition offers people a measure of protection and makes it easier for them to participate since it helps diffuse individual responsibility.[8] In other words, when a group is the source of the opposition, it's unlikely that narcissists will focus their entire wrath on a single individual, much less make that rage stick. And that's an important selling point since getting people on board to challenge the narcissist – especially early in the game – is often extraordinarily difficult.

Second, there are alternatives to the group itself taking action, especially if a majority of the membership lack the gumption to challenge the leader in the first place. For instance, group members can present their case to the narcissist's boss or some other person of authority within the organization and ask them to intervene on the group's behalf. Of course, this approach has risks of its own, not the least of which is that the group might be perceived as doing an 'end run' around a superior, a move that may be interpreted as driven by political motives. In fact, the group might be asked if they have brought their concerns to the leader directly. If the answer is no, the follow-up question is likely to be 'Why not?' As a result, we feel that the end run approach is something that is best used as a final, last-ditch option. On the other hand, in some cases there may literally be no one to end-run to, such as when the narcissist is also the owner of the firm or the CEO. In that case, the group can only appeal to outsiders, like the board of directors in a publicly held company, investors, or the press. Again, these are all risky strategies, especially if there is plenty of 'situational inertia' present. In other words, challenging the narcissist will be more difficult in certain contexts. For instance, challenging a narcissist may be more difficult if the firm is doing well or if the narcissist has been specifically given a mandate to 'lead change'. These types of circumstance help anchor and solidify the narcissist's position independent of his or her behaviour.

Another alternative is to take a legalistic approach. The narcissist's threats and rages may fall within the definition of harassment (sexual or otherwise), menacing, or even assault, as defined by either the law or company policies. In that case, the group members may, collectively or individually, choose to file a complaint through the firm's human resource department or independent legal counsel. Such a move invariably means that a slow, difficult and painful process will ensue, one where the final outcome is by no means certain. It also means that the group needs to document the narcissist's extreme behaviours and the harm that they cause very carefully and that members must be prepared to share their 'testimony' when necessary.

Despite these costs, the legalistic option also offers potential benefits. For instance, once under way, it will be very difficult for the narcissist to stop or entirely derail the process itself, especially if the firm has a well-developed set of grievance procedures and a good case against the narcissist can be made. It will tie up and slow down the narcissist if nothing else, and will broaden awareness of his or her behaviour. A legalistic approach also exposes and takes advantage of some of the narcissist's weaknesses – like a notorious lack of attention to detail. Narcissists tend to see themselves as 'owning the world', so doing their homework has little value or appeal. The due process of legal or grievance procedures requires an extraordinary grasp of detail and an ability to present information in a timely, accurate and diligent fashion. Those requirements put narcissists in something of a bind. As the process proceeds, the narcissist will find it increasingly frustrating, 'unjust' and anger-provoking, all of which makes it more likely that he or she will lash out irrationally, fail to respond in sufficient detail, or otherwise trip up. Which specific legal avenue to pursue depends on the company's culture and the clarity and fairness of its policies. As we'll see later, in firms with narcissistic cultures, internal complaints may carry little weight – leaving only external options.

Our final response about the risks associated with forming coalitions to stop narcissistic abuses has to do with the stakes. If you've diagnosed things correctly and you really are facing a narcissist, then there's a damn good chance your group, your unit, or even your organization could be in real trouble. Put another way, **failing to act** could prove an unwise career move! If you end up being seen as an accomplice of a narcissist, unwittingly or not, you'll bear some of the responsibility for the destruction and havoc that ensue. In fact, we've seen situations where purges and recriminations have taken place after the narcissist has moved on or been forced out, with many of the 'collaborators' paying the price. It may be cold comfort, but at least by standing up and joining colleagues to oppose narcissistic rages, you'll be able to look at yourself in the mirror and say, 'I'm doing the right thing.' And sometimes owning the true moral high ground is enough.

ME, MYSELF AND I
Raging bulls, part 2

When my boss felt threatened in any way, he got abusive in a hurry. He was like a psychic vampire – you could be having a great day and he could come along and suck the life right out of you with one of his famous blow-ups. Once we were nearing the deadline for a major project. My stuff was under control, so I decided to head home. I'm just about out the door, when he sees me and starts shouting, 'Don't you know how important this project is to me? Get back to your desk, you lazy son of a bitch!' I was stunned but said something about my part of the project being basically done. He stormed off with this parting shot: 'I hope you're not fucking with me!'

Auditor, public accounting firm

Recently, a minor software glitch briefly shut our computers down. I was already working on the problem when the VP-Finance comes running up to my desk, shaking his finger in my face and shouting so the whole department can hear, 'Hurry up and get the goddam system back! I'm losing money because of you! Make sure this never happens again!' People in the department spent the rest of the day talking about the whole thing. It was really embarrassing.

Information systems manager, insurance company

My boss is the owner of the company. He's a real tyrant who is set off by the smallest and most unpredictable things. He screamed at one person in my department who didn't have the answer to a question at his fingertips that he was a 'big dope'. Another time he yelled at a woman whose mother had died for not touching base every day when she was out of the office. When she returned to work, the first thing he did was start screaming in her face about how she 'lacked commitment'.

Marketing specialist, privately held durable-goods manufacturer

The president of our company would become insulting and hostile when the least little thing wasn't going well. He'd start slamming phones down, slamming doors and swearing at us. He would threaten to 'fire someone' daily and 'fire everyone' weekly. Before going into one company-wide meeting, he told me to 'smile more so employees don't think we're losing money'. After the meeting, he started yelling at me because I was 'smiling too much' and said that 'if you can't get it right, maybe you should just wear a bag over your head'.

Vice-president, plastic-container manufacturer

Interpersonal Tactics for Responding to Narcissistic Rage

In this section we make some interpersonal suggestions for dealing with narcissistic rage. Some of this advice may help you execute the coalition strategy we've described above. It may also be useful for responding to – or preventing – the one-on-one explosions of narcissistic temper that are all too common. But first, a word of caution. We are not going to cover every single thing that might be done if you encounter managerial rages. Not every temper tantrum comes from a narcissist. Executives can have short fuses for a variety of personal or situational reasons. In those cases, tactics oriented toward increasing leaders' self-awareness, developing better anger-management skills, or acknowledging the leader's status (to defuse rage) have some value.[9] But the equation is different with narcissists in our opinion. Fundamentally, you have two choices.

Avoiding tactics

Avoidance is one option. Standing up to narcissistic rage is tough. That's especially true when you're on your own, either literally or figuratively. Perhaps you're in a group full of people with jelly for backbones, people who are unable or unwilling to stand up for themselves. As a consequence, avoidance – either refraining from doing anything to prompt narcissistic blow-ups or somehow 'evacuating' the context when they occur – may be the best choice. Avoidance requires that you identify the triggers that typically spark a tantrum, a difficult undertaking since even inane issues can be interpreted as 'threatening' by narcissists. Nevertheless, the goal would be to avoid creating situations, bringing up issues, making comments, or expressing ideas that might be perceived as threats by the narcissistic leader. If certain situations or issues are unavoidable, then the objective should be to find another poor sap to be the messenger! Avoidance certainly can be a viable strategy, at least in the short term. But it requires walking on eggshells and does nothing to impede the narcissist's destructive march over the long haul.

Plus, once you're on the receiving end of a tantrum, the corollary of avoidance is the slippery slope of appeasement and apology. For example, you could let the narcissist 'vent' and let all their emotion out. Once the tirade is over, a follow-up that might further defuse the immediate anger could run something like this: 'This sounds really important to you and I'm very sorry if I did anything to cause this problem. What can I do to help? I'll give this my full attention.'

Unfortunately, this kind of approach ratifies the narcissist's obsessive need for dominance and validates the use of tirades to get it. Ultimately, that will only cause more problems later.

Putting a stake in the ground

Instead, a better option – if you can handle it – might be to play a particular kind of 'hardball' with the narcissist. This is akin to the group-oriented approach we advocated above. But since you're standing alone this time, you must be able to call on your internal strength and interpersonal skills at a moment's notice. Over the long term, however, this firmer approach has a better chance of flushing narcissists out and pushing them over the edge. Your example may also inspire colleagues to take a stand. Again, what we are suggesting is not for the squeamish. You'll need good interpersonal skills, political acumen and self-confidence. And be prepared: narcissists have spent their lives being abusive and getting away with it. Never underestimate them!

In any event, the basic idea is to show strength rather than weakness in the face of narcissistic rage. This involves a variety of verbal and non-verbal behaviours – followed up by good contingency planning. We want to be clear, however, that we are by no means advocating 'fighting back' in any conventional sense. In other words, don't respond to rages and tantrums with emotion-laden arguments, personal accusations (eg 'you're lying'), complaints, whining, or excuse-making. These moves rarely work anyway, but in this case they're tantamount to sinking to the narcissist's level. They also implicitly display weakness since you're signalling to the narcissist: a) 'you got to me'; and b) 'I'm desperately looking for a way out.' The narcissist will pick up on these cues and move in for the proverbial kill. Instead, when you are ambushed by a raging narcissist, hold your ground. From a non-verbal perspective, we mean that literally:

- **Stand or sit erect.** Do not lean away from the leader, push your chair back, or allow yourself to be backed up as he or she bores in on you.
- **Make direct and sustained eye contact** with the narcissist during the tirade. You can take all the punishment (short of physical assault!) that the narcissist can dish out.
- **Avoid 'submissive non-verbals'** (eg slumped shoulders and panicky expressions). Try to remain as emotionally expressionless as possible.

Remember, the narcissist is exploding to re-establish dominance: cowering in the face of rage confirms the tantrum 'works'. But you also need to show strength verbally. How you do that will depend on the nature of the narcissist's tirade. Here are some general suggestions:

- **Whatever you say, speak firmly.** Project enough volume to be heard clearly by the leader and any witnesses.
- **Stay as calm as you can.** Strive for an emotionally 'cold' and controlled tone.
- **Avoid being too tentative with your words** (eg stay away from 'maybe', 'I'm not sure', or other qualifiers).
- **Use respectful, but not overly solicitous language.**

From a tactical perspective, look for opportunities to interrupt the tirade. Used well, interruptions can slow down or partially blunt the narcissist's runaway anger without making it seem like you're caving in. In fact, interruptions allow you to wrest at least some control over the confrontation back from the narcissist. Here are some specific examples of useful interruptions:

- **Interrupting to 'seek clarity'.** If you're not sure what the underlying issue is or what the narcissist is yelling at you about, use that confusion to interrupt: 'Wait a second. Please slow down. I don't understand what your exact concern is. Could you give me some more background here please?'
- **Interrupting to 'restate' or 'agree'.** Deliberately interrupt to either restate the obvious (eg 'It's clear that you're angry because this is important to you') or agree with something generic or innocuous (eg 'I agree completely with you when you say that we should put the welfare of the company first').

▪ **Interrupting to express your 'openness'.** We don't recommend interrupting to acknowledge the leader's power, accomplishments, or status directly. But you could interrupt to indicate your willingness to hear the narcissist out and to profess your desire to understand exactly what it is that he or she is trying to say. That shows respect, but not submission.

▪ **Interrupting to escape dangerous anger.** If the narcissist's anger is extremely intense and you fear a complete loss of control or a physical attack, interrupt to leave the situation. Firmly state that you are excusing yourself until the narcissist can calm down and have a professional conversation (at which point you'd walk away). If the narcissist pursues you like a mad dog, try putting both hands in front of you, palms out, and state: 'STOP! Your behaviour is unacceptable. I cannot have a discussion with you under these circumstances.' Again, walk away: leave the floor or the building if you have to.

Another tactic that's useful for demonstrating strength is to express your disagreement, either during the tirade or after it fizzles out. Your objections might be about the narcissist's general conclusions or specific points. In either case, there's a fine line to walk. The trick is to express disagreement without directly saying that the narcissist is off his or her rocker. This means using careful phrasing (eg 'I don't agree with that point/perspective/conclusion' or 'I have a different view/perspective/opinion'). Asking for more information while expressing disagreement can also be effective (eg 'At this point, I'd have to disagree with that conclusion, but perhaps you can explain things a bit more for me'). But avoid inflammatory language that personalizes the stakes (eg 'you've miscalculated', 'your idea won't work', 'I don't think you've analysed this completely', etc).

Contingency planning after the tantrum is over

Of course, expressing disagreement – no matter how carefully crafted – may prompt even wilder swings from the narcissist. In fact, there are many things that can go wrong when you try to 'manage' narcissistic rage. And even if you think you've handled things pretty well and have got out of the episode with your skin intact, you should still prepare for a counterattack. That may involve manipulation and exploitation of various kinds, as discussed in the last chapter. The bottom line is that if you weren't seen as an enemy before, you probably will be now.

As a consequence, you should:

- **Create a written record of the episode.** Documenting what happened might prove very important later.
- **Share the gist of the episode with carefully chosen colleagues or superiors.** Broach the issue in terms of your surprise, and ask for perspective (eg 'He just came after me out of the blue the other day . . . I still don't understand it. . . does this make any sense to you? Am I missing something?'). Describe offensive behaviours without characterizing them (eg 'He called me an idiot at one point'). Doing so lets people form their own conclusions (not a problem since the behaviour is so odious anyway!) and you avoid appearing whiny. Your goal is to let the informal network spread the word about the narcissist's outrageous behaviour. You can also solicit advice about what to do next, including whether to send a memo to the narcissist, talk to other people, or take other steps.
- **Consider following up in writing.** Stylistically, your writing should project strength, but not be inflammatory. There are a couple of options for content. If you're unclear about the issues or couldn't get a word in during the tantrum, you could use that as an excuse to ask for more information. Coming up with a polite request for information should be easy since the narcissist is hardly likely to make cogent arguments during a tirade! Besides creating a paper trail, the narcissist's response (or lack thereof) may serve to underscore his or her lack of attention to detail. A stronger approach would be to use the memo to express your disagreement with the narcissist's points or conclusions, while emphasizing that your only concern is the best interests of the company. Stronger still would be to express concern at the unacceptable way you were treated and indicate that you do not expect the narcissist to repeat the behaviour. Depending on which option you choose (especially the latter two), it might also be wise to state that your intent is not to undermine or embarrass the narcissist.
- **Consider what moves to take if the abuse continues.** This might include sending copies of correspondence to higher-ups or other authorities. It might also involve more openly soliciting allies. For instance, you could ask someone to act as a mediator or go-between when dealings with the narcissist are required, the idea being to minimize contact and interaction in the near term. This is really a coping strategy and it has limits. If the narcissist is a direct superior, then finding someone to act as a mediator may be impractical.

Are you part of the problem?

Many of the suggestions we've made for responding to narcissistic rage are difficult to pull off, even by someone with good skills. However, you can rehearse and practise these responses. And by working for a narcissistic leader, you'll no doubt have plenty of reason to do just that!

But this is also a good time to look at yourself in the mirror, especially if you have a history of not responding well to narcissistic rage. Ask yourself, 'Why do I put up with this nonsense?' Rages, tirades and tantrums certainly involve the most obvious – and arguably the most damaging – behaviours that a narcissist can perpetrate. If you're someone who has been putting up with this kind of abuse for a long time, then the failure to break that cycle may say more about you than anything else. Reversing things starts by developing greater self-insight. Here's some food for thought. As we said in an earlier chapter, some people become the willing 'enablers' of narcissism over time. Others are actually attracted to abusive narcissists. Are you?

For instance, individuals with weak self-images and strong dependency needs may find comfort in the role of sycophant. They want to please and can tolerate being the objects of narcissistic rage. Why? Because at some level, they feel that they deserve the abuse or are 'being taken care of' by the boss who is also a parent figure. But not all subordinates bring these tendencies to the table from the beginning. Sometimes repeated exposure to narcissistic tantrums teaches subordinates to see themselves as dependent and weak. In other words, subordinates begin to believe the narcissist's lies and start accepting the blame that comes with the abuse. As their self-doubt rises, subordinates may conclude that any chance for success or improvement depends on the narcissistic leader. And, given their current 'inadequacies', subordinates may believe that they deserve the verbal and emotional floggings that the narcissist administers. Of course this state of affairs – what experts sometimes refer to as 'learned helplessness' – blinds subordinates to what really drives the narcissist. In effect, they have been set up to fail by the narcissist's grandiose scheming and unsustainable vision.[10]

CHAPTER TAKE-AWAYS

▦ Over time, narcissistic rages can effectively destroy the ability of a group to function effectively and make good decisions. The destruction of the group process often occurs in five predictable stages.

▦ The group's passive reactions to initial rages are the first stage. This makes it difficult to support a challenger when he or she stands up to the leader, especially when the narcissist reacts with intensified rage, which is the essence of the second stage. Ironically, the group often rallies around the narcissist and reject the challenger in Stage 3, mainly as the result of fear. In Stage 4, that forces the group into a role where they must appease and apologize for the narcissist, which has a chilling effect on any remaining opposition. Stage 5 is marked by endgame convulsions where performance problems flare into the open.

▦ Several options exist for arresting or reversing the impact of narcissistic rage on groups. Perhaps the best option is to form a coalition with other group members to present a collective challenge to the narcissistic leader. Other approaches include asking other authorities in the firm to intervene on the group's behalf, or filing a formal complaint about the narcissist's behaviour. Complaints can be filed either internally (eg with human resources) or externally (eg through the legal system, governmental institutions, or other public entities).

▦ One-on-one strategies for dealing with narcissistic tantrums include: a) avoiding triggering events, however those are defined; and b) playing interpersonal 'hardball'. Avoidance strategies are by definition short-term and do nothing to get at the root of the problem.

▦ 'Hardball' tactics are about showing strength rather than weakness in the face of tantrums. That includes standing your ground both verbally (eg speaking firmly) and non-verbally (eg standing erect and making direct eye contact). Interruptions can be used strategically to disrupt the flow of narcissistic rage and to reassert some control over the tantrum. For instance, you can interrupt ostensibly to gather information, restate what's already been said, agree with innocuous points, express your willingness to listen, or escape extreme episodes of rage. Expressing disagreement in a non-inflammatory way is another option for showing strength.

▦ Once the rage has subsided, contingency planning is vital. The details of the incident should be recorded. Sharing the gist of the incident with a few carefully selected individuals will help spread the word about what happened. It is also wise to prepare a memo to send to the narcissist with one or more of these themes: a) soliciting more information about the narcissist's concerns; b) expressing disagreement with the narcissist's positions; and c) expressing concern about the abuse that was endured. Be prepared to take more severe steps should a backlash ensue.

Finally, assess yourself. Perhaps you have certain personality traits or behavioural tendencies that make enduring narcissistic tantrums and tirades palatable. Or maybe you've suffered so much narcissist abuse that you've learnt to doubt yourself. Developing these self-insights could help you break out of a self-defeating cycle.

Chapter 5

Responding to excessive impression management

ME, MYSELF AND I

Taking off. . . on the backs of your employees

I used to work for a station manager at a major airport who was obsessed with his own image. The staff often joked about how shocked we would be if he actually thought about something other than himself for more than one minute a day. Usually it wasn't a laughing matter. As a supervisor, I spent way too much time talking down gate agents after their frequent run-ins with the station manager before they'd go back to work. If I didn't do this, the agents would take out their frustrations on the passengers. Almost always, the station manager caused conflicts because of something that he felt would reflect badly on him. He was always saying that 'I have to take action to protect my image'. After one incident, I had to send a gate agent home because she was so upset and angry. The station manager had complained about her appearance, telling her that she was 'fat', 'sloppy' and that her 'poor presentation' made him look bad to his superiors. He then told her that if she wanted to get anywhere, she should 'go buy an exercise bike' and concentrate on improving herself! The woman was 16 weeks pregnant at the time.

Gate supervisor, major US airline

BLOWHARDS AND BRAGGARTS

Optimism. . . is a mania for maintaining that all is going well when things
are going badly.

Voltaire

Back in Chapter 2 we talked about some of the strategies that narcissistic
leaders use to create favourable images for themselves. For instance,
common moves include credit-stealing, exaggerating accomplishments
and sweeping problems under the rug. In this chapter, we focus on
these and other tactics that narcissists use to accomplish their
impression management goals. And those goals are critical to the
narcissist's sense of self. In fact, impression management is an obsession
for narcissists – something vital for keeping their dreams of glory intact.
For many narcissistic leaders, it would not be inaccurate to say that
impression management is often their real full-time job. They become
experts at 'fawning upward' or putting an interminably positive spin on
everything they're associated with, even when the facts suggest
otherwise.

Of course, adding grist to the narcissistic mill are a lot of experts
proclaiming how essential it is to blow your own horn these days. They
argue, with some justification, that performance alone won't cut it. It's
the corporate equivalent of the tree falling in the forest paradox: if no
one's there to hear it, does it really make a sound? So if you're doing
outstanding work and your higher-ups don't know about it, all the
righteous indignation in the world won't get you that promotion.
Instead, you've got to stop whining about how overlooked you are and
start getting your message out where your seniors can hear it. So start
bragging!

Buttressing this argument is the idea that it's harder to get noticed
nowadays. In recent years, companies have been generally running
lean, even to the point of corporate anorexia. As a consequence,
managers in some firms are now responsible for four or five times as
many subordinates as they were in the past. That makes it harder for
managers to have the kind of sustained contact with people that will
lead to real understanding about their accomplishments – hence, the
argument goes, the need to get in their faces and tout yourself! The
'team thing' has also arguably increased the need for self-promotional
chutzpah. Teams are everywhere: there are work teams, cross-functional teams, project teams, virtual teams, steering committees, and so

on. But how do you snare some credit for yourself in a team environment? The short answer, it seems, is by aggressively speaking up. Acting as spokesperson for the team usually means getting the lion's share of the credit, often at the expense of the rest of the team members.

Then there's the growth of 'knowledge industries'. In traditional manufacturing firms, performance was pretty easy to measure and failures fairly difficult to hide. Usually, objective measures of quantity and quality were available (eg counting how much defect-free product you shipped). That's not the case in fields like consulting where 'performance' is often based on highly subjective judgements. As one expert put it, in knowledge industries, 'if you're doing a good job, God knows if anyone knows it'. Once again, that means you need to define yourself as a superstar and then market the hell out of yourself![1]

Impression management has developed to the point where various styles of self-promotion have been described, the idea being that you should brag in a way that best suits you and your corporate culture. That might mean an endless stream of publicity-seeking behaviour or sustained networking to tout your skills and accomplishments. Then there's a 'Napoleonic' or 'conquering style' that could appeal to many narcissists. The idea is to brag about what you're going to do before you do it (eg 'within six months, I will revitalize the firm and increase sales 50 per cent'). This makes you look more like a hero than flogging your past successes would. Some might argue that this is a risky move: if you fail, you look like an ass. But a clever narcissist can pump up the 'difficulties' of the 'challenge' if things start going south or taking longer than expected – winning sympathy and points in the process for 'setting high standards' (eg 'I would have met my original time-frame for revitalizing the culture, but I underestimated the entrenched resistance from the deadwood in this company'). Likewise, narcissists can manipulate information such that partial successes, Pyrrhic victories, or even outright failures are sold as 'big wins' to important constituencies.

And that's really the bottom line when it comes to impression management: there's plenty of evidence that it works pretty well, especially in the hands of a skilled practitioner. For example, in recent years improving corporate governance has become a popular cause in the US. Proponents argue that if boards of directors were more independent – as opposed to being loaded with the CEO's cronies – they could do more to rein in the excesses of CEOs and other senior executives. And, as we've seen, there's often more than enough narcissism to worry about in the executive suite! But more independent directors may simply cause CEOs – narcissistic or otherwise – to crank up their impression management machines to get what they want. One study found that as the independence of the board increased, the more CEOs relied on impression management tactics to protect their perquisites and limit the board's influence. Specifically, this involved a combination of persuasion and ingratiation, a sort of 'frenzied sucking up'. The most interesting thing is that such manoeuvres seem to work. The CEOs forced to deal with more independent boards tended to have more lucrative compensation packages than those that didn't.[2]

In the next section, we'll explore some of the impression management tactics that can be used by narcissistic leaders in more detail. Then we'll tackle the thorny issue of how to respond.

IMPRESSION MANAGEMENT TACTICS: TOOLS OF THE NARCISSIST'S TRADE

What Matters Most: Perception or Reality?

Clearly, narcissistic leaders have a variety of impression management tactics to choose from. But before we discuss specific tactics, we'd like to provide some background on why impression management often works. To begin with, it's helpful to remember that leadership can be thought of as a relational phenomenon. That's a fancy way of saying that 'leadership' only exists in so far as there is a solid bond, a relationship, between a leader and a subordinate. So leadership develops as that relationship develops.

Over time, the precise nature of this relationship depends on several factors, including how comfortable the leader is with the subordinate. Often, it's the perception that shared values and attitudes exist that 'lead' to a comfortable working relationship. In fact, many top executives look for comfort when hiring key subordinates. Here's what Starbucks CEO Howard Schultz had to say on the subject: 'I look for the same kind of qualities most people look for in a spouse. . . To me, they're just as important as skills and abilities. I want to work with people who don't leave their values at home but bring them to work, people whose principles match my own'.[3]

Of course, those 'principles' can be admirable (Schultz says he looks for 'integrity and passion') or repulsive – as is often the case with pathological narcissists. As we've said, narcissistic leaders tend to surround themselves with fawning sycophants while trying to project an image upward that both buttresses their egos and is consistent with what their superiors want to hear.

All of this raises the question of whether what matters most is form or substance – perception or reality – when it comes to leadership. Are 'real' relationships between leaders and subordinates what matter? Or is it the manoeuvring of subordinates and superiors into **perceiving** those relationships or principles – which don't necessarily exist – that counts as 'leadership'? It's at this point that impression management issues swing into view. In fact, there is a school of thought among scholars that argues that 'leadership' is nothing more than a social construction. In other words, people interpret their surroundings, their experiences and their relationships in terms of the leadership concepts and dimensions that they already embrace. As a consequence, this perspective would say that it isn't leader behaviour *per se* that matters, but the individual's perception of it . Some of us have romantic views about leadership and as a result we interpret a leader's behaviour as 'charismatic' – a rallying point to follow. Others with a more jaundiced view of the world may see exactly the same behaviour differently, as smarmy, unbridled emotionalism that is inherently dishonest.

We bring this up for two reasons. First, we think this perspective, while controversial and perhaps a bit extreme, reminds us that leadership is ultimately about what followers are willing to accept. Second, it's a perspective that certainly dovetails with how narcissists tend to operate, especially when it comes to impression management. Listen to what one advocate had to say about what it would mean to view leadership as a 'social construction': 'Rather than search for the right personality, one would search for the opportunity to create the right impression. Reputations would be more significant than actions. Rather than being concerned about engaging in the right practices, one would be concerned about creating the right "spin". The creation and sustenance of interpretive dominance regarding leadership would have the highest priority'.[4]

We dare say that this is an approach to leadership that few narcissists would argue with! To be fair, of course, this constructivist approach isn't intended to promote narcissistic leadership. But it does underscore the potential power of impression management to make a difference in how leaders are viewed. And since narcissists have a strong vision and agenda for themselves, it's an irresistible tool as well.

Narcissistic Impression Management: Shaping Perceptions For Personal Gain

Indeed, what's interesting is that the skilled use of impression management tactics can create perceptions – and lead to relationships – that are extraordinarily difficult to change, even in the face of contradictory behaviours. This can account for the disturbing observations that many of us have made about the world of work. It can explain why certain individuals always seem to get ahead, regardless of their performance – like the narcissists whose biggest talents are stroking their own egos. Likewise, we can all name people who are hard-working and gifted, but who never seem to catch a break. They remain trapped in corporate backwaters, toiling away anonymously. Perhaps their only real sin is *naïveté* when it comes to corporate politics in general and impression management in particular.

In any case, these workplace truisms reflect the power of perceptions and how they create self-fulfilling prophecies in leader–subordinate relationships. Research suggests that leaders tend to categorize their subordinates, often placing them into one of two camps. A lucky handful will enjoy an in-group relationship with the leader and are thought of as trusted insiders. Usually, this is based on perceived similarity in values and attitudes. Perceived similarity increases the likelihood that the leader and subordinate will feel comfortable with each other. Over time, subordinates in this role are assigned desirable jobs and end up with a disproportionate share of available rewards and resources. In return, the in-group subordinate is expected to be loyal and act as a sounding board for the leader.

The other alternative is to suffer in an out-group relationship. This unappetizing prospect leaves the subordinate exposed, with little concern or coaching coming from the leader. In essence, the subordinate is relegated to the leader's mental scrapheap – someone not worth the time of day, much less to be trusted. As a consequence, the leader expects little from out-group subordinates and may rely on coercion to manage them.[5]

Now let's insert the narcissistic leader into this discussion. When dealing with subordinates, complete subservience and a willingness to sacrifice 100 per cent for the narcissist's self-absorbed fantasies are what constitute a 'good working relationship'. Subordinates who are competent and stick up for themselves will find themselves on the outside looking in. In many cases, the result is a polarized set of subordinates, with intense bitterness manifested by those in the out-group toward their in-group counterparts. We received many comments about this aspect of life under narcissistic leaders in our surveys. The gist of subordinates' feelings involved incredible resentment about the favoured – and undeserving – treatment that the leader's favourites received. One out-group manager had this to say about his in-group brethren: 'Whenever the boss got in trouble, he'd assign one of his favourites to clean up the mess. We used to refer to this as "sending in the clowns".'

Needless to say, polarized relationships among subordinates undercut teamwork and co-operation. Plus, as their morale sags, out-group subordinates' performance may also drop precipitously. The irony is that poor performance and 'bad attitudes' will merely confirm the leader's original assessment and justify the continued abuse of out-group subordinates).[6]

But all of this also has important implications for managing superiors' perceptions. Narcissistic leaders definitely want in-group relationships with superiors and other powerful constituencies, hence the relentlessly positive spin they put on things going up the line. In fact, that assertive approach is consistent with what many experts recommend. They suggest that sitting around waiting for superiors to come up with their own judgements isn't very smart. Instead, they argue for taking the bull by the horns and selling yourself to superiors early to increase the chances of obtaining that coveted in-group status. And impression management tactics can prove quite useful for convincing people that you have the 'right' values, attitudes and work habits.

Types of Impression Management Tactics

In this section, we'll highlight some specific impression management tactics. These can be used by anybody. But they can be extremely destructive in the hands of narcissists because their motivation is so intensely selfish and all-consuming.

Self-promotional tactics are used to project a positive aura to important people. The targets are usually superiors or other powerful groups (eg major shareholders, customers and officials). In short, the idea is to make yourself look good to get what you want (eg a promotion, resources, a larger empire, or respect). Common examples include bragging about your successes, exaggerating your accomplishments and name dropping in a way that links yourself to other successful people (sometimes referred to as 'BIRGing' or Basking In Reflected Glory). The trick, of course, is not to be seen as a completely self-interested individual whose only goal is to be a walking self-marketing campaign. Anything that arouses suspicion – you're too blatant or you start bragging at predictable times, like when promotions or other 'goodies' are on the table – invites people to investigate your specious claims. Nevertheless, studies show that job candidates who can execute such tactics well are seen as better interviewees and are more likely to be hired, regardless of their actual job-specific competencies and experiences. Clearly, this is an illustration of form counting more than substance![7]

Exemplification is another impression management tactic that can be misused for personal gain. On the surface at least, exemplification is subtler than outright self-promotion. Behaviours designed to make you look like a selfless organizational citizen fall into this category. For instance, trying to look dedicated when superiors are around is a type of exemplification (eg working hard and showing up early, or at least claiming that you're doing so!). Appearing to live up to the firm's stated values also fits the definition of exemplification.

Take fairness as an example. Many companies embrace the idea of fair and open management, where leaders make their policies transparent and apply them equitably. Narcissistic leaders may try to project an image of fairness, even though being fair in any real sense is the last thing on their minds. After all, if having a reputation for fairness carries a lot of cachet, it can help you get what you want, a point not lost on politically savvy narcissists. To capitalize on this, a narcissistic leader might announce that all merit-pay decisions are based on performance-based criteria that are uniformly applied, even if it's the underperforming lap-dogs who actually land the biggest raises. And studies suggest that managers can in fact help build their own reputations just by 'looking fair' rather than actually being fair.[8]

Better still might be behaviours designed to project an image of self-sacrifice. Used judiciously, this can be an effective option for narcissists. For example, volunteering to perform unpleasant tasks (especially if they are short-term or not that bad!) makes you appear selfless and may also give you an opportunity to showcase important talents and skills (especially if your own subordinates can be ordered to do the bulk of the work behind the scenes). Once again, not having your true motives detected is the key. A narcissist who is reasonably skilled might be able to pull it off and impress the right people. But truly self-sacrificing behaviour is something that the narcissist will avoid. For example, few narcissists are likely to give up their time and energy to work the extra hours needed to help a colleague (read 'potential rival') successfully complete a critical project – even though pitching in could greatly benefit the company.[9]

On the other hand, **other-focused tactics** are designed to polish someone else's image. 'Bootlicking' behaviours fall into this category – things like flattery, agreeing with someone and offering to do personal favours. Usually, direct superiors are the target because they have the ability to give the narcissist what he or she wants. Again, such tactics can work. For instance, studies have shown that **ingratiation behaviours** directed at superiors – such as expressing agreement and praise – lead to better performance appraisals. But narcissistic leaders who overuse these tactics (or lack subtlety in doing so) risk being seen as duplicitous 'suck-ups' or worse.[10]

This raises the question of which impression management tactics are the most effective (with 'effective' being defined as getting what you want with the fewest costs). The answers are complex, and depend on the narcissistic perpetrator's skills as well as the situation (eg how suspicious is the target, and does the perpetrator have a history of relying on impression management tactics when problems occur?). But studies imply that if you have to pick, other-focused tactics are the safest bet. Why? Because other-focused tactics may do more to create positive perceptions (liking, affection, etc) in the target than anything else. Let's face it, we're all susceptible to flattery, as insincere as it often is. Whom would you rather be trapped on a desert island with: someone who tells you how wonderful you are, or a braggart and know-it-all?[11]

Consider this situation. Gloria is a narcissistic manager who has spent months 'getting to know the CEO'. Much of that time has been spent flattering and buttering up the CEO for the sole purpose of landing an open division VP slot (something that would be a huge promotion). These other-focused tactics gradually cause the CEO to like Gloria and to increasingly view her as someone with similar values and attitudes. As a result, she gets the job over more competent and experienced rivals.

On the other hand, had Gloria just relied on self-promotional behaviours, she might have come across as being too self-absorbed for her own good, especially if the CEO did some homework and knew that Gloria's subordinates were the real cause of 'her' successes. In Figure 5.1 we summarize how other-focused tactics are thought to work when a superior is the target. The general message – for narcissists or anyone else for that matter – is that 'bootlicking' can pay dividends.[12] And that's also a reason why narcissistic leaders sometimes get themselves into trouble. They tend to be better self-promoters than bootlickers. After all, bootlicking is a bit inconsistent with the Napoleonic vision that many narcissists have of themselves.

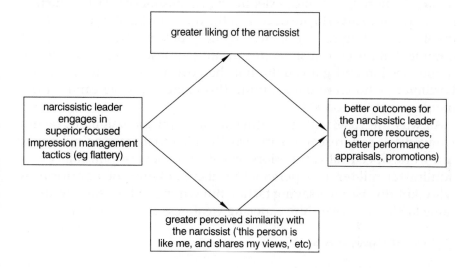

Figure 5.1 Superior-focused impression management tactics: How they work for the narcissistic leader

Face-saving

Up to this point, we've focused on the positive side of things. What about when things screw up, fail, or are otherwise going badly? The narcissist can't tolerate having any negatives stick and will eschew making overt apologies. Of course, finding a scapegoat to blame is a tried and true narcissistic strategy that we've mentioned before. A more sophisticated approach, however, might be to offer face-saving accounts. These manoeuvres include exclaiming your innocence, making excuses and providing justifications.

For instance, the narcissist could state his or her innocence when faced with a débâcle by: a) denying the negative event ('No, the client has not terminated our account'); or b) deflecting responsibility elsewhere ('Yes, the account has been terminated, but that's not in my bailiwick – go and see so-and-so if you want answers about that'). Needless to say, sometimes the responsibility for a disaster is simply too obvious to sidestep completely. In that case, excuses might be the better option. For example, a narcissistic leader could explain that yes, the firm is bleeding money because of a product recall, but that: a) the product was designed on someone else's watch; b) no one could have predicted the fault in advance; c) prior consumer complaints were 'unintentionally' ignored; and/or d) extenuating circumstances existed, such as lack of funds to investigate or correct the problem. Finally, justifications involve admitting responsibility for the problems that occurred, but arguing that the ends justified the means (eg 'Yes, I tampered with the union election and got caught, but the goal was to dump the union hardliners who were bankrupting this company – we can't let the monkeys run the zoo').

As was the case with the other impression management tactics we've discussed, research supports the idea that face-saving moves can work. Specifically, superiors will attribute less responsibility and administer milder, less personal punishments to poor performers who skilfully use face-saving tactics. But when used repeatedly, these same tactics can wear thin, exposing weakness and incompetence.[13]

Going off the deep end

Once again, 'skilful' is the operative word here. Many narcissistic leaders do incredibly well for a long period of time because they are practised and polished impression managers. But in many cases, the house of cards eventually crumbles because their towering egos and personal fantasies get the better of them. As a result, narcissistic leaders simply take things too far:

> My boss would routinely lie to customers and employees about the successes of the company. He would make up awards and citations for articles in trade publications that did not exist.
>
> *Manager, software and database marketing firm*

In fact, one common thread running through our employee surveys is the extent to which narcissistic leaders engage in excessive – and destructive – impression management. In particular, credit-stealing appears to be pervasive, with narcissistic leaders routinely purloining subordinates' efforts and presenting them as their own. Absconding with subordinates' ideas, work and successes appears to be a convenient way for narcissistic leaders to boost their own images. And judging by our feedback, there's nothing infuriates subordinates more than having their efforts stolen out from under them. Take a look at the accompanying 'Me, myself and I' box for some choice examples of narcissistic thievery.

ME, MYSELF AND I

The narcissist as thief: Taking credit where it isn't due

My boss Alex is a tremendous credit-stealer. He consistently assumes credit for anything successful in the group. I remember one idea I presented to him about a product enhancement that would increase our business. In the next monthly team meeting, Alex told everyone that my idea was a brainstorm that he 'had on a drive home'. He did the same thing when someone on his sales staff came up with the idea of creating a new product manager position.

Programmer, software company

The director of our facility regularly took credit for the accomplishments of subordinates. Once, a new employee created a lead for a large potential account. This was a client where the director had been unable to generate any interest. When the new employee actually set up a meeting with key decision-makers, the director called the VP of sales and said, 'You won't believe what just happened. I got a meeting with ABC Corp!' The conversation continued with the director discussing the details of how to proceed with the potential customer. Not once were the contributions or abilities of the new employee mentioned.

Manufacturing manager, automotive parts supplier

Our boss has a very inflated opinion of himself. He wanted to show his superiors that he was real knowledgeable and on top of everything. We did all the work, found all the answers and made all the corrections, but he always took the credit and never mentioned us. He also liked to brag that he could do this or that and make his bosses believe anything he wanted. I can remember being in one meeting with him where the topic was quality. He started dropping names of books on the subject that he used to prominently display in his office. Later I asked him if he had read any of those books and he said, 'Nah.'

Manufacturing supervisor, medical imaging firm

This plant manager would encourage employees to develop patent ideas. But when somebody would bring something forward, he would immediately assign the development of the idea to his own direct reports. If questions came up, his subordinates would go back to the employees who generated the idea and force them to answer questions, work out the problems and sweat all the details. That way, he could avoid any risk if things went wrong and deflect any criticism when things weren't working out. By keeping tight control over the process, any patents that were awarded always went to him and the members of his team.

Engineer, electrical equipment manufacturer

If we presented a new idea, she would punch holes in it and make us feel like it wouldn't work. Then she would turn around and sell the exact same idea as hers to her boss.

Call centre employee, commercial bank

Our boss would make certain that anyone he put forward for promotions or rewards always knew that he was the one responsible for their achievement. He would say things like, 'Remember, I got you the Rookie of the Year award.'

Sales representative, pharmaceutical company

Before leaving this section, we want to revisit sandbagging, an idea we introduced in Chapter 3. Sometimes impression management involves deliberately trying to look bad, like projecting an image of being overworked or lacking in the resources needed to do your job well, something you might do if you're competing for a coveted promotion and you want to convince your enemies that you're a weak opponent. This strategy is designed to lull competitors into letting down their guard and exerting less effort. Studies suggest that sandbagging is most likely to occur in competitive situations where the outcomes are uncertain. That's often the reality when narcissists are fighting to build their empires – guaranteed victories are rare (and narcissists are fundamentally insecure). On the other hand, sandbagging is an inherently risky and limited tactic that is probably best used as a one-shot attempt to lull opponents into a false sense of security. Using it too often will tag the narcissist as devious and underhanded.[14] However, this remains an area where more research is needed. We don't really know very much about the factors that elicit the desire to create bad impressions.[15]

LIMITING NARCISSISTIC IMPRESSION MANAGEMENT

Up to this point we've reviewed impression management processes and a variety of specific tactics. That review should help you recognize impression management behaviour and as such gives you some ammunition to deal with narcissistic excesses. But harbour no illusions about the difficulty of this task. Ultimately, the key is to accurately diagnose intent. And ferreting out ulterior motives is a tricky business. Nevertheless, you need to distinguish between the honest use of impression management (eg you desire to be seen as a good citizen because you really believe corporate citizenship is critical) and tactics used in a manipulative and purely self-serving manner. The bottom line is that impression management tactics aren't inherently bad. They're a fact of life in corporations and, at least to some extent, a necessary one. Of course, pathological narcissists engage in impression management for their own gain, no matter what the cost to the company or to colleagues. That means that you need to be a discriminating 'audience member' to limit the fallout from narcissistic impression management.

Enhancing Your Audience Skills

As we've said, understanding impression management tactics and how they work provides an important inoculating effect. In other words, you're less likely to be duped by a narcissist's impression management tactics. But there's more to it than that. A skilled narcissist will assess the audience's needs and view of the world and then tweak his or her performance accordingly. And remember that narcissistic leaders can be very good at spotting weaknesses in others that might serve their dramaturgical ploys (eg dependent subordinates with weak self-concepts who look for leaders with larger-than-life attributes to 'take care of them').

In a nutshell, narcissistic leaders can be quite good at telling audiences – including subordinates – what they want to hear. They may use ingratiation or self-promotion tactics to play to audience stereotypes about leaders, even down to dress and physical demeanour.

The implication is that you need to know yourself first and foremost. What are your blind spots, your needs and your view of leadership?[16] That could help you detect whether or not you're the target of a narcissist's impression management strategy. Likewise, are you in a situation that is tempting from a narcissist's standpoint? Major changes, a crisis, scarce resources, unclear goals and ambiguous policies are all environmental factors that represent openings for narcissistic impression management (eg to engage in credit-stealing and other self-promotional behaviour that can damage subordinates).

The point is that with careful observation, you can spot clues suggesting that the behaviour you're seeing is driven by narcissistic motivations. For instance, does so-called 'selfless' or self-promotional behaviour only occur when:

- superiors are 'watching'?
- reward opportunities pop up (like promotions or someone's annual review date)?
- performance criteria are subjective (and thus easier to finesse)?
- competent rivals for power, influence and resources are present (threats exist)?
- the corporate culture appears to value such behaviour?

Likewise, how would you assess the quality of the impression management behaviour? Narcissistic leaders trying to impress people with exemplification are unlikely to do as much homework, put out as much effort, or generally stay as engaged as people motivated by truly unselfish goals. Although narcissistic leaders may volunteer for highly visible jobs, tasks, or committees, they're likely to do the minimum and provide little in the way of real value-added behaviour.[17] 'Walking the talk' and being a real role model is no picnic: it requires persistence, consistency and hard work. In fact, one study found that 'world class' leaders tended to use legitimate exemplification extensively and were seen as more effective, considerate, charismatic and inspirational as a result.[18]

Screening Out Narcissists in the First Place

There's also an obvious way to take our 'be a better audience' argument one step further: use the same basic principles in the hiring process to weed out narcissistic executives. Experts claim that the screening criteria typically used to hire executives actually allow a significant number of pathological narcissists to sneak through. Narcissistic leaders often excel at schmoozing up to superiors and making themselves look good. They may project a veneer of confidence, charm and charisma, which, when combined with a healthy dose of assertiveness and ambition, fits the recipe for 'successful executive' in many companies. No wonder that narcissists often make exemplary interviewees).[19]

Later, if narcissists are exposed as insecure fakes and manipulative charlatans, companies are often eager to get rid of them in a way that minimizes collateral damage (eg lawsuits and public embarrassment). That might mean giving the narcissist glowing references to any interested firm. This enables narcissists to hop from job to job, creating a house of mirrors around themselves that throws off a blinding image of glamour and success. Head-hunters also contribute to this mess by placing too high a value on candidates' self-presentation skills.

So if you find yourself in a position to influence your organization's hiring policies or are fortunate (or unlucky!) enough to be appointed to an important search committee, here are some suggestions for flushing out the narcissists that may come your way:

- Adopt a balanced hiring philosophy that looks for the factors that predict leadership success as well as the factors that can lead to failure, like extreme narcissism.
- During the interview process, ask candidates to talk about the difficult problems, conflict-ridden relationships, or battles they've faced, and how they were tackled. Look for answers suggestive of narcissism, such as: 'My subordinates weren't up to the task', 'I did so well that I became the target of jealous rivals', or 'I won that fight because I was the best.'
- If you find yourself liking a candidate quickly, ask yourself why and look for red flags ('What is it about this person that I'm so taken with after just a few minutes? Is he/she too nice, too cordial, too ingratiating?').
- As part of the selection process, administer personality inventories that screen for narcissistic traits.

Fighting Credit-stealing

But what if you've become a victim of narcissistic thievery? As we suggested earlier, credit-stealing seems to be an all-too-common part of the narcissist's repertoire. In this section, we'll explore what you can do in response to such behaviour and how you might lessen the chances of a repeat occurrence.

Reactive strategies

Perhaps the best technique for fighting back after your ideas or work have been stolen is to get the word out. There are a variety of ways to do that. You could write memos explaining the situation to other superiors or human resource managers if the violation is severe enough. But you run the risk of being labelled a troublemaker or whiner. It may also expose you to a backlash from the narcissistic leader, especially if your memo kicks off a more formal grievance or investigatory process (which could cause public embarrassment, cost the narcissist a coveted promotion, or threaten his or her empire, etc). However, as we've said in previous chapters, this formal approach could still be your best option, especially if you're prepared to endure a slugging match and have documented your case well. Plus, you might be able to trip the narcissist up in the process (eg the narcissist might not have covered his or her tracks, or may lash out irrationally in self-defence).

A more subtle strategy would be to share the reality of the situation and the circumstances surrounding the theft informally with a select group of colleagues, including any direct evidence of your contributions (eg documents, drawings, position papers, or designs). This could be done among peers, subordinates, or managers in other units. The idea would be to let the grapevine carry your message forward. Over time and with repeated episodes, people should begin to realize that you are the real 'power behind the throne'. Of course, this approach still risks a backlash, especially if word circulates back to the narcissist that you're waging a low-level campaign to expose the theft. Plus, it's hard to control the dissemination of information in this case (some of your conduits may distort your message or fail to follow through). There's also no automatic imperative for anyone, including your intended audience, to do anything about it. On the other hand, a formal complaint typically requires some kind of response.

Nevertheless, an informal approach can work quite well. In fact, that seemed to be the preferred route for employees in our surveys. Few reported much success with formal complaints registered with human resources or superiors (we received many 'got nowhere' types of comment). Here's a good example of the informal strategy in action:

> I was transferred into this woman's department and soon realized that the tracking of costs wasn't being done. I developed a spreadsheet on my own initiative that calculated net profits, tracked costs, and how long it took to get work finished. She figured out what I was doing and told me to turn in the spreadsheet to her at the end of the month. After nosing around, I became convinced that she was going to steal credit for the spreadsheet and present it up the line as her own. She had pulled similar tricks with other subordinates.

As the end of the month neared, I printed up some copies of the spread-sheet program and showed them to some of my co-workers. One of them took the spreadsheet to the senior VP and explained to him that I had developed it on my own. The VP was surprised, but called me up to compliment me. The department head got wind of what happened somehow and thoroughly bitched out the co-worker who had taken the spreadsheet forward. The co-worker was told she'd be fired if she ever did anything like that again and that all ideas coming out of the department were 'mine to use as I see fit because I'm the department head'. She then started a policy that no employee could leave the floor (to go to another department or visit the senior VP) without her permission! She also began to monitor me constantly. Luckily, I was promoted a few weeks later to the senior VP's staff.

Manager, financial services company

While this example highlights a successful outcome, it also underscores the risks and dangers associated with challenging the narcissist. It inti-mates that having a receptive superior or other audience is a prereq-uisite for any informational campaign. Sometimes, however, a receptive audience is unavailable, as when the credit-stealing leader also happens to be the owner of the firm. In short, if there is no receptive internal audience, you really only have two choices: a) take your message to external constituencies such as the press or legal counsel; or b) take your contributions and willingness to work to another organization that will appreciate you.

Prevention strategies

There are some steps that can be taken to protect your future efforts from being appropriated by narcissistic leaders. First, be assertive prior to undertaking a major project or work effort. Ask everyone involved to sit down and hash out who will do what, including who will take credit for which pieces of the work and how (eg giving briefings within the company and writing professional papers). Then put the whole thing in writing, ask everyone to sign it and share it with the narcissistic leader and any other higher-ups who might be interested. If sharing the document is too risky (a backlash or other threats are likely), then wait until games start being played before hauling it out. In either case, having such a document and being able to disseminate it would make the case for credit-stealing that much easier to prove.

A broader approach would be to propose that procedures be put into place that acknowledge individuals for their efforts when major contributions to important projects, inventions and so on are required. For instance, a written record could be kept that lists each person's contributions as the work is done. Once the effort is complete, a summary of those contributions – countersigned by the contributors and their respective managers – would be submitted as part of the final report or product. This would serve as a formal verification of individual employee contributions and would make credit-stealing more difficult.

Of course, the main hurdle will be selling the process and getting buy-in. For instance, whom would you send the proposal to? Human resources? A sympathetic executive? Another alternative might be to send it through the company's suggestion system, assuming a viable one exists. Then there's the tone of the proposal itself. It should be devoid of blaming or anything that smacks of whining, anger, or bitterness. Instead, the proposal should be pitched as something that's in the company's best interest. The recognition that the proposed procedure generates will ensure the commitment, enthusiasm and best efforts of employees. Sounds pretty good, doesn't it?

But being able to put a process like this into place may depend on the culture and values of the company. And if narcissistic leaders are already in place and thriving, those values may be suspect. Ideally, you'd want to have the corporate mind-set of a company like PSS/World Medical, a medical supplies distributor with over 80 branches in the US and Europe. Put simply, the company believes that bad branch leaders are its worst enemy. And it expects employees to promptly identify them and explain why they're bad. The senior executive team listens and, if they agree with the diagnosis (which they usually do), the leader in question is swiftly removed. 'Removal' can mean termination, retraining, or reassignment to a less demanding job – it depends on the nature of the leadership problem. Driving this process, which is taken very seriously, are two of the company's most important corporate values: a) always communicate without fear of retribution; and b) fire leaders for dishonesty, not for having abilities that fall short of the job. This 'whistle-blowing' culture would be a tough place for a narcissistic leader to survive.[20]

A Final Thought: One-upping the Narcissist

In some ways, impression management is about one-upmanship and trumping your competition to seize the glory for yourself. With that in mind, we'd like to suggest – tongue in cheek of course – that the ultimate way to bring narcissists to heel might be to give them a dose of their own impression management medicine. We end this chapter with what one of our survey respondents had to say on that score:

> My boss was the general operations manager and he had carefully crafted his persona. He was 'the king' and we were expected to know our place and never raise any 'undiscussables' that might embarrass him. Around his corporate superiors, he was into this major sucking-up behaviour. But the rest of us were treated like serfs. In walking around the operation, you would see him and extend greetings. He would look at you, ignore you and walk on by as if you didn't exist. The irony of this came out after he had been on a vacation trip to New York City with his wife. I overheard him complaining that after a Broadway show, he and his wife were having dinner in a very nice restaurant. He noticed an 'old friend' of his, Lee Iacocca, getting up from a nearby table and starting to walk out. He stood up to go over and say hello. Lee brushed right by him, ignoring him; it took him by surprise and totally deflated him. He couldn't understand how Lee could do that to him since they had worked together on a project years before.

Department manager, automobile manufacturer

CHAPTER TAKE-AWAYS

- For a variety of reasons, impression management is more important and more prevalent today than ever before. This plays to narcissistic leaders' self-aggrandizing tendencies.
- Generally speaking, impression management behaviour takes advantage of perceptions, including the biases, attitudes and beliefs that already exist in the minds of the audience.
- Impression management includes a variety of tactics, including self-promotional behaviour, exemplification and other-focused behaviours like ingratiation. Face-saving and credit-stealing are also prominent tactics used for selfish purposes, and are commonly used by narcissistic leaders to excess. Deliberately trying to look bad may also serve a narcissist's agenda under certain circumstances (ie sandbagging).
- Fortunately, there are ways to limit narcissistic impression management, including:
  a) becoming a more sophisticated audience (eg increasing your knowledge of impression management, knowing your own blind

spots, being aware of situational factors that prompt impression management behaviour and being able to assess the quality of the tactics used);

b) watching for impression management ploys and narcissistic tendencies when recruiting managers.

To combat credit-stealing, getting the word out about your real contributions is a good reactive strategy. That could involve an informal process using the grapevine, or a more formal written effort to set the record straight. Both options carry risks and neither is foolproof. Long-term prevention is also tricky. Alternatives include trying to clarify responsibilities and credit-sharing steps before embarking on a major project and then putting that understanding in writing. A broader version of this involves trying to establish a corporate policy for officially submitting a list of individuals' contributions at the conclusion of a project. Such steps should make it more difficult for narcissists to get away with credit-stealing.

Chapter 6

Responding to poor administrative practices

ME, MYSELF AND I

In the line of fire: Life in a narcissistic administration

It was impossible to avoid our president because he came 'looking for you'. He would say that it was his job to 'make sure people are doing what they are supposed to do'. He constantly interrupted business meetings and phone conversations or just sat in your office or stood in your doorway until you stopped working. Then he would either criticize something about your work or talk about how much he paid for his new tie, his Jacuzzi, his maid/lawn service and other useless crap. I finally spoke with him privately about his behaviour, but I suffered negative consequences. This included getting additional 'busy work', having to make last minute and unnecessary revisions on my reports and being forced to work longer hours. It also went beyond me. Members of my staff, including my accountants, administrative assistant and secretary, were also 'punished' in similar ways for my 'direct confrontation'. Eventually, these things hurt the performance of my department to the point where I either had to go public and fight back or get out. I ended up resigning.

Accounting manager, plastic container manufacturer

When things were going well we would go weeks without seeing or hearing from our boss, who was the superintendent of manufacturing. No communication, sharing of information, or even a friendly hello would occur. If a problem developed, he would be your new office partner. Often he would take over the situation completely before we even had a chance to try fixing it on our own. His reasons were always, 'you wouldn't have fixed it', 'you don't know how to fix it', or 'I can't waste time teaching you something you can't learn.'

Engineering manager, automobile manufacturer

This guy was one of three partners who owned our 200-employee company. He would spend every day roaming around the manufacturing floor watching people instead of doing his job. If you were in the bathroom more than a few minutes, he could come in after you yelling, 'Stop screwing around and get back to work.' If you talked to the next person while working, he would start screaming, 'I'm not paying you for talking!' If you made a mistake on a machining operation, he would scream at the top of his lungs, threatening to fire you in front of everybody and name-calling, like 'you stupid asshole'!

Machine operator, steel components manufacturer

My boss liked to force people to attend irrelevant meetings and perform volunteer activities. He had an inflated sense of self-importance and wanted to show employees that he could get them to do anything he wanted. One time he asked me to 'volunteer' to sell government bonds in the department. I refused, saying I had already done things that I considered inappropriate at his request, such as buy wedding cards for his secretary. I told him that none of those tasks fell within my role as an engineer. His face turned all red and he yelled, 'This would have been good in your job review!' I replied that he was threatening me and that I didn't see the connection between selling bonds and my engineering performance. He angrily said, 'Watch it, I can make you do it', then turned and left my office. He found another engineer to sell the bonds.

Engineer, electrical equipment manufacturer

Our department head would post false performance statistics when corporate management visited. He would also capitalize expense items to show better short-term performance. A few of us knew about these things and we were always in utter disbelief when they happened. Somebody finally wrote an anonymous letter to the CEO about them. To make a long story short, they slapped him on the wrist and told him to apologize to the entire department. He promised to do so, but never actually did. After that, the bastard cracked down on us hard. He would publicly humiliate anyone for taking initiative or making a decision on anything, no matter how small. One guy was chewed out for making a decision whose maximum impact on the company was about $80. It made a bad place that much worse.

Product line supervisor, electrical and hydraulic components manufacturer

WHY NARCISSISTIC LEADERS MAKE LOUSY MANAGERS

Narcissistic leaders exhibit poor administrative practices. To be blunt, they are lousy managers. But what exactly does this mean?

Experts widely agree that management involves at least four main functions: planning, organizing, leading and controlling. As you might imagine, some managers are very good at two or even three of these functions, and fewer still are skilled in all areas. But, as far as narcissistic managers are concerned, it's four strikes and you're out. Why is this? First, they tend to be very poor planners. We'll show how projects are often overblown, with very little attempt made to prepare for roadblocks along the way. Their organizational skills are also lacking. This is easy to understand when you find that they try to juggle a dozen or more initiatives at once. They fly in and out of the projects wantonly, often at the most inopportune time and with little background information.

Parachuting in and out is bad enough, but when they do land temporarily they're not content to stick with a delegation decision. They take this momentary focus of their effort to interject opinions, issue edicts and altogether control the agenda – without having the necessary information. So, while you may think narcissists have a leg up on the 'controlling' function, in fact they are not properly controlling at all. Perhaps this is because they often have no real strategy to start with. How can you ensure that performance meets or exceeds your plans if there are no plans, except the implicit one of personal advancement?

Problems in planning

In Chapter 7, we'll be considering how the strategic vision of the narcissist often contains fatal flaws. Here we'll focus more on the operational aspects of planning. These include the decision-making styles and problem-solving approaches of the narcissistic leader. They can easily be seen in everyday interactions with the narcissist and are often a source of frustration. Consider the following quote: 'Normally, my boss and I would get along well. But if I surprised him with a problem and he had to make a quick decision, he would get red in the face. You could see it creep up his neck. Suddenly, there would be a lot of tension in the air. He'd lose his temper and start shouting'.[1]

This quote might be typical of the frustration that those who work for a narcissist face every day. A root cause of this typical narcissistic reaction is probably the lack of planning. As we mentioned, narcissistic leaders tend to be very poor planners. The many projects they take on – or more precisely that they assign to others – are often too big and poorly executed, with very little effort made to contingency-plan or otherwise prepare for problems along the way.

Some of the planning chaos we see with narcissists results from their belief that they can successfully juggle a dozen 'initiatives' at once. The constant search for the next big, hot project that will increase their fame and fortune is all that is important, as illustrated in the following quote:

Early on, people thought Dan was very energetic. But I was kind of suspicious of him from the start. He knew nothing about our industry and made no effort to learn it. All he did was trot out his long list of initiatives he wanted to move on and some of them were just crazy. It got to be a joke. Every meeting he'd trot out his list and it had a new business 'idea' on it. He'd want to get into every nutty scheme he'd run into at all those meetings he'd attend. But he had no idea whatsoever whether or how we could do it. When I was in New York for a seminar, I ran into a guy in a bar who used to work for Dan. He noticed my name tag and struck up a conversation. We got to the topic of Dan pretty quick, and he chuckled when I told him that my job basically was to run behind Dan and clean up the messes he'd make from starting the next big direction. This guy had it right when he said, 'Dan throws anything and everything up on the wall but he ain't going to help make it stick. You end up exhausted because of his stupidity!'

Product Development Manager, machine tool company

Obviously, new ideas and concepts are important; they deserve a complete and full analysis. But that's precisely the trouble with narcissists. They may have pet projects that they will execute come hell or half of Georgia, but it will all be without doing their homework from an operations standpoint. The narcissist often bounces in and out of whatever projects survive after being thrown up against the wall. And this relates to another administrative deficit for many narcissists – organizing.

Organizing Issues

Organizing is also a very important administrative function. It subsumes issues such as the chain of command, dividing up tasks and decision authority, among other things. One issue that takes on an over-arching quality in this category, particularly for narcissistic leaders, is delegation, the process of assigning responsibility and authority for getting things done to someone else. A lot has been written about dele-gation, particularly on managers' unwillingness to delegate.

Managers may fail to delegate for a variety of reasons. They may be used to doing things themselves, lack faith in subordinates' ability to do the job well, or worry about being blamed if things go wrong. Of course, the last reason intersects with the narcissist's agenda.

On the other hand, managers sometimes delegate too much. Excessive delegation might occur because managers can't say no to a vocal employee and want to avoid conflict. Managers may also delegate excessively when they have too many irons in the fire and believe that somehow anything that they're associated with will simply 'happen'. Again, this last explanation is one that often characterizes the behaviour of narcissistic leaders. Overall, narcissistic leaders tend to vacillate between the two extremes, often at the most inopportune times. Let's look at these two extremes and when they tend to occur.

The delegation thing

At first blush, narcissists may seem like ideal 'new age' managers. In fact, many portray themselves as big advocates of empowerment and cutting through bureaucracy. They may even try to set the tone with speeches about letting people 'run their own show'. The trouble is that narcissists haven't a clue about what delegation really means. Delegation isn't just throwing tasks and projects at subordinates. It involves a series of carefully planned steps, including up-front devel-opment work, clear assignment of tasks, the granting of power and authority to subordinates and setting specific objectives.

But narcissistic leaders tend to 'dump' rather than delegate. And, to an extent, they have to. They start so many different projects with little background planning, that they may be unable to truly delegate. Instead, they barely have time to parachute in momentarily to provide the 'needed direction', which often means issuing edicts, changing directions or shoving their views at others, sometimes without the necessary knowledge or skills. As a result, narcissists are rarely interested in the details of executing anything and tend to 'delegate' responsibility for doing the real work to others.

Indeed, narcissists may prefer this style. They love a large yard to play in: grand visions need grand stages. But this pulls them further away from the ability to stay on top of their growing empires in any real way.[2] For example, narcissists are good at keeping their own bosses at arm's length so they can do their own thing. In fact, we'll argue in later chapters that there are some problematic corporate conditions that attract narcissists. These conditions often result in narcissists being given a very long leash by their superiors. This leaves them time to do what they like doing best – advancing their own self-interests – even if that is done outside the sphere of tasks directly related to their jobs. That can free them up to get involved in time-consuming professional associations, organizations, or boards, and sometimes even to run their own side businesses.

There are plenty of examples where narcissistic bosses dabble in pet interests while subordinates are left to take care of the real work. One company we know of even got sucked in by the 'dazzle in the dabble' when they hired a new VP, who managed to sell himself based on a lot of glitzy, non-traditional activities that bore little relation to the job at hand. He bragged of electronics businesses he had started, a patent he had received, his role in assisting other ventures and even his 'management' of a private island. Fortunately, his piloting experience allowed him to fly there directly to perform his 'duties'. Missing from his comments were descriptions of his experience of managing and developing people. They were missing because he had no such experience. Unfortunately, despite these and several other warning signs, he was hired. Within a year, clear signs of narcissism had emerged. Over time, his performance tanked (along with his unit's) and turnover skyrocketed. In his third year he was let go.

When extreme micro-management is most likely

The extreme delegation that we described above lasts only as long as things seem to be going well. But eventually, narcissists' lack of attention to detail catches up on them. When you pile on all their other traits – the manipulation, the impulsive and abusive behaviour, and the self-promotion – you'd have to say that narcissists are unlikely to have a committed set of employees waiting to go that extra mile when the crunch comes. Or if they do, subordinates will be of the blind puppy variety, perhaps willing but unable (ie incompetent loyalists).

When a crisis emerges, narcissists will swing into extreme micro-management. The most intense attention will be focused on pet projects, activities, or tasks where they feel psychologically vulnerable, and where failure or weakness will cause embarrassment and blame to rest at their doorstep. Narcissistic leaders cannot afford to have their fantasies and veneer of omnipotence ripped away: it would expose long-repressed self-doubts and self-loathing.

How exactly a situation unfolds depends on the magnitude of the problem, the extent of the personal threat and the narcissist's prior track record (eg does he or she have a string of perceived successes to fall back on, or is this another in a long line of flops, setbacks, or highly criticized moves?). But there are likely to be some common themes when narcissistic leaders reinsert themselves into situations in a big way. First, narcissists are often rapid-fire thinkers and decision-makers. So, if they feel pressure, they are likely to jump in quickly and start 'doing'. Even if completely wrong, they'll quickly size up situations and charge off to deal with the issues.

Of course, decisiveness in the absence of real analysis and information can do more harm than good. In addition to being extremely annoying, narcissistic leaders who become 'your new office partner'– to quote one of our survey respondents – tend to go off half-cocked. Their goal, after all, isn't to do the right thing or even fix problems *per se*: it's to save face and protect their images – right now. That's why in areas of special concern to them, narcissists may take significant action before subordinates even find out they're no longer running their own shows. When they do communicate, narcissists will issue hasty, incomplete and often inaccurate directions on how to get things back on track, based on 'gut feel' or intuition. And you can expect those directions to be wrapped in anger, intimidation and threats. They may also try to cut deals, cajole and mislead. In short, you can expect to see the entire range of narcissistic behaviours on display. Specific micro-managing tactics will include second-guessing, overturning, or bypassing subordinates altogether, on even the smallest decisions. The guiding principle will be, 'How does this reflect on me?'.

Problems in leading

Delegating (or not delegating) is one thing, but what happens after the narcissist vacillates between these two styles? When things go wrong, narcissists will inevitably look for somebody to blame. Obviously, leaders should clearly communicate expectations, and we've already indicated that narcissists often fall short here. But another component of leading is to accept responsibility for problems and to provide accurate feedback to those with whom you work – hardly a strong point for narcissists! In fact, their strengths lie in the opposite direction. A common narcissistic strategy is to float or foster rumours that can soften people up to their way of thinking. As one employee put it: 'They put out messages on the rumour mill that there are going to be layoffs. There probably won't be any layoffs. They just put the rumours out there to get people to work harder and to shift blame.'

Alternatively, narcissists may present a tale of gloom and doom, recite a set of negative (but incomplete) facts and let listeners 'reach their own conclusions' about whether their initiatives will help the firm avoid imaginary or exaggerated problems.

Even when they get their way, narcissists will be more than willing to set you up for the fall that may result from a failure in their programme, sometimes under the guise of delegating. For example, it's often part of their leader style to hold positive feedback or useful information in reserve, as illustrated in the following example:

> My boss Bob thinks he's an expert delegator. It's true that he leaves me completely alone once he's given me an assignment. That part is fine, or it would be if he would really let me in on what he expects, and why he's asked me to do something. He'll send me a memo from someone else with a scribbled 'Would you take care of this, Bill?' note on it. If I plough ahead on my own, half the time it turns out that he had a completely different idea about it. Or I'll run into some static from people whose toes I've stepped on, only to find out that he knew there might be some tender toes around. According to him, it's my job to find out about things like that, but if I do go check with him before I get started, he'll patronize me as if I were a kid who had to be told to put his shoes on before he laces them up. Oh, Bob's a real expert all right – at getting across that he wonders why in the world he ever made me his deputy.[4]

Or, as another employee put it: 'There's nothing worse than having to smell out which direction we're currently supposed to be going, and then being yelled at when I guess wrong'.[5]

Leading by example

There is a lot said about leading by example – but a narcissistic example is rarely a good one. The narcissist seems to be saying that there is him or her, and then there is everybody else, the 'little people'.

Sad to say, but when leaders really act like leaders, people notice because it's a relatively rare event. When hard times hit at Nucor, a steel company in North Carolina, some years ago, the then president Ken Iverson took a 60 per cent cut in pay. As one compensation expert said at the time, 'It makes a real difference if employees see that their CEO is willing to take it in the shorts along with them.' Herb Kelleher, CEO of Southwest Airlines feels the same: 'If there's going to be a downside, you should share it.' When Southwest had some hard times a few years ago, Kelleher went to the board to cut his salary by 20 per cent, and the salary of officers was cut by 10 per cent. He also leads by trying to understand the employee perspective and intently listening to employees' direct feedback, something a narcissist would never do. But apparently even Kelleher has limits. As he said: 'I don't mind their tracking dirt across my rug, but I just wish they'd stop calling me shithead in front of the customers.' But just joking in this way illustrates he 'gets it' when it comes to leading.[6]

Lack of Proper Controls

We've already described narcissistic leaders as people who enjoy exercising power to serve their own interests, and who have no compunction about manipulating others to foster their personal agendas. These characteristics alone would suggest that control systems, if they exist, might easily be bypassed by the narcissist when convenient. Or, alternatively, narcissists might apply control systems in a rigid or manipulative way when it proves advantageous.

One area of abuse is the chain of command. Narcissists are often quite skilled at violating the chain of command up the line even while simultaneously enforcing it rigidly among subordinates. This undercuts the authority and credibility of subordinates' direct reports – something that they are then held accountable for later!

Another key control lever is the human resource system. Among other things, this refers to performance appraisal systems, development and measurement of standards, and rewarding above-standard performance, all of which can be abused and perverted by narcissistic leaders for their own purposes.

Before we leave this section, consider this. Many corporations are going electronic with their control systems, for everything from finances to human resource management to communications. And therein lies the potential for many high-tech forms of abuse. In fact, there's already considerable discussion about the techno-tricks that savvy narcissists can play with caller ID, voice mail screening, blind carbon copies of e-mails, and electronic scheduling (eg someone's intranet schedule lists eight important people at his or her key meeting, when only four will be there).

One executive with arguably narcissistic tendencies developed this little scam. When subordinates commit to a project deadline, he sends them an e-mail acknowledgement. Next, he spends less than a minute to write a quick follow-up note that asks a couple of general questions that will require considerable time and effort to answer. Now here's the catch. The executive programmes his computer to send these notes to subordinates just a few days before the agreed-on deadlines. The notes are automatically postmarked between midnight and 2 am, which makes it look as though the executive is up working into the wee hours. To many subordinates, the executive is scary – he appears to be on top of everything. Others wonder about the timing and suspect games-manship, but they can't prove which e-mails are 'live' and which aren't. At least not yet. And what about the distrust and cynicism that such scams may be breeding? Here's what the perpetrating executive had to say: 'What's the big deal? I'm not really misleading anyone. I'm just using the network to be there when I can't. Do you really think I'd be a better manager if I personally sent the e-mail at midnight the week before?'[7]

Yes, we do. And a more honest one to boot.

Summing Things Up

In summary, there are several distinctive management practices that characterize narcissistic leaders. Whether you look at their 'skills' in the areas of planning, organizing, leading, or controlling, there are often some very serious deficits. Each of these skills brings you back to a management 101 class – the basics that most managers should be aware of and should work on mastering. Yet narcissists have great difficulty in doing so. Or, alternatively, they have mastered the 'dark' side of their craft by perpetrating abuses in these areas. Regardless of the reason, living with their management practices is one of the most irritating and annoying aspects of working for narcissists.

STRATEGIES FOR DEALING WITH POOR ADMINISTRATIVE PRACTICES

So what can be done to deal with the poor administrative practices of narcissistic regimes?

Disperse Decision-Making and Planning

An organization-wide emphasis on sharing input and planning provides a number of possible benefits. These might include methods for various groups to have input into strategic planning, such as improvement/quality committees, bottoms-up communication tactics, and 360-degree feedback. Will these input methods work? Will they prevent narcissists from consolidating power and wreaking havoc? In many cases, the answer will be no. All the methods mentioned can be perverted and abused by narcissists already in the corporation.

Nevertheless, these mechanisms act as hurdles that narcissists must clear. And sometimes they will. As we have shown, narcissists can find ways around input filters of the type we're suggesting. And more insidiously and dangerously, they are also quite good at co-opting these input mechanisms to their advantage. This is more threatening because to higher-ups it can appear that the input mechanisms are working and that things are going well. But the more checks that are in place, the more likely it is that narcissists will eventually be tripped up. In our view, this process is akin to what safety experts say about home security. If narcissists want to get into your 'house', an alarm isn't going to stop them. At the same time, having an alarm gives them less time to loot the place.

Form Coalitions

Narcissistic leaders are often adept at undercutting people and playing sides off against each other. As we have documented, this can happen in any number of ways, making coalitions or partnerships with potential allies a reasonable countering strategy. This can be personally dangerous, especially if your coalition decides to confront the narcissist directly at some point. After all, we've pointed out that even the mildest of suggestions is likely to be viewed by narcissists as unacceptable criticism.

Build Information Networks

Building information networks can aid and abet more subtle approaches. One of the best weapons in the narcissist's arsenal is control over information. Narcissistic leaders are especially good at manipulating information, perhaps better than anybody around them really understands. But the truism that information is power cuts both ways. Make contacts with managers in other groups and feel them out on the administrative issues of concern, as we discussed in Chapter 3. This is a tricky process because, as you'll recall, the narcissist has probably tried to play one (or more) of the groups against another. In fact, in later chapters, we'll point out that strongly divided camps or fiefdoms are an invitation for the narcissist to take or consolidate power in the first place.[8] Nevertheless, if you start an information pipeline flowing, it will help in the process of exposing narcissistic abuses and countering narcissistic lies and disinformation.

Consider Playing Hardball Yourself

On the other hand, people can resort to more hardball tactics, risky as that can be. This prompts an obvious criticism: aren't you sinking to the narcissist's level? Not necessarily. Plus, employees who have spoken to us about this topic have suggested that sometimes drastic steps are the only real option, apart from quitting outright.

This includes many of the 'guerrilla' tactics discussed in previous chapters. We won't rehash all the details here, but we will briefly mention a few of the more important hardball strategies for dealing with administrative abuses. For instance, you can report the narcissist's misdeeds to higher-ups (either anonymously or not, depending on both the severity of the narcissist's behaviour and the likely backlash). If there are no higher-ups (eg your boss is the owner) or they've been co-opted (eg the board are all cronies of the CEO), then some sort of outside intervention or whistle-blowing is an option.

Lying Low and Getting Out

Finally, quitting is always an option, though perhaps not a very fulfilling one. Quitting can leave you feeling powerless and defeated. But you can try to seize the moral high ground by spilling your guts on the way out: at least that way you can walk away with a clear conscience. If the company chooses not to act on your information, then that's its responsibility.

Then there's the often-mentioned strategy of lying low. Although not without some problems of its own (eg you have to lie pretty low to get off the narcissist's radar screen, and it can deflate self-esteem and build cynicism over time), lying low also has distinct pluses. Staying out of the fray allows you to focus on looking around for a new job, within or outside the company. It also decreases your profile as a target for narcissistic abuses. Overall, lying low may put you in a better position to get out quickly before you get fired – or before things go so badly that your suffering increases to the point where taking more unpleasant action becomes irresistible. But in the final analysis, how long you can lie low depends on:

▦ your own mental toughness and coping skills;
▦ how closely you have to work with the narcissistic leader;
▦ your job and career options;
▦ how much power and influence the narcissistic leader has;
▦ how much power and influence you have;
▦ how much power and influence potential allies have.

CHAPTER TAKE-AWAYS

▨ Narcissists are notoriously bad managers – one of the most irritating things about working for them day in and day out.

▨ Among other things, narcissists are particularly poor planners, organizers, leaders and controllers, the four classic aspects of management.

▨ Narcissists plan badly. The many projects they take on – or more precisely that they assign to others – are often overblown, with very little attempt made to prepare for roadblocks along the way.

▨ Narcissists are poor organizers as well: they float in and out of projects at unpredictable times. The same is true for their delegation decisions. On the one hand, they are notorious for dumping (not truly delegating) lots of details. On the other hand, when their pet projects come under scrutiny, narcissists reverse gears and become intolerable micro-managers. This flip-flopping may be their most important management deficit.

▨ Suggestions for dealing with the poor administrative practices of narcissistic leaders include direct and indirect strategies. Putting policies and procedures into place to involve more people in decision-making can help. Opposing the narcissist by forming coalitions or creating an information network to expose abuses are also options. Sometimes, however, external whistle-blowing may be necessary. Finally, subordinates can lie low until the narcissistic leader leaves, or until they can find a suitable job elsewhere.

Chapter 7

Responding to flawed visions and perceived infallibility

ME, MYSELF AND I

Narcissistic infallibility: Making a bad problem worse

I work for a publicly held company. Our president believes in growing the company by acquiring other privately held companies. He thought this was ideal because he didn't have to deal with getting approval from a company's shareholders. What he would do instead was get to know the family owners of these private companies and convince them to sell over a period of time. It got around that if you wanted a fat price for your company, you could simply approach our president, act friendly and flatter him. Unfortunately, the 'relationships' our president developed caused him to overlook serious ethical flaws in many of the owners of the companies we acquired. We were left to deal with the mess and expense of things like pollution cleanup and replacing unlicensed software in these companies.

Manager, food processing company

On a big reorganization project he was managing, my boss made two or three really bad decisions. They involved his deliberate efforts to increase the scope of the project. He became extremely angry when several members of our team tried to talk him out of it and share their concerns about the risks. A bigger project would make him look good, but was needlessly expensive. Although the decisions to enlarge things created major problems once the project implementation started, he never referenced his mistakes.

Supervisor, consumer products manufacturer

VISIONS FROM HELL

You run a company according to good, sound business principles. But what are good, sound business principles? Good, sound business principles are what the president says they are.[1]

Harry V Quadracci, co-founder and president, Quad/Graphics

If you're not familiar with Harry Quadracci and Quad/Graphics, consider this. The printing firm that Quadracci co-founded in 1971 had over $1.4 billion in sales in 1999 and is the largest privately held printer in the US. Quad/Graphics also has a strong culture and is known as a great place to work for its over 11,000 employees. Clearly, Quad/Graphics is a success story. So why this quote in a chapter about flawed visions? To put it simply, these words underscore the damage that pathological narcissists can do when they reach senior leadership positions.

Granted, how much power and discretion a top leader actually has over a firm's fate is a complex issue. Real discretion is a function of things like the firm's internal organization (eg culture, size and resources available), its external environment (eg the strength of competitors, growth potential in the industry and market demand stability) and the characteristics of the top leader (eg his or her ego, ambition and political acumen). Nevertheless, senior managers typically have enormous discretion, especially relative to junior counterparts.[2]

That fact alone certainly attracts narcissists to senior executive jobs. And the more discretion on the plate, the more narcissists believe they'll be able to play the corporate equivalent of swashbuckling hero, doing exactly what they want and earning plenty of fame in the process. That's fundamentally what discretion is for narcissists – a big window of opportunity to change things and cover themselves with glory. As you've probably surmised, this will become a self-reinforcing situation. In fact, the narcissistic tendency will be to grab as much discretion as they can get once they land a top slot. So, putting a narcissist in a senior position is likely to increase the degree of discretion already inherent in the job. Having discretion is what enables narcissists to write their own rules and disguise their personal vision as a corporate one.

Of course, inflicting a self-focused vision on a company may propel it into the proverbial pit. And stopping a narcissistic vision will prove difficult, especially for subordinates. First, you're up against a high degree of managerial power, as we've just mentioned. Plus, as we've said before and will say again, change seems ubiquitous these days, making the supposed need for 'vision' in business stronger than ever. Combine those perceptions with a narcissistic leader in a senior position and you've got big trouble. Today, firms are expected to have a 'vision for the future', and narcissists can easily use that vision as a cloak or cover story for their own need fulfilment. The visions that narcissists create for their companies are reflections of their own flawed and bifurcated personalities. Fundamentally insecure, they compensate by pursuing delusions of grandeur, and operate as if they possessed a kind of infallibility, where nothing and no one can harm them. Toss in some decent interpersonal skills – including the ability to charm and turn a phrase – and you'll often find plenty of employees who willingly follow the narcissist's dream. Just like lemmings running off a cliff.

Our Vision for This Chapter

So here's how things will unfold in this chapter. First, we're going to sketch out how bad narcissistic visions can be for the bottom line. For instance, research suggests a connection between narcissistic leadership and flawed acquisitions. Next, we'll explain in some detail how narcissism infects the process of creating and implementing a corporate vision. After all, before you can combat narcissistic 'visioning', you should fully understand what you're dealing with and be able to spot the warning signs, including how subordinate needs can once again make them co-conspirators. Finally, we'll address the issue of how to cope with narcissistic visions. That's a tall order, especially if the company is privately held and there's a narcissistic owner at or near the top. And public companies are no picnic either, even though there are more potential leverage points to work with (eg outside investors and greater government regulation).

Visions of Narcissistic Grandeur. . . and Acquisition Pain

Research has found that people tend to be more accurate judging others' performance than their own, especially on important or 'ego-involving' tasks. Specifically, most of us suffer from what experts call 'a self-serving bias' when evaluating our own abilities and performance: we think we're a bit better than we actually are. Many experts will tell you some self-serving perceptions are normal, if not healthy. But some people are excessively and unrealistically positive about their abilities and accomplishments. And guess what? Studies suggest that those people are likely to be narcissists. Put another way, narcissistic personalities tend to project high self-regard and infallibility, in part to live up to grandiose images of themselves and their strong desire to feel superior. Especially interesting is that as the stakes rise – when the job at hand is very ego-involving and failure would prove devastating – narcissists may puff themselves up and exaggerate their omnipotence even more.[3]

We've brought these ideas up here because they help explain the grandiose scheming and 'visionary excess' that we see in the corporate arena. In fact, we'd argue that one of the best places to see this in action is in the merger and acquisition game. It's one area where many narcissistic leaders get to play out their fantasies. Of course, acquisition fever has been running hot in the US for some time and, increasingly, European firms are taking the same road.[4]

So how many times have you heard this story line recently? A CEO comes along with a grand vision, absolutely convinced that once an 'underperforming company' is acquired, his or her 'management skills' will turn the place into a money tree. In many cases, excessive narcissism is driving these acquisitions. After all, the CEO is typically the executive with the most discretion when it comes to acquisition decisions, including what price is offered. And it turns out that there's good evidence linking CEO egotism to acquisition decisions.

The fact is that all too often CEOs end up overpaying to acquire a target company, in some cases shelling out an enormous premium to the firm's actual market value. And instead of rolling in the profits generated by the 'synergies' that the acquired firm was supposed to provide, the CEO and the acquiring company often end up no better, if not worse, off. The reality is that acquisitions rarely result in significant improvements in the long-term profitability of the acquiring firm. Actually, declines in the acquiring firm's profitability are more likely. And, as the cost of the acquisition increases, so do the odds that the deal will blow up in the CEO's face.

This doesn't necessarily mean that such acquisition snafus are the result of narcissism. A cynic might argue that sheer stupidity is a better explanation. But that's too simplistic. There's little doubt that a variety of factors may explain failed acquisitions (eg unexpected economic turmoil). Nevertheless, research suggests that many CEOs become irrational as the acquisition process unfolds, ignoring information about potential risks. Buoyed by their own egos, they are swept up in the euphoria associated with taking control of the target company.

Obviously, exaggerated self-confidence is the wellspring of narcissism. It's what propels narcissistic leaders on their flights of fancy and is necessary to keep repressed insecurities at bay. As a consequence, CEOs who suffer from these narcissistic excesses are often willing to throw piles of cash at a firm because of their mistaken belief that they can turn the acquisition into a testimonial for their own greatness. In essence, they assume that the high price they pay up front will eventually be paid back by all the money they'll be able to squeeze out of the acquired firm – once it's 'properly led'. That basic assumption turns out to be the key driver of many ill-advised acquisition decisions.

What's fascinating is how research actually connects CEO narcissism to acquisition prices. In one study, researchers created an index of CEO hubris and investigated what role it played in 106 public acquisitions that cost $100 million or more each. This index consisted of three basic parts, considered below, all of which predicted the CEO's willingness to overpay for the acquisition in question.[5]

'If we're doing well, I'm the cause'

As we've said earlier in this book, narcissistic leaders tend to be credit-stealers. So if the organization is reasonably successful, it stands to reason that a CEO with narcissistic tendencies will take personal credit for it, even if more objective success factors are present. Put simply, the narcissistic CEO wants to believe that 'since I'm here, it must be me'. In fact, an analysis of annual reports over a two-decade period found that senior leaders consistently portrayed themselves as the reason why good things happened in the company, but blamed periods of bad performance on 'outside' or 'environmental' factors.[6] In any event, firm successes build up the reputation and stature of the CEO, deserved or not. This simply fuels the narcissistic craving for glory and adoration: the CEO can do anything and achieve everything. Consistent with this was the finding that the better an acquiring firm had done in the previous 12 months (as measured by shareholder returns), the bigger the premium the CEO was willing to pay to buy the target company's stock.

Hyping the leader: The media's role

The second part of the index involved media praise. As we noted back in Chapter 1, the business media often paint larger-than-life pictures of top executives, portraying them as corporate heroes and romanticizing their accomplishments. The study counted the number of articles about CEOs published in major newspapers and business magazines in the three years leading up to the acquisition. The result? As the number of favourable articles increased, so did the acquisition premiums paid! In fact, just one highly favourable piece was associated with a nearly 5 per cent increase in the premiums paid (ie about $50 million on a $1 billion transaction). You can do the arithmetic if a dozen glowing reviews are on the table! Once again, the idea here is that media exposure stokes narcissistic fires, fuelling the CEO's ego and reinforcing perceptions of infallibility. The bottom line is that CEOs end up believing their own press.

'I'm paid a bundle, therefore I am'

The final piece of the puzzle involves CEO compensation, one of our favourite topics! Unlike the average employee, CEOs often wield considerable influence over their own pay packages and those of top lieutenants. As a consequence, the ratio of the CEO's pay to that of the second-highest-paid executive is arguably a good indicator of the CEO's self-importance. And wanting to be the highest-paid as the 'top dog' certainly is consistent with the narcissistic behaviour pattern. Once again, as pay differentials rose (with some CEOs earning over 100 per cent more than the second-highest-paid executive), so too did acquisition premiums.

What about the board?

You may be wondering where the board of directors are in this picture. They certainly do play a role, but not always for the good. In fact, the connection between CEO narcissism and overpayment for acquisitions was strongest when board members weren't doing enough to protect shareholder value. This lack of diligence tended to occur when directors were mostly insiders – people more likely to be controlled or co-opted by the CEO. And board diligence could be undercut substantially if the CEO also chaired the board.[7]

Finally, who are the big losers in all of this? First, shareholders of the acquiring company are often losers: its stock often drops after an acquisition, sometimes precipitously. Adding insult to injury is the fact that CEOs' power and discretion can protect them if things go badly after an acquisition. For example, a form of ritualized scapegoating can occur. In essence, CEOs can pressure company directors into quitting, thereby creating the impression that they've been hamstrung all along by incompetent directors.[8]

CEOs may also be able to protect their treasure chests. For instance, in 1998 a group of executives at Cendant Corp. was accused of overstating the company's income by some $500 million. Not surprisingly, the firm's stock took a nosedive, wiping out $26 billion of shareholders' value. This all occurred after CEO Henry Silverman had acquired Cendant, with the alleged fraud taking place on his watch. Mr Silverman also stood to lose a lot financially. He was sitting on a $600 million paper loss since his 46 million stock options had fallen in value from around $800 million to a mere $200 million. But the company's board decided to reprice some of his options. One expert described the Silverman situation this way: 'The shareholders don't have that option for their investment. Why should he?'[9]

Then there are the employees who have to live through the turmoil associated with an acquisition, who may lose their jobs if things don't work out. Of course, the CEO's reputation can suffer too when things go awry. As one ex-CEO put it, 'You're remembered as the CEO who made the lousy acquisition'.[10] Needless to say, that possibility won't stop many chief executives from carrying out their acquisition plans. Take a look at the accompanying 'Me, Myself and I' box for some examples of CEOs who arguably wanted to 'make a big splash' to cap their careers.

ME, MYSELF AND I

Going Out with a Bang

We [CEOs] are all building monuments.

Ralph S Saul, former CEO of Cigna Corp.

While it may appear ludicrous to frame an acquisition in terms of the CEO's retirement date, that's often what seems to happen. As retirement looms, many top executives may be driven less by business imperatives than by a desire to go out with a bang – to leave a memorable and lasting personal legacy. They often seem compelled to make that last big splash. As one consultant put it, 'A desire for immortality causes chief executives to do deals on the back end'.

In a recent three-year period, over 70 per cent of the CEOs involved in large merger and acquisition deals were more than 60 years old. But it isn't age *per se* that we're talking about here: CEOs are older by definition. What's amazing is how often looming retirement dates and megadeals seem to coincide. For instance, just before he retired at 70, Thomas Murphy, former chairman of Capital Cities/ABC Inc, sold the firm to Walt Disney Company for $19 billion. And consider drug giant Novartis AG. The company is the product of a $27 billion merger between Ciba-Geigy AG and Sandoz AG, whose CEOs at the time, Alex Krauer and Marc Moret, were 65 and 72 respectively. In fact, one former Sandoz employee was quoted as saying that Mr Moret 'wanted to wrap things up nicely' by pulling off the merger before he retired.

But creating a lasting legacy isn't easy. Even if a deal is successful, the legacy can prove elusive. Retired Squibb CEO Richard Furlaud might be a case in point. In 1989, at the age of 66, he helped orchestrate Squibb's merger with Bristol-Meyers. Several years later, Mr Furlaud said that when calling his 'legacy' – Bristol-Meyers Squibb – 'the telephone operators don't know my name'.

Then there's the obvious problem of having your megadeal legacy wiped out by difficult problems that pop up later

But such cautionary tales are doing little to curb executives' appetites for mergers and acquisitions. In fact, complex three-way mergers are becoming increasingly popular. For example, in 1999 Alusuisse Lonza Group agreed to become part of a three-way deal with Canada's Alcan Aluminum and France's Pechiney. A few years back these kinds of deals would have been shot down as being too bold and too audacious. But no longer.

Of course, the risk of running into major problems on such complex deals is enormous. And as the number of companies involved increases, so does the potential for clashes of ego. That's especially the case if one or more of the companies is an unwilling partner. In fact, some experts say that the thorniest issues in complex acquisitions are always about managerial egos, whether or not the executives involved are retiring. Who the big boss of the new combined company will be is usually the subject of a considerable amount of infighting and acrimony.[11]

HOW NARCISSISTIC LEADERS ABUSE THE 'VISIONING' PROCESS

In this section, we'll describe in more detail how narcissistic leaders at senior levels create visions to serve their own selfish ends. Granted, narcissistic managers in all ranks can hide behind visions and use the 'need for change' to manipulate and abuse subordinates in the name of self-interest. But there are many reasons why narcissists in senior positions can pull this off more easily than those lower in the ranks. Obviously, senior positions come with more power and discretion, as we mentioned earlier. But another 'starting gate' advantage that senior-level narcissists possess is that relatively few people have a close-up view of their behaviour on a day-to-day basis. Plus, the actions (or inactions) of senior leaders tend to have delayed and indirect effects on the firm in any case. The upshot is this. Studies find that in the absence of precise information, people will simply assume that the performance of the firm is due to the leader's managerial panache. Middle-level managers, in contrast, are surrounded by subordinates, peers and superiors who can observe and quickly draw conclusions about the efficacy of their behaviour.

As a result, senior leaders are more likely to get the benefit of the doubt. Their relative isolation also allows them to control and stage their public behaviours more carefully for maximum effect. That can be quite helpful when executing a vision. For example, a narcissistic VP who wants to galvanize support and earn glory in the process could take advantage of (or manufacture) a crisis and then take highly visible actions to 'solve' it. Research shows that the dramatic approach gains more personal credit for the leader than engaging in more deliberate and less visible steps behind the scenes, which might have prevented the crisis in the first place.

That may explain why everyone knows who Lee Iacocca is: the 'saviour' of Chrysler and embodiment of the phrase 'heroic leader' (at least to some). But how about the name Philip Caldwell? Ring a bell? Probably not. Yet both men were CEOs in the 1980s, Iacocca at Chrysler and Caldwell at Ford. Iacocca's approach was more dramatic. He made a series of highly public moves: acquiring American Motors, doing TV commercials to promote his vision, orchestrating government help and capping things off with his autobiography. Likewise, when Caldwell became CEO, his company was in dire financial straits. But Caldwell's leadership was much less visible than Iacocca's. Caldwell pushed cultural and strategic changes at Ford behind the scenes, including a team-based approach to product development (which led to the highly successful Taurus). As a result, Ford steered itself to record profits in the mid-1980s: it was the only US car company to increase market share during that time. Despite Caldwell's relative obscurity outside the US motor industry, he was arguably as successful as Lee Iacocca.[12]

Charismatic Change and Narcissistic Visions

Perhaps another difference between Iacocca and Caldwell was charisma. Many of the most successful 'strategic visionaries' are judged to be charismatic by followers. And charisma seems easy to identify. We can all name larger-than-life leaders who possess tremendous skills, including the ability to inspire unbelievable effort to create positive change. Nelson Mandela and Franklin Delano Roosevelt would probably be on many lists. And ratings of leader charisma tend to be positively related to objective measures of firm performance.[13]

But charisma is a complex, two-edged sword. For every Abraham Lincoln, there's an Adolf Hitler. Most scholars view charisma as a unique interaction between the leader's skills and behaviours, subordinate needs, and the context.[14] Our view is that charisma is something we 'give' leaders as opposed to something they possess. In short, we see leaders as charismatic when it suits our own needs (eg the leader is someone we identify with or want to please). Those needs intensify if people feel vulnerable or are otherwise dissatisfied – say because the company is in a financial crisis and jobs are at stake. Of course, a narcissistic leader with some key skills (eg impression management, information manipulation and rhetoric) may be able to prey on such fears and convince subordinates that they can escape the current situation by following the leader's flawed vision.[15]

And that's really the crux of the issue for narcissists: how to get people to go along with their selfish agendas. All charismatic executives influence subordinates by tapping into their sense of self-worth, or lack of it. Again, the context can make this job easier. If a company is in trouble and the way out is unclear, the workforce will become angst-ridden and laden with self-doubt. This makes the idea of a charismatic hero who will rescue them all the more attractive.[16] But instead of trying to rally people by expressing confidence in them, narcissistic charismatics encourage dependency. They want people to identify with them personally, not with the company or the 'mission' *per se*. They crave adoration and want weak and dependent followers who offer unquestioned loyalty and obedience.

A vision can help narcissists accomplish these goals. First, narcissistic leaders can articulate an idealized goal for the future that's a huge change from the status quo. The trick is that only they are capable of seeing that future and leading people to it. This in itself is a warning sign that the vision is narcissistic. Plus, many experts argue that the vision should be seen as extremely challenging, but still within the realm of possibility.[17] But the narcissistic leader's vision often requires a leap of faith in the religious sense, because it's impossible to achieve without the narcissist's godlike powers. Of course, gods are different from the rest of us, making the unconventional and outlandish behaviours we talked about in earlier chapters more acceptable. In many cases, you'll see a Jekyll and Hyde type of performance, with unmitigated boldness, risk-taking, confidence and enthusiasm on the one hand, combined with 'wrath of God' abuse aimed at anyone who doesn't appreciate the leader's brilliance and foresight – especially when things start going wrong.

How far the act plays out depends on the level of the narcissist's skills and prior track record, which are intertwined. Impression management skills are among the narcissist's best weapons, as we've seen. Those skills can make previous Pyrrhic victories – if not outright defeats – sound pretty damn good. Plus, they can be used to disguise or deflect attention away from the leader's real motivations.

Sweating Over the Details and Narcissistic Vision

But ultimately, developing and executing a successful vision is hard, difficult work.[18] And as we've said, sweating over those details is something that narcissistic leaders tend not to be interested in. And why should they be? There's no need to do your homework when you project 100 per cent confidence and act as if every idea that tumbles out of your mouth will work simply because you said it!

In fact, some of the most successful visionaries are individuals who have spent enormous energy involving others in the development of the vision. They are also people who know that visions are fundamentally long-term propositions that require persistence, patience and objectivity about risks. Interestingly, it's questionable whether charisma has to be part of this equation at all, even in a crisis. Some experts studying this process note that many visionary leaders lack charisma: they aren't larger-than-life figures whose excesses we have to forgive.[19]

Former Motorola CEO Robert Galvin is a good example of what we mean. Galvin doesn't fit the rabble-rouser persona associated with many charismatic leaders. But there's little doubt that Galvin created an environment where Motorola could transform itself. In the early 1980s, Galvin concluded that Motorola was ill equipped to deal with the threat coming around the corner – an onslaught of tough Japanese competitors. Galvin had personally visited many of these firms and came away scared. And Motorola had become slow and complacent.

Over the next few years, Galvin tried to instil recognition of this threat. In the process he challenged assumptions about how Motorola was doing things and invited criticism. Galvin spent endless hours wandering around Motorola talking to employees about what was wrong with the firm and how it operated. Eventually, Galvin decided that the company's management and decision-making processes were key problems.

The next step was to manage the creation of a new vision. Once again, Galvin spent an enormous amount of effort trying to convince his senior managers to let go of their past successes, and figure out ways to deal with the Japanese threat. Galvin was also adamant that the people under him should flesh out the details of the vision and how to implement it. That was a smart move because it helped involve people and gained their commitment. The vision that emerged involved embracing constant corporate renewal. Instead of setting specific economic targets, the goal was to make Motorola an adaptive company, one employee at a time.

To implement and institutionalize the vision, Galvin supported new initiatives designed to 'shake the box'. Among the better-known examples were Motorola's Organizational Effectiveness Program (designed to help risky new inventions get developed quickly), its Six Sigma Program (designed to achieve a 'zero-defect' manufacturing environment) and Motorola University (where millions are spent annually to train employees).

Thanks to Galvin and thousands of Motorola employees, the firm enjoyed double-digit growth through the mid-1990s. But nothing lasts forever. By the late-1990s, Motorola had lost its way again. The firm was roughed up by industry changes, strategic blunders, managerial infighting and a new breed of foreign competitors, such as Finland's Nokia. Despite ongoing problems – such as the failed Iridium satellite project – Motorola seems ready to tackle the new millennium with vigour. At the helm is Bob Galvin's son Chris, who became CEO in 1997. His key themes are familiar: renewal and innovation. Clearly, the years ahead will be interesting ones for Motorola.[20] But even as an observer, Bob Galvin still takes the longest view: 'Motorola will be a $10 trillion company by 2040. You can't do that by selling a few more cellular phones – you have to get into new lines of business.' And the only way Motorola can create those new businesses is by encouraging employees to think counter-intuitively and by listening to any idea with potential.[21]

STOPPING THE NARCISSISTIC VISIONARY . . . OR AT LEAST NOT GETTING BURNT

We've said a lot about illusions in this chapter. But we're under no illusions about how difficult it may be to stop a narcissistic leader's flawed vision. In many cases, the most prudent thing you can do is to get out quickly. If your assessment is correct and things are going very wrong, going elsewhere will ensure that you – and your reputation – are not associated with a débâcle.

Know the Warning Signs

Nevertheless, there are options for sticking things out and trying to slow down the narcissistic vision machine. The first step involves recognizing what you're dealing with, a theme we've hit many times in this book. And some things bear repeating! In this case, you need to know the warning signs indicating that the vision or mission your company has been asked to pursue is the product of a narcissistic mind, and that employees may be receptive to it. Ask yourself these questions – a lot of 'yes' answers may mean you're in big trouble:[22]

- Is the company facing a severe threat or crisis that has raised employee anxieties and created self-doubt about their skills and ability to cope? Is the leader surrounded by a cohesive group of subservient lieutenants who share his or her views?
- Are employees otherwise inexperienced or dependent? Are they looking for someone to make decisions for them, and to guide and nurture them? Are they ready to idolize someone? Do they seem to suspend critical judgement when a potential 'hero' comes along?
- Is the vision closely tied to the leader's own persona, reputation, or past successes? Does it seem like a giant attention-getting device that merely builds on the leader's previous dreams? Does the leader personalize the vision when presenting it, essentially saying that only he or she can make things happen? Are employees asked to believe in and serve the leader as a result? Does the leader paint an exaggerated picture of how the marketplace and other constituencies will react to the vision?
- Does the vision strike you as bold, but not thought through? Does it seem too big, or too unrealistic? Does the leader neglect to mention risks or what might go wrong? Does the vision ignore obvious costs,

environmental forces, or internal constraints, which would preclude its accomplishment?

▓ Does the leader seem incapable of detecting market changes that would affect the vision? Does the leader seem unable to grasp the time and resources required to implement the vision? Has the leader failed to involve others in the development of the vision?

▓ When challenged on the vision, is the leader's response incoherent, autocratic, or irrational? Does the leader fail to explain how the challenges will be overcome, or what steps will be taken to figure them out? Is the leader's tone dismissive or threatening?

▓ When problems occur, does the leader first seem to be in denial? As problems persist, does the leader blame employees for letting him or her down? Do abusive behaviours typically follow, with many employees internalizing and accepting blame? Do some employees concoct a track record that justify the abuse? Do they refer to the leader's perfection or special attributes as excuses?

▓ Are the other symptoms of narcissistic leadership that we've described in earlier chapters present?

Some Action Options

If you conclude that there's a narcissist taking your firm on some visionary flight of fancy, what can you do about it other than exit? Part of the answer depends on where you are in the company and what your reputation is. The higher up you are and the more influence you possess, the better your chances. It's hard to knock down the vision from the mailroom!

Play devil's advocate

One thing everyone in the company can do is step back and try to be more clear-eyed about where things stand. Rhetoric aside, how does the vision stack up to reality? If you have doubts and concerns, investigate and document them. Then express them. Of course, there are many ways to do that. For example, if you are the lone dissenter in the group of managers surrounding the narcissistic leader, consider speaking up. At least you'll be on record if things go bad. And there are ways to raise questions that steer discussion, rather than putting threatening issues directly on the table immediately (eg lead off by asking a rhetorical question like 'I wonder how we could do better?' or 'How are our competitors handling this kind of thing? Is there anything we can learn from that?').

Alternatively, you could seek advice from relevant experts, either inside or outside the company. You could then bring that dissenting information to the group yourself (eg by presenting independent analyses of your situation) or ask outside experts to present it. But as we discussed in previous chapters, challenging the narcissist – even in a subtle fashion – risks a backlash. That risk has to be weighed against the possible benefits, such as being able to sway some minds. However, the odds won't be too good in a group where most of the members support the narcissist, out of either loyalty or self-interest. And narcissistic leaders typically listen to no voices save their own.

As a consequence, we've heard plenty criticism of these suggestions: that it's unrealistic for lower-ranking managers to take on the narcissistic leader, especially when the odds of success are poor. Plus, such managers are likely to be abused if not fired in the process. But our rejoinder is this: if your assessment is correct and you do nothing or keep silent, you're dead anyway. What's better, to be associated with a corporate disaster or to take the hits that go with standing up for what you believe? At least standing up allows you to look yourself in the eye when you get up in the morning. The other point we'd make is that your real target is not the narcissistic leader, but the people surrounding him or her. There's always the chance that you can win enough converts to stop or slow the runaway vision.

There are other options too, many of which we've touched on earlier. For instance, there are indirect, informational strategies aimed at spreading the word (about the flawed vision in this case) or at building a coalition to fight back behind the scenes. We won't rehash the details here, but suffice it to say that you could share your concerns (eg that the vision fails to account for key threats or to take advantage of major opportunities) with important players and constituencies, either inside or outside the firm. Whistle-blowing can be done informally or put in writing – both have pros and cons. Of course, there are behavioural options as well (sabotage, slow-downs, deliberately failing to execute, etc). Although dangerous, these can prove quite effective, especially if executed in a co-ordinated way.

The Executive Team: A Prevention Strategy

The best approach with narcissistic visions is not to let them get rolling in the first place. How? A glib answer might be not to put narcissists in management roles. And there are ways to screen out narcissists in the hiring process, as we discussed back in Chapter 5. Other glib answers are: a) don't hire weak, dependent employees; and b) don't let the company get into such trouble that employees become paralysed with self-doubt and thus more open to a narcissistic saviour.

But let's face it, most companies hit serious trouble at some point in their life cycles and hiring practices are never perfect. The real trick is to create a corporate environment that makes it more difficult for narcissistic leaders to abuse 'the vision thing', especially when the company is floundering or facing a crisis. Granted, these are long-term issues that have to be addressed over time. One option is to implement a team-based approach for decision-making among top managers.

We know mentioning 'team' and 'executive' in the same sentence will cause many eyes to roll and heads to shake. And there's reason to be concerned about teams, executive or otherwise. Most of the time, teams aren't nearly as effective as we'd like to believe. So we understand if people think that 'executive team' refers to some kind of ponderous, high-level 'committee' that:

- will have managers spinning their wheels to reach consensus and 'act like a team' on every issue;
- will be a colossal waste of time that prevents the firm from capitalizing on opportunities or beating back threats;
- requires managers to change their styles to be warm and fuzzy team players all the time.

But that's not what we're suggesting. It's true that top managers have very little time as it is to make decisions, much less spend it just on building group harmony. But that's precisely the point. The CEO can't do it all. Viewing the CEO as the 'great leader' who must make all important decisions and who determines whether the firm succeeds is a perspective that encourages narcissism. So where does that leave us? Experts suggest that effective executive teams require a balancing act between individual decisiveness and interpersonal synergy. That means being able to distinguish between situations or issues that require a truly collaborative effort and ones that don't, where the CEO makes the tough call alone. In other words, 'teamwork' and 'team effectiveness' aren't always synonymous. Here are some specific suggestions for building the kind of senior executive teams we're talking about:

- First, don't assume that the top executive group has to 'act as a team' all the time.
- Look for roles where executives can collectively assume responsibility (eg at Nordstrom, a US department-store chain, senior executives collectively perform the 'job' of chief operating officer, handling internal company operations).
- Look for 'pieces' of the firm's overall strategy that can be handled collectively or handed off to the individual executives with the most appropriate skills.
- Keep the elements of effective groups in mind when organizing the executive team (eg keep it small, look for complementary skills, set mutual working expectations and hold people accountable).
- Choose executives who can adapt and be flexible from a style perspective (eg team members have to learn to shift between their team and subordinate roles without undercutting the CEO's final authority).

Studies suggest that while executive teams are difficult to pull off in practice, they can make better strategic decisions, especially in areas where the CEO lacks knowledge and appropriate skills. Important tasks – like developing and implementing a vision – are also less likely to be neglected or executed badly. Furthermore, executive teams can help resolve thorny succession problems, especially in large, diverse organizations (something we address in more detail in Chapter 8). Finally, keeping the rest of the company informed about how the executive team operates helps blunt narcissistic excesses because it fosters a culture of openness, fairness and collaboration.[23]

Here's a case in point. Katherine Hudson is the CEO of US-based Brady Corporation, a $500 million manufacturer best known for its high-performance labelling and sign systems. When she took over a few years ago, she found a firm full of units and managers who competed against each other. Politics were rife and information rarely shared. Working with other senior executives, Hudson rewrote the corporate values statements to focus on collaboration and openness. Next, to attack the self-focused, competitive and 'us versus them' mind-set that existed, the trappings of executive power were removed, including managers' reserved parking spots. All employees were also put on a salary. But perhaps the cleverest idea was to take the executive team 'public'. The senior management team now invites a cross-section of all employees – nearly 10 per cent of the entire workforce – to corporate strategy sessions. The idea? To share information and allow people to watch how the decision-making process works at the top. Brady is now a more successful and innovative firm, thanks in part to the executive team and the changes they've inspired.[24]

CHAPTER TAKE-AWAYS

- Narcissistic leaders project high self-regard and infallibility. And as the stakes rise, they tend to puff themselves up even more. This can help explain their grandiose scheming and visionary excesses, including those seen in various mergers and acquisitions.
- Narcissistic CEOs are willing to throw cash at a firm because of their mistaken belief that they can turn the acquisition into a testimonial for their own greatness. For example, CEOs who are the subject of favourable articles in the press usually pay higher premiums to buy companies. The media exposure stokes narcissistic fires, fuelling the CEO's ego and reinforcing perceptions of infallibility.
- Instead of trying to rally people by expressing confidence in them, narcissistic visionaries encourage dependency. They crave adoration and want followers who offer unquestioned loyalty and obedience. A vision can help them accomplish their goals. How far they get depends on a variety of factors, including their skills (especially in impression management) and prior track record.
- There are signs that warn that a vision may be inspired by narcissism. These include: a) that the vision is closely tied to the leader's own persona, reputation, or successes; b) that the vision is extremely bold, but neglects implementation details, risks, obvious costs, environmental forces, or internal constraints; and c) that when problems occur, the leader blames employees for letting him or her down.
- Options for combating narcissistic visions include investigating and documenting your concerns, which might involve consulting with outside experts and asking them to share their views with key managers or constituencies within the company. You could also do this on your own, through a variety of formal (eg memo) or informal (eg grapevine) mechanisms.
- A prevention-oriented strategy would involve using an executive team to make major decisions. Such teams require a balancing act between individual decisiveness and interpersonal synergy.

Chapter 8

Responding to the failure to plan for succession

ME, MYSELF AND I

Want to eliminate the 'succession problem'? Just crush competence and initiative

My boss was the president of an upscale grocery-store chain. It was a family-owned business. How he managed to come out on top, I don't know. He kept all of his siblings in menial positions that had no line into management. The outside managers that were brought in never lasted more than three years before being driven away. As managers started to prove themselves, the president would start picking on them for small things until they couldn't take it any more. In one case, he was rifling through a manager's office because he 'needed a file'. He became upset because he couldn't find it and threw the manager's materials, papers and files, including everything on his desk, all over the floor and down the stairs leading to the office. He then demanded that the mess be left for the manager 'responsible for the missing file' to clean up when he returned. After he left, one of the other managers was told to make an announcement to every employee in the building to leave the mess as it was. Within a short time, the manager whose office was trashed quit. Because of this kind of harassment, there were no designated successors available and none in the pipeline. That was just the way he wanted it. I'm looking for a new job myself.

Store manager, retail grocery chain

Our 'leader' put together a 'succession plan' for our group, but never actually did anything to implement it or pursue individual development. The real goal of the plan was to show his superiors that he had a plan. There was never any intention on his part to use it. When employees became too productive or too assertive, he would feel threatened. Instead of developing these people, he would find a way to knock them down. If they resisted, he would run them out. In one case, he fired someone for 'insubordination' who happened to be an assertive individual and who was also the most productive person in the quality assurance department. That decision effectively shut down the department for six weeks, until he could hire a slave more to his liking.

Quality technician, chemical company

To get ahead with my boss, you had to be young, stupid and never challenge him. His closest subordinate was a young, weak and unskilled 'yes man'. We all had more experience and longer lists of accomplishments, but he went straight to the top. He was promoted seven times in two years from an entry-level position to the number two person in charge.

Software programmer, software/database marketing firm

I worked for her in an entry-level position where I seemed condemned to doing her dirty work – even emptying her trash. I often tried to offer my own suggestions or opinions on matters. These were met with extreme defensiveness or ridicule in every case. After repeated requests on my part to learn more complex things (she would always say I was not ready), I managed to transfer to another division. This embarrassed her. She told me I was wrecking my career and that I would fail. After that, she barely spoke to me again. Eventually, she moved up to corporate and I was brought back to replace her. When she left the company a short time later, I replaced her again. In both cases, she left absolutely no instructions or guidelines, and made no effort to hand over her office in an organized fashion. I always found her employees to be brain dead. They did no thinking on their own since she had told them that only she had the answers. She really wanted all her people to look up to her as a hero. I must have been crazy to follow her twice!

General accounting manager, manufacturer of power transmission equipment

IS THERE ANYONE TO HOLD THE FORT?

Maybe we should have said, 'Is there anybody *good* to hold the fort?' If a narcissist is running the place, the answer's likely to be 'no'. To narcissistic leaders, succession is a dirty word. Grooming someone signals that you're not indispensable and omnipotent after all. Somebody else has something to offer. And, horror of horrors, what if you find out in the process that your junior executive-in-waiting actually has a mind of his or her own? The 'succession problem' from a narcissistic perspective is not about finding and developing someone decent to take your place. If anything, it's about making sure a weak loyalist will step in, someone you can control if you decide to hang around. The result, of course, is that when you leave, die (perhaps murdered by your subordinates!), or disappear, your legacy will be a unit or company that's paralysed because: a) it's unclear who is supposed to step into the breach; or b) the heir apparent is one of your chosen lap-dogs who isn't worth a damn.

The irony of all this is that there's a burgeoning literature on how important things like good succession planning, management development and mentoring are for the long-term health of corporations. For instance, executives who have had a positive experience with a mentor are more likely to become mentors and be interested in truly developing their subordinates than executives who haven't.

But the view from the trenches isn't always so rosy. For every encouraging story about a powerful mentor who serves as teacher, role model and skill developer, there are examples of mentors who manipulate their protégés because they want to be seen as brilliant and inspiring. In such cases, a good argument can be made that the mentor is the one getting more out of the deal, at the protégé's expense. And mentoring experts warn that this fantasy life is a two-way street, with many protégés seeing their mentors as dominant, all-powerful parents, whom they are desperate to please. That can make both personal development and a sense of independence more difficult to achieve. One protégé seemed to reflect this slippery slope in describing her mentor as someone who 'had invented me'. In fact, it should come as no surprise that some experts have suggested that mentoring relationships can be fodder for a variety of narcissistic impulses and fantasies.[1]

So let's take a moment here to revisit a few narcissistic themes that are especially relevant to our focus in this chapter, managerial succession. Narcissistic leaders use their power to dominate and manipulate subordinates for their own selfish ends. They aren't interested in receiving suggestions and input from others, especially any implying criticism. Instead, narcissistic leaders thrive on the limelight and their own sense of self-importance. Not surprisingly, narcissists are insensitive to subordinates' needs and aspirations, except when they want to manipulate them.

Clearly, narcissistic leaders create an unhealthy developmental context in which the growth of potential successors is stunted if not extinguished to begin with. Narcissists attract and retain uncritical loyalists, who often have severe self-concept and skill deficits of their own. Dissenters will be eliminated and the narcissist will entertain only what he or she wants to hear.

In this chapter, we'll take a closer look at the succession planning process and how narcissism can wreak havoc with it. We'll also document the damage that poor succession planning can do. Finally, we'll offer some advice about how to develop and protect a legitimate succession planning process. As was the case in Chapter 7, you'll find that most of these suggestions go beyond what a single individual could be expected to accomplish, unless he or she is highly placed or has tremendous influence in the corporation. In other words, the best defence against narcissistic corruption of the succession process really revolves around the company's culture, policies and procedures.

SUCCESSION: A MESSY MYSTERY

There's arguably nothing more important to a company – and its employees – than who sits in leadership positions. And there's always plenty of turnover in the executive ranks. In fact, turnover at the very top may be accelerating as an entire generation of leaders approaches retirement. In 1997, almost 20 per cent of the CEOs at large US firms were over 62 years old, nearly double the 1993 figure. Plus, between 1998 and 2010 the number of managerial positions in the US is predicted to jump 21 per cent. Fortunately, the trailing edge of the baby boomer generation are hitting their mid-40s, so there should be an adequate talent base in the short run. But others worry that managers are less willing to put up with nonsense from their superiors than they used to be. With retirement accounts fattened by a rising stock market, more managers in the 55–64 age range seem willing to walk away than ever. In 1970, over 80 per cent of that age group were still working. But in 2000, only 66 per cent are expected still to be in the corporate game. And, as 2010 approaches, even the youngest of the baby boomers could be leaving in large numbers.[2]

While these figures may be somewhat overblown, they do under-score the importance of succession issues. In fact, many experts argue that succession decisions are important 'adaptive opportunity mecha-nisms' for corporations. Put more colloquially, new leadership blood supposedly helps firms change for the better. And some argue that outside blood is best, especially if the firm is suffering or in crisis. Outsiders are thought to be more objective than insiders, less committed to the firm's current failed or losing strategies (and therefore more likely to embrace needed changes) and less likely to put up with the various insider deals, scams, or quid pro quos that hamstring corporate performance.[3]

Of course, in many cases the reality is quite different. Rationality rarely rules. In fact, the track record on succession leaves much to be desired. Instead of a clear, organized and systematic process, succession too often resembles the crusades – bloody, mindless affairs driven by planet-sized egos. The blood-letting can be driven by the leader (who may want to crush up-and-coming rivals before they become threats) and by potential heirs (who may wage brutal wars against each other to win the right to succeed the boss). In other words, narcissism reigns supreme.[4]

Throw in an acquisition process and you have an even bigger mess. In an acquisition context, 'an aura of conquest' often envelops the players and drives succession-related decisions. As you saw in Chapter 7, the whole point of an acquisition, at least to a narcissist, is to experience intense feelings of dominance and superiority. When narcissistic feelings of disdain and inferiority are expressed toward executives in the acquired company, the executives tend to leave quickly and in droves rather than suffer. One senior manager who resigned shortly after his firm was acquired described his new leaders this way: '"We bought you. You belong to us. Fill out our forms. Come to meetings in our offices. Put our name on your stationery. If you want to go to the bathroom, ask us." They didn't quite put it that way, but that's the way I heard it.' Such departures can leave a huge management gap in the acquired firm, complicating integration efforts and potentially undercutting firm performance over the long term. The fact that acquisitions rarely produce the expected returns may reflect, at least in part, the influence of narcissism in general and the large-scale exodus of acquired managers in particular.[5]

On the other hand, a crisis may prompt a different set of succession problems, with narcissistic leaders fighting tooth and nail to hang on. For example, narcissistic leaders will scapegoat junior executives, especially those that are weak and unable to fight back effectively. That way, the narcissist survives while subordinates are sacrificed.

But at some point – crisis or not – a successor proves inevitable. In that case, narcissistic leaders often want to control the process to ensure that only a weak, but loyal, successor will take over. This allows them to pull strings from behind the scenes (say from a seat on the board). This goal may be more attainable to the extent that the narcissist: a) has been able to cultivate a subservient board; and b) has managed to keep competent executives from having much exposure to the board (which could make the narcissist look expendable).

Needless to say, the company can get hurt in the process. For example, studies suggest that in the absence of a crisis, outsiders hired into senior management positions tend to fail, and their companies do less well than if insiders are hired. The reason? Passed-over managers take their rage out on the outside interlopers, causing them – and the company – considerable grief in the process. Other studies show that when the CEO has extensive influence over the board of directors, performance criteria can become 'decoupled' from the succession decision.[6]

The 'bail out' process we referred to above isn't limited to mergers and acquisitions. Sometimes the announcement of a leader's departure sparks especially brutal succession battles. Afterwards, the losing candidates may leave in droves, causing massive internal headaches and triggering a domino effect of new, expensive searches and succession battles down through the ranks. Some firms in this situation have tried retention bonuses to salve the losers' wounded egos. But if the wrestling match involves narcissistic managers willing to bludgeon their way to the top, then power and glory will matter more than a payoff. In short, they'll leave unless they win the job they want.

Of course, sometimes you have narcissism on both ends. On one side is a narcissistic CEO who hangs on too long and trashes potential successors in the process, especially those that shine a bit too brightly for comfort. On the other side are narcissistic managers willing to push, fight and ultimately take their game elsewhere if stymied.

Sometimes leaders refuse to put a succession plan into place. In fact, one survey found that less than 30 per cent of CEOs who had been on the job for at least 10 years had given any thought to a successor, much less spent any time grooming one.[7]

So let's say Disney's Michael Eisner is killed riding Thunder Mountain. Or that Herb Kelleher dies because one of his Southwest Airlines jets crashes – and he's on it. What would happen next? While it's anyone's guess about how succession issues would play out, there's little doubt that the companies involved would experience plenty of turmoil and plunging stock prices in the short term. Plus, there's a good chance that the turmoil would actually be prolonged without a clear succession plan. That could result in significant setbacks in the marketplace as competitors zero in to take advantage of a distracted company.

And ironically, the more success a company has, the more the CEO is given the credit, and the less pressure there often is to plan the succession. For instance, Southwest CEO Kelleher leads one of the world's most admired airlines, one that's been profitable for more than 20 years straight. But at least through mid-1999 there was reportedly no obvious succession plan in place, much less an heir apparent. Part of the problem is that Kelleher is one of those larger-than-life figures who embodies the company he helped create. Kelleher has managed to create a firm that is a direct – and highly successful – reflection of his own vivacious and outgoing personality.

But the point we want to make here is that because the corporate culture is Southwest's primary competitive advantage, the next CEO virtually has to be an insider. And none of Southwest's current executives measure up to Kelleher on the flamboyance meter. Some think Southwest is in for a very rough ride unless Kelleher manages to clarify the succession picture. Those concerns were heightened recently when it was announced that Kelleher had prostate cancer.[8]

However, even if a clear succession plan is in place, few people inside or outside the company are likely to know about it. Firms tend to be reluctant to discuss succession issues in any case, mainly to avoid public battles, divisiveness and infighting among potential successors. For instance, General Electric CEO Jack Welch is said to place a high value on succession planning and puts enormous effort into developing senior leaders, so much so that GE is a favourite hunting ground for corporate recruiters. But Welch doesn't talk about the process or which executives are in the running to succeed him when he steps down in late 2000. Some claim that the field has been winnowed down to two: Jeffrey Immelt (head of GE medical systems) and W James McNerney (head of GE aircraft engines). But since no one at GE is talking officially, the rumour mill is the only game in town.

IMPROVING THE SUCCESSION PLANNING PICTURE: KEEPING NARCISSISTIC LEADERS AT BAY

In this section, we turn our attention to improving the succession process in ways that will limit narcissism. As we mentioned, most of our suggestions will involve policy, procedural and cultural issues that need to be dealt with on a company-wide basis. That's especially true for the first part of this section, where our focus will be on senior leadership. In fact, we've already touched on some procedural issues that are relevant in previous chapters. For example, putting procedures into place designed to screen out managers with severe narcissistic tendencies is certainly something of value in the succession process. That advice was presented back in Chapter 5 and we won't repeat it here. But there are some additional points that we would like to offer that could help reduce narcissistic interference in the succession process and prevent narcissistic managers from rising through the ranks in the first place.

Improving Succession at the Top

CEO succession is a complex issue. There's the issue of finding somebody worthy. Then there's the problem of how to handle things once a successor is found. For example, some experts advocate making an announcement about the chosen successor as soon as possible. That kind of communication can refocus efforts on the transition process. Advance notice may be helpful if the successor is following a successful founder or an otherwise 'legendary' CEO. Abrupt transitions can, among other things, slash investor confidence (ie stock prices).

But the succession endeavour is much more challenging if the current CEO is narcissistic, and determined to obstruct or manipulate the process. And even when narcissistic CEOs have left their positions, they may not really be gone. In fact, they sometimes manage still to run things after stepping down, if not lying in ambush to take out their successors.

So what to do? As we've suggested in previous chapters, a good first move might be to step back and diagnose the current leadership situation. That will help dictate how quickly the company needs to move to implement some of the ideas presented below. Look for these warning signs of narcissistic trouble:

- Is the CEO not doing well? Is he or she acting belligerently or irrationally, or manifesting other narcissistic characteristics? Is the company suffering as a result?
- If the answers above are 'yes', have some board members failed to notice or chosen to ignore the behaviours?
- If the search for a successor is already under way, has the CEO: a) been allowed to control the search process or demanded to run it personally; and b) stated that he or she still wants to keep the CEO job?

Of course, if many of these warning signs are present, re-establishing control over the succession process will probably be difficult. In this case, it might be wise to ask a board member – or better yet the majority – to approach the narcissistic CEO and request that he or she: a) relinquish control of succession to the board; and b) set a specific retirement or resignation date, which the board will then enforce. Much will depend, however, on how many board members are willing to stand up to the narcissistic leader. And, as we discussed in previous chapters, forming coalitions behind the scenes with other board members or investors first might be necessary. Likewise, an intermediate goal might be to prompt even more irrational behaviours from the narcissistic leader, who will tend to lash out when threatened. That could help drive more people away from the narcissist and engender support for a coup.

But as you might suspect, prevention is the best medicine. Steps should be taken to prevent the succession process from being hijacked by a narcissistic CEO in the first place. That means that the board will have to play a strong, independent role in the selection of a successor. In fact, the board can supply invaluable pressure if a narcissistic CEO needs to be pushed. And typically such CEOs do need to be, since thinking about and grooming a successor is simply too threatening. For narcissists, succession planning is about as attractive as writing a will. Below are some suggestions for carrying out an effective succession process – one that will limit narcissistic influences. An important prerequisite for these suggestions is that board members are selected for their independence as well as their expertise. The board must be largely free of undue influence from the CEO for the recommended process to work. Granted, this is a tall order and may strike you as a chicken–egg type of paradox. Nevertheless, the board is the key to preventing narcissistic CEOs from pushing through weak successors whose only real 'strength' is devotion to the narcissist. Fewer weak candidates will be brought forward, much less make it past the scrutiny of the board, if these policies are followed:

- **Make the board ultimately responsible for succession planning outcomes.** For example, in 1997 Campbell Soup Co.'s board put a succession committee in place to handle the transition from retiring CEO David Johnson. All committee members were outside directors. The committee identified internal candidates and hired a search firm to recruit outside candidates. After narrowing the combined list of over 20 candidates to five, the committee embarked on a whirlwind of intensive interviewing that involved many company constituencies. In the space of a few months, the committee met 15 times. Eventually, insider Dale Morrison was tapped as the new CEO. Many critics have suggested that Campbell's process is an outstanding model that other companies should follow.
- **Link CEO pay to helping with the succession plan and grooming of high potential talent.** For instance, Ralston Purina Co. tied a portion of ex-CEO William Stiritz's compensation to helping the board find a worthy successor.
- **Nurture a succession culture where talented managers are rotated through developmental assignments to enhance skills.** That's essentially what Whirlpool Corp. is trying to do. It has a huge room, referred to as 'the bunker', where all 500 of its top managers are tracked. Pictures and names of managers are tacked up on the walls, which are illustrated by regions of the world where the company does business. The only discussions allowed in the room are about management development and succession planning, including the assessment of the progress being made by the managers whose pictures decorate the walls.
- **Have board members meet internal candidates regularly in several settings, then review and assess them relative to promising outsiders.** That's something that General Electric CEO Jack Welch insists on. Promising executives are routinely asked to present to the board of directors and to meet with them in a variety of social and business settings.
- **Have the board and CEO meet regularly to discuss succession issues, including crisis situations (eg who takes over if the CEO drops dead).** That's what happens at Corning Inc., where board

members are expected to digest fat briefing books on promising candidates for all senior executive positions before meeting regularly to focus on succession issues and management development.[9]

Improving Succession and Management Development Across the Company

Of course, succession at the top is simply the most visible part of an issue that has an impact on management down through the ranks. The ability to institutionalize good succession planning and management development practices throughout the company is arguably the best long-term weapon for preventing narcissistic leaders from gaining a foothold anywhere. The next two sections offer some suggestions.

Make leadership development important – then measure and reward

This means that the company has to identify what leadership skills, abilities and attributes are most necessary. Next, systematic efforts should be made to develop and measure them across the board. In fact, all managers should be drilled on the importance of developing subordinates and identifying successors. That's how many of the best companies thrive – by identifying, harnessing and developing their managerial horsepower, and then spreading it through the company. Here's what General Electric CEO Jack Welch – whom many consider a passionate advocate of corporate-wide leadership development – had to say on the subject: 'This is all about moving intellectual capital – taking ideas and moving them around faster and faster and faster.' Indeed, Welch has said that the most important challenge facing GE today is 'globalizing the intellect of the company'. Many GE managers spend an incredible amount of effort on leadership development and related 'people issues'. Even in overseas subsidiaries, far from the company's Connecticut headquarters, GE managers often report that people development eats up 30–50 per cent of their time. Welch also set a good example, personally reviewing the progress and talents of some 3,000 high-potential employees annually.[10]

But strong measurement and reward systems are needed to underscore and institutionalize the importance of leadership development. For instance, the US Army promotes soldiers based on the successful completion of specific assignments, the demonstrated mastery of certain skills and the learning acquired at designated schools and

ME, MYSELF AND I

Give it up. . . for good

Now here's some real succession planning of the personal kind. Your retirement date looms. No more CEO, no more perks. And you have to give up your seat on the board of directors when the big day comes, right? Well, maybe not. Boards of companies as diverse and as well known as Dupont, Procter & Gamble, and USX all have had ex-CEOs as board members at some point. Granted, there are cases where it might be prudent to keep the ex-CEO around to tap his or her intellect and experience. Intel might be a case in point, where ex-CEO Andy Grove still serves on the board. But Grove developed a close partnership with his successor, one that recognized both the new boss's authority and a mutual freedom to agree to disagree at times.

Unfortunately, Grove's role as ex-CEO is unusual. Real partnerships with successors are still all too rare. More common is the situation where the ex-CEO interferes with – if not runs – the company from his or her board seat. And sometimes the ex-CEO decides that absence makes the heart grow fonder. In short, the CEO's role becomes simply too precious to be without. And if you're still on the board as ex-CEO, it's the perfect platform from which to mount a palace coup and retake the throne from your unlucky successor.

This underscores what many critics have been saying: that company directors would be wise to think carefully before allowing an ex-CEO to remain on (or near!) the board. That's especially true in the following circumstances:

- **Most of the board was appointed by and is still loyal to the ex-CEO.** That makes independent thinking unlikely, especially if the ex-CEO is still sitting there and offering opinions – as most tend to do!
- **The ex-CEO has done a lousy job of grooming a successor.** This suggests that the ex-CEO will find it tough to give up power and has narcissistic tendencies. Keeping that person on the board invites meddling and interference.
- **The company faces a major crisis.** In this case, the new CEO shouldn't have to tiptoe around making needed changes because doing so might imply criticism of the old regime.

But isn't there a way to have your cake and eat it too? What if the ex-CEO does have some valuable perspectives or insights to share? What then? Former Citicorp CEO Walter Wriston – who resigned from the board when his successor took over – offered this straightforward advice: 'If the new CEO wants to tap the perceived wisdom and experience of the retired CEO, a telephone call or a quiet meeting does not require a board seat.'[11]

training programmes. This is something of an irony (and the subject of Chapter 12) since narcissism is no stranger to military leaders, even among those seen as highly successful (eg General George S Patton, Jr of Second World War fame).

Managers should have a significant part of their compensation tied to how well they provide subordinates with challenging assignments, developmental feedback, skill-building experiences and appropriate training opportunities. These developmental moves should be tied to a specific career counselling plan developed jointly by managers and subordinates, with markers in place to indicate whether the subordinate is ready to move on to the next level. At General Electric, for example, all managers rank their staff members on leadership skills and their ability to contribute to the company's 'organizational vitality'.

Of course, the appropriate use of these criteria and assessments also needs to be measured if managers are to be appropriately rewarded for their leadership development efforts. For instance, what the job managers are doing in nurturing talented subordinates can be evaluated using a carefully implemented 360-degree feedback system in combination with other yardsticks (eg types of training subordinates attended, how much developmental feedback can be documented, improvements in key skills areas, and the number of quality job rotation and challenging project opportunities provided).

Create a leadership development infrastructure

But creating a leadership infrastructure goes beyond measurement and reward systems. We've alluded to training and skill-building opportunities as being important parts of the leadership development picture. But those things don't just happen by themselves. Companies need to design developmental opportunities and then put processes into place for tracking managers into them on a systematic basis. For example, that could involve things like formal mentoring programmes, assessment centres (where the primary goal is developmental rather than performance appraisal) and personal growth programmes (eg self-awareness workshops, team-building training, etc).

And those opportunities should begin immediately. At General Electric, many new hires are put into leadership development efforts right out of the gate. For instance, new engineers are sent into a two-year leadership development programme that weaves together three eight-month projects with classroom work on leadership and project management, among other things. High-level executive training takes place at GE's leadership development centre in Crotonville, New York. This campus-like environment provides a forum for managers from different parts of GE to work on problems and hone leadership skills. It also helps build the relationships and personal networks needed to bind the pieces of global companies together. This commitment to leadership development may explain why General Electric has been described as having a 'massive iceberg of leadership ability'.

Finally, the process of designing and putting a sophisticated leadership development and succession-planning infrastructure into place will require resources, time and guidance. Creating, empowering and charging a steering committee for leadership development is one way to get things off the ground. A standing committee or facilitator may also be necessary to help co-ordinate leadership development and succession planning efforts across the firm over the long haul. Without these mechanisms, leadership development efforts will probably be haphazard and vary dramatically from manager to manager.

Helping Yourself

At this point you're probably thinking, 'Yeah, yeah, all these examples are great. But they don't apply to my situation.' In other words, what if you don't work in a company where the conditions are ripe for leadership development, and you're not in a position to influence them directly? What if your boss isn't supportive: he or she is narcissistic or just doesn't see how leadership development fits into day-to-day operations, much less the bottom line? What if the corporate culture doesn't emphasize learning and development? What if job assignments have no developmental criteria and there is no integration between tasks, training and succession planning?

If that's what you're living with, then you're on your own. But there are things that you can do to develop yourself, without help from the company or your boss (or perhaps in spite of them). Here are some things you can do – or at least push for – on your own:

■ **Develop your own career plan – where do you want to go and why?** How might you be able to get there? What important skills or attributes are missing or need development? Obviously, developing a good plan assumes a certain amount of self-insight on your part. That in itself might be something to improve on.

- **Try focusing and concentrating on doing a better job of monitoring yourself.** How do you react in certain situations? Why? What makes you uncomfortable, nervous, or fearful? What does that say about you? Remember that narcissistic leaders are good examples of what not to do. Don't emulate them!
- **Find some self-help tools and put them to work.** Once you've identified some things to work on, there are plenty of books, videos, computer programs and training courses that you can pick up and use on your own. Selecting appropriate materials, however, will take some work. There's a lot of junk out there and stuff of dubious value. But if you take the time to look for quality and do your homework, you might find something helpful. Just keep 'caveat emptor' in mind!
- **Look for ways to develop yourself informally on the job:**
  - **Approach peers or other managers who might be willing to serve as informal mentors.** Such mentors can play a variety of useful roles: offering advice, coaching, protection, exposure, etc.
  - **Volunteer for assignments, tasks, or projects that will stretch your skills or expose you to new learning opportunities.** Offer to help other people out, even if it means doing things that fall outside the scope of your job or unit.
  - **Seek out feedback from as many people as possible.** Ask them what mistakes you've made, what skills you might improve, and how you might help yourself grow.
  - **Work on triangulation – trying to view things from multiple perspectives.** Keep in mind that leadership situations are usually complex. Even if the answers appear easy, implementing them rarely is.[12]

CHAPTER TAKE-AWAYS

- Narcissistic leaders aren't interested in succession planning or developing subordinates. Doing so means they must share the limelight. It also risks exposure by a competent subordinate. In short, narcissists find succession issues immensely threatening.
- Succession battles at the top are often driven by narcissistic excesses. There can be plenty of narcissistic resistance from CEOs (who want to keep their jobs and destroy or undercut successors) as well as from potential successors (who are willing to do anything to nab the job they want). Even after a successor takes over, CEOs sometimes manage to hang on to their board seat, a good platform for causing mischief if not regaining their jobs.
- Studies tend to confirm that ego and irrational factors drive succession processes in many firms. And in many cases it's the company that ultimately gets hurt.
- Many top leaders refuse to even think about succession issues, much less plan for it. Among those that do, secrecy often rules about potential successors, which ostensibly discourages infighting and destructive competition among potential heirs.
- Recommendations for improving succession at the top include: a) working to include independent people on the board of directors; b) making the board responsible for succession planning, including running the search process; c) Linking CEO compensation to succession planning efforts; and d) nurturing a culture where succession planning and management development are valued.
- Suggestions for improving succession and leadership development across the company include: a) making leadership development a core value; b) measuring and rewarding managers for their developmental efforts with subordinates; and c) creating an infrastructure that systematically provides developmental opportunities.
- Strategies for developing yourself include: a) creating your own career plan; b) raising your self-insight by more closely monitoring yourself; c) searching for various self-help tools to improve areas of weakness (eg books and videos); d) informally looking for developmental opportunities on the job (eg seeking out people who might be mentors, volunteering for activities or projects that will stretch your skills, and seeking out feedback whenever possible); and e) trying to view things from different perspectives.

Part 3

Reining in the threat of narcissistic leadership

Chapter 9

How pressures for change and faddism encourage narcissistic leadership

ME, MYSELF AND I

Change and fads: The narcissist's best friends

Our company decided to move to team-based management. After receiving special training and being 'put on notice' to do more, my boss started to 'preach' teamwork, empowerment and openness. What he actually did was to twist the whole thing around to serve his own purposes. He avoided participating in discussions with other members of the executive team. Instead, he'd rant and rave at his management peers in front of our department, calling them vile names and ridiculing their intelligence. His idea of a 'team' was to shape the department into believing that 'only our guy's the real thing, so it's us against the rest of the world'. If you didn't go along and demonstrate complete loyalty, look out! He used a recent company decision to implement a 360-degree feedback system as a way of enforcing conformity. After he got the first set of survey results about himself, he called each of his reporters into his office to 'discuss' their ratings and comments. The meetings were 3–4-hour-long searches for 'who said what' along with a rationalization of any bad behaviour. When the second survey was distributed six months later, only four of ten people in the department responded. Of those, three circled only positive ratings to avoid confrontation. Since I was the only person who answered honestly and provided written commentary, I was subjected to a six-hour meeting in his office where I was screamed at and told that my ratings were 'bullshit'. While he was running things, we had 50% turnover per year in our department. He wasn't fired until our company was purchased and a new management team was brought in that focused on real issues.

Manager, food ingredient manufacturer

My boss manoeuvred himself into a position where he could act like he was a critical contributor to the corporate renewal strategy. Everything he did was sold as somehow tied in with that strategy. What it allowed him to do was to spare no expenses or resources (human and/or financial) to pursue pet projects that would make him look good. It also allowed him to refuse to provide even adequate support for peers and subordinates and hoard it for himself and his agenda.

Production manager, off-road machinery manufacturer

Over the last few years, our company has tried to become more 'globally competitive' and 'lean and mean'. The big change was to put much higher emphasis on cutting costs than in the past. There was pressure to come up with new products that were cheap to make and to cut costs out of existing products. Our boss took advantage of that. On one project to redesign an existing product, we weren't making enough progress and were behind schedule. Additional team members needed to be allocated to the project. The boss refused, saying it would completely use up the budgeted hours. We were convinced that he thought he could score points by finishing the project under budget. At the same time, he was allocating resources and manpower to rush through a design for a completely new product. He wanted to offer the new design to top management as a 'global product'. It was what they wanted to hear.

Product development supervisor, consumer products firm

MAKING IT EASIER FOR NARCISSISTIC LEADERS

The last several chapters described the characteristics of narcissistic leaders in considerable detail as well as the damage that they can do. We've also talked about how subordinates can respond to narcissistic leadership. But now we'd like to step back and put the narcissistic leader into broader context. As we said in Chapter 1, narcissistic leadership is more common that many of us want to believe. But why are these stories about narcissism so common? What are the larger effects of narcissistic leadership? What can companies do about it? And to what extent? Should we want to completely extinguish all traces of narcissism in corporations? These questions are the subject of the last section of our book, 'Reining in the threat of narcissistic leadership'.

For instance, Chapter 10 will examine how specific aspects of organizational culture – 'the way we do things around here' – create opportunities for narcissistic leaders. In Chapter 11, we'll talk about the cynicism such leaders can create among employees, and strategies for re-energizing morale after a narcissist moves on to new pastures. Finally, Chapter 12 will remind us that narcissism is not automatically pathological. In fact, an argument can be made that a modicum of narcissism in the leadership ranks can be beneficial under certain circumstances. The tough part is distinguishing between 'enough' and 'too much'.

In this chapter, we start the process by considering how companies inadvertently encourage narcissistic leadership. That was a point not lost on our survey respondents. Many of them blamed their firms for not doing anything to control narcissistic leaders and argued that company-wide efforts had the best chance of limiting narcissistic excesses over the long term. As one of our survey respondents put it:

> Narcissistic leaders are like child abusers. One generation breeds the next. Companies must take steps to break the cycle.
>
> *Engineer, metal fabrication firm*

Unfortunately, many companies do exactly the opposite. They help perpetuate, if not strengthen, the cycle of narcissism. We've touched on some of the relevant issues already, like runaway executive compensation and the 'winner take all' culture often found in US firms. In this chapter, however, we'll talk about how pressures for organizational change contribute to narcissism. We'll also discuss how the 'change' that results from jumping on the latest management fads also encourages narcissists, or at the very least provides them with potential openings to exploit.

Hyping Change

It's traditional to start most discussions of change by essentially saying, 'Wow. . . change in today's business world is dramatic.' You know the spiel. The pace of change is dizzying, economic shocks are frequent and unpredictable, international competition is super-intense, the only constant in today's business is change, blah, blah, blah. Obviously, these clichés are a reality for some companies and industries. At the same time, however, this particular pitch is one-sided and has turned 'the unprecedented rapidity of change' into a knee-jerk phrase that's tossed out like rice at a wedding. Endlessly repeated and overused, it becomes trite. The fact is that change has always been with us. Economic upheavals are nothing new: sooner or later, we all get hit. Likewise, threats from foreign competitors have been there in one form or another for decades if not hundreds of years. Indeed, one could argue that the many economic confederations and organizations created over the last 30 years have acted to reduce or buffer the impact of change in the 'global economy'. Indeed, a serious analysis of 'internationalism' and 'globalism' has led some to conclude that it's an issue with much less substance than meets the eye.[1]

So we understand if you're a bit jaded when you read about change. Plus, it's an annoyingly hard subject to avoid. Change is an ubiquitous topic in the popular press. You wouldn't be alone in feeling that it's all a bit too much, a bit too over the top. And if you've been around long enough, you might remember that many predicted changes – in business or other spheres of life – simply never materialized or caught on. In the 1950s everybody was going to have the 'kitchen of tomorrow' that could produce futuristic food instantly. All of us would have picture phones in our homes by now. Besides being in the late Stanley Kubrick's 1968 film, *2001: A Space Odyssey*, where are they (we'll grant it isn't 2001 yet as this book goes to press)?

The point is that there's been a long and relentless history of predictions about change. And the new millennium has whipped the change prediction business into a frenzy. A recent *Business Week* cover story touted '21 ideas for the 21st century'.[2] Those 'ideas' (read 'predictions') included the 'end' of superstar (read 'narcissistic') executives as we know them. Why? Supposedly, the increasing prevalence of work teams, flat hierarchies and so on will make the individualized leader obsolete. Talk about wishful thinking! What this overlooks is that 95 per cent of the time companies are doing just that – talking about teams, empowerment and so on, while the reality is often business as usual.

Even the vaunted Internet, which has 'revolutionized' business, communications and God knows what else, has been oversold. Granted, the Internet is wonderful in many respects, but it's hardly the model of efficiency or organization. The phrase 'garbage in, garbage out' comes to mind. No wonder there's so much cynicism about change.

So yes, it is a brave new world, but probably not the one we expected. And yes, we've all been affected by change, but not always for the good. Nevertheless, a serious student of prognostications might say that there's credence in the old saying, 'The more things change, the more they stay the same.' That's certainly the case with predictions for the future, most of which turn out to be wrong. All of this is our way of saying that the 'need for change' should be taken with a pinch of salt. Instead of getting caught up in the hype about change and mindlessly embracing a variety of fads and fixes, companies need to analyse their situations carefully and craft their own solutions. There's simply no substitute for doing your homework.

Real Pressures for Change

Of course, when faced with real pressures, companies do need to respond. Sometimes this requires that the organization change to compete better in its environment. That kind of change – like losing weight – often takes years. General Motors, for example, has been 'changing' for decades – a not uncommon time-frame when large firms and ossified corporate cultures are involved.[3]

There is a variety of unplanned and planned forces that can create pressure for change. Many environmental events that demand change are unplanned. Consider the effects of governmental regulation. In the 1980s a US judge ruled that AT&T had to divest itself of several business interests, including their local phone service companies. These were peeled off to form seven separate regional companies, and nearly a million employees were affected by the ruling. One executive likened this process to 'taking apart and reassembling a jumbo jet while in flight'.[4] Ultimately, today Microsoft finds itself under assault by the US government for 'anti-competitive' practices. Where this takes Bill Gates and Microsoft remains to be seen.

Of course, sometimes a **dramatic event** will effect a change on all industry members, such as has happened in the nuclear power, oil and airline businesses. Several years ago, environmental groups targeted the food industry for their use of polystyrene food containers. A campaign was launched against McDonald's, a large user of the containers in its fast-food operations. Initially, McDonald's responded with a recycling programme for the 'clamshell' style containers. Later the firm abandoned the programme and moved to a quilted paper wrap solution.[5]

Clearly, **economic competition** can lead to intense, unplanned pressures for change. For instance, automotive parts companies have often felt blindsided by cost and quality pressures from competitors. Other industries have also felt this kind of surprising and unwelcome pressure. That's certainly true in software and telecommunications, where rapid technological advances allow firms to close gaps or leapfrog each other quickly.[6] Regardless, companies react in a variety of ways. Some find ways to strike quickly to bring out new products or dramatically improve quality and internal efficiency. Others fight back by partnering or merging with companies that possess complementary strengths. And others, sadly enough, simply succumb.[7] There are many other **unplanned** forces for change, including organizational catastrophes, strikes and sabotage.

On the other hand, some changes are **planned**, in that they somehow involve a deliberate and conscious attempt to change some aspect about the business. Usually, these occur in response to a perceived performance gap or weakness, perhaps something that is anticipated to hurt the firm enormously, but isn't doing so yet. As a result, a firm may decide to plan a new product, restructure the organization, reengineer business processes, introduce new technologies, or carry out a host of other possible moves. Planned change efforts tend to be more proactive and are designed to position the firm better for the long run or to take advantage of anticipated trends. Recognition of some of these important trends and the related effects on your business doesn't necessarily require a tea-leaf reader, since many can be empirically established. For example, we know about the 'work at home' trend and the rise in 'e-commerce'. But, if you're a house-builder or furniture-maker, it's less certain how these trends might affect your business. Further, some important events are extremely difficult to predict. Consider the relatively rapid fall of the Soviet Union. While some experts predicted its eventual demise, no one predicted the precise timing, much less fully understood the specific impact this would have on certain businesses (eg aircraft-makers or defence-related firms).

Our view is that unplanned or crisis scenarios certainly provide outstanding opportunities for narcissistic leaders, especially if they have good interpersonal skills and can convince followers that they have charismatic or larger-than-life tendencies. However, planned changes may offer the best opportunities for the largest number of narcissistic leaders (after all, there are many more narcissists in the ranks than there are CEOs). In fact, since these change efforts typically extend over a long period and are often poorly executed, they offer the time and space for the more forceful traits of the pathological narcissist to be brought to bear.

Why Change is Tough and Ambiguous

Uncertainty is a big part of the equation linking change and narcissism (and a theme that we'll continue in the next chapter). Organizational change – whether big or small, planned or unplanned – is a tricky and ambiguous business. First, if it is foisted upon you, it's easy to be caught off guard and unprepared for a calculating and prepared narcissist who rushes in to take advantage. Second, the need for planned change has to be anticipated accurately – and that isn't easy. Even if it is, decisions have to be made about what specific changes are necessary to meet anticipated needs. Basically, change is part science and part art. Only a handful of leaders and companies are very good at repeatedly recognizing and implementing necessary change. Even then, after they've succeeded a few times, firms usually end up stumbling over their own built-up hubris. Witness Motorola's recent struggles: it is a company well known for successfully anticipating change and dealing with it throughout the 1980s and early 1990s. In the early 1980s, the company recognized the developing threat that Japan represented and over the next several years successfully reinvented itself. Motorola had to relearn some of those lessons in the late 1990s as nimbler competitors like Finland's Nokia started taking advantage of the company's drift.

Interestingly, some have suggested that the ability constantly to adapt is the only thing that separates the long-term corporate winners from the losers.[8] While there is probably a lot of credence in this view, we don't want to debate it here. Instead, our point is that whether it's a major one-off event or a daily occurrence in your firm, change is tough to plan and even tougher to go through. And people are generally uncomfortable with uncertainty, particularly when so much money and so many livelihoods are often at stake. Organizational changes may involve the important features of everyday work, including:

- allocation of resources;
- performance measurement/appraisal;

　job responsibilities;
　decision-making capability or scope;
　company structure and/or reporting systems.

Each of these changes in itself – let alone in combination – can invite the highly political activities of a narcissist. Many of these activities were highlighted in earlier chapters. Under pressure of organizational change, however, political shenanigans can be taken to new levels by narcissistic leaders. For example, a firm under pressure may face declining resources, as costs are cut and budgets realigned. This might go hand in hand with a new performance measurement technique to get a better handle on things. The special manipulation and exploitation skills of narcissists, in combination with their abilities to manage impressions, can take them a long way under these conditions, as our opening 'Me, Myself and I' box suggested. Likewise, change – even when planned well – is a rollercoaster that inevitably increases ambiguity. A lot of new questions arise that aren't easily answered. What exactly is the mission of our new group? How does it interact with other (new) divisions? What exactly are my new job responsibilities? When will we get some answers? People can be impressed with a leader who brings apparent order to confusion and, as we know, the narcissist is more than willing to do that.

NARCISSISTS CAPITALIZE ON THE VALUE PLACED ON CHANGE

The Clarion Call for Change

Our discussion above warns that narcissists might take advantage of the real need for change to exploit the organization for their own personal goals. An even more insidious problem is narcissists' ability to capitalize on our belief in the need for change – whether it's the right change or not – to gain personal advantage.

We documented above that today's firms have an almost unquestioned belief in the value of change, and that a major theme in popular business writing is 'constant change'. In fact, change has become an axiom of modern management. If it's an unquestioned canon, what better way to disguise an agenda of personal advancement? Who could argue with a new leader who says things like, 'We want to enact some positive change in our company' or 'We're going to do things differently and better right now?' Or what about the call for change that comes in the form of crying wolf ('The future of our company and all of your jobs are at stake')?

We think it's important for us to say that many of these calls for change are probably warranted. Who wants to argue that a firm should rest on its laurels and keep doing things the same old way? But perhaps when it comes to some things – like culture – there can be merit in stability. Many businesspeople strongly believe in the concept of organizational culture. Culture refers to an enduring set of beliefs, values and ways of doing things that define a company. Experts believe that the development of a strong, positive culture is the key to continued corporate success. Southwest Airlines, for instance, is a US company best known for it's people-oriented and fun-loving culture, an idea rarely associated with airlines in the US (or anywhere else for that matter). In a service business, that culture is a competitive advantage that can't be duplicated easily – it's the main reason why Southwest is the only US airline to enjoy uninterrupted profitability for over 20 years. And 1999 was no exception, with Southwest enjoying double-digit increases in profits despite rising fuel prices.[9]

Johnson & Johnson is another example of a firm with a strong culture. The Johnson & Johnson way of doing things is exemplified by their long-standing credo, a distilled statement of their culture. This statement emphasizes product safety and ethical business practices, ideas that have endured for over 70 years since Robert Johnson first put them into print. Many experts, within and outside the company, have suggested that this philosophy provides the foundation for the company's success and its ability to weather some strong challenges. For instance, when its pain reliever, Tylenol©, was poisoned on store shelves some years back, the result was a nationwide scare in the US. Johnson & Johnson quickly pulled all of the product off store shelves. While this cost the firm millions of dollars, it also brought praise for crisis management and eventually strengthened customer loyalty. A strong, stable corporate culture provides direction for the firm and serves as a stake in the ground for expected behaviour.

So, on the one hand, change is revered. On the other hand, a strong, positive and stable culture is also valuable.[10] Ironically, stability can even be important for a change advocate. Some experts suggest that, once resistance to a change effort is overcome, new views and values (culture) must be 'refrozen' in place, to bring about a sense of stability. So, for all these reasons, we have a healthy respect for both change and stability. Unfortunately, much of the appreciation for stability gets lost when narcissistic leaders jump on the change bandwagon. Stability gets in the way of the narcissist's personal agenda. And if you question the methods used or, more fundamentally, the need for change in the first place, there's little doubt that you're placing a nice big target on yourself for the narcissist to zero in on. Take a look at the accompanying 'Me, myself and I' box to see what we mean.

ME, MYSELF AND I

In harm's way: Attempting to deflect a narcissistic change agenda

I took the new VP's invitation for feedback on the organizational change plan seriously. That was stupid. It happened during a weekly meeting of operations managers. As usual, there was no agenda. I anticipated the meeting would unfold as it had on the last three occasions – a supposedly participatory brainstorming about the VP's 'plan' for the division. At lunch after the first couple of meetings, there was a good bit of grumbling among all the managers about the form and appropriateness of the VP's plan, let alone the nature of the meetings. Someone pointed out that the meeting was actually participatory – the VP spoke and we 'participated' by nodding our heads! After the third meeting, we sat around griping again. One of my more vocal colleagues suggested the VP's 'plan' was nothing more than a few general ideas that had been rejected the previous year. Now, while we waited for the chronically late VP to show up for the fourth meeting, the bitching was openly flying fast and loose.

Going into the meeting, I was prepared to bring up a few issues. I had done some research on several elements of the plan in terms of feasibility and cost effectiveness. My research showed that a few parts of the VP's plan had credence and, with some modifications to better reflect market realities, might actually work. When he arrived to start the meeting, the VP immediately said he would forge ahead to discuss the implementation of his plan – if there were no objections. I raised my hand and said that I supported the basic elements of the plan, but wanted to discuss some constraining details that required some tweaking and fine-tuning of the effort.

The VP took this as a direct challenge. He briskly shot back, 'You'd better give your numbers another look, they're wrong', and went right on lecturing us about the plan. When I raised my hand again, he lost his temper. Before I said a word, he angrily stated that he was hired to bring 'positive changes' to our 'tired organization'. He wanted to know if we really represented 'more of the same old crap this place is known for'. No one said anything after that. Once the meeting was over, he asked me to stay and lit into me like nobody's business. At the end he coolly asked if I really wanted to continue my career in management. If so, he told me to go back to my office and 'think about how you can make that happen'. I got the message and so did everybody else.

Department manager, educational services firm

FADS, CONSULTANTS AND NARCISSISTIC LEADERSHIP

In this section, we examine how faddism and the burgeoning consulting industry aid and abet narcissistic leadership. We'll start by asking you to reflect on the following all-too-familiar scenario.

Management author and speaker Allan Kennedy had just given a 50-minute pep talk on organizational culture to a group of high-powered executives at a large corporation. They paid $10,000 for the show and it was pretty slick. Kennedy, a former principal at McKinsey & Co. and co-author of a prominent business book (*Corporate Cultures*), had given the presentation hundreds of times before. 'By now, I've got an act that could play on Broadway,' he said.[11] And he was right. His 'critics' gave him rave reviews – the executives' enthusiasm surprised even Kennedy. At dinner, the CEO pronounced, 'This corporate culture stuff is great'. He turned to one of his charges and ordered, 'I want a culture by Monday'. And he was serious.

Of course, this is hardly news. All too often, executives hang on every word that spills out of the mouths of management gurus, no matter how banal. They chase the latest fads and fixes without the slightest bit of evidence that what they've grabbed hold of has any more staying power than the hula-hoop. Most alluring are the newest buzzwords and quick fixes, especially if a few other 'big name' firms are already on board.[12]

Of course, this feeds into our previous discussion of change. Many fads are simply pedestrian management thinking that have been repackaged by gurus and sold as 'new, dramatic ideas'. You're probably well acquainted with the recent cast of labels here (eg reengineering, knowledge management, etc). Nevertheless, while the management consulting industry has truly come into its own in the 1980s and 1990s, it's also easy to name management fads in every decade since the Second World War (see Table 9.1).

Table 9.1 Some management fads by decade

1950s	1960s	1970s	1980s	1990s
computerization	T-groups	experience curve	theory Z	total quality
quantitative management	centralization/ decentralization	zero-based budgeting	intrapreneuring	supply chain management
diversification	matrix management	portfolio management	restructuring	downsizing rightsizing
management by objectives	conglomerations		1-minute managers	reengineering
	managerial grids			

Adapted from Byrne[13]

In actuality, many companies have found some fads useful. In other words, there's nothing automatically wrong with the fundamental concepts underlying popular management techniques. The problem occurs when such techniques aren't investigated fully or implemented in a sustained and serious fashion, but are instead really knee-jerk reactions to what others are doing or merely superficial ploys that allow management to claim they are dealing with tough issues. When used as gimmicks they can do more harm than good.

Let's look at 360-degree feedback systems as an illustration of what we mean. The mechanics of such systems involve giving the manager feedback from peers and subordinates as well as from superiors. In fact, you'll recall that one of the examples in the 'Me, Myself and I' box that opened this chapter focused on how one narcissistic leader used 360-degree feedback to his advantage. So how did that happen and why was he able to get away with it? The basic answer is that 360-degree feedback has arguably become just another management fad. These systems are often implemented abruptly for no other reason than management's desire to be 'fashionable', or to create an impression that the firm is more 'open' than it really is.

In fact, there is a disturbing lack of performance-based thinking and measurement when it comes to 360-degree feedback systems – just like there often was for TQM and a host of other often thoughtlessly implemented management fads. The major implementation driver in many cases is simply the knowledge that other companies 'are doing it'. Little effort is made to understand the problems other firms experienced or what their outcomes were (or should have been) with 360-degree feedback. The reality is that companies should first analyse how 360-degree feedback might help achieve bottom-line objectives, including what type of system is best able to accomplish that (eg should 360-degree feedback be used as a management development tool, performance appraisal vehicle, or both?). In lieu of that, 360-degree feedback systems can become a political weapon used by narcissists to push their agendas, impress superiors with their 'innovativeness' and browbeat subordinates. What this creates is a picture of yet another management fad run wild – one that leads to more employee cynicism.[14]

As we showed in Table 9.1, fads have been with us for some time. What's alarming, however, is the increasing frequency with which 'new' theories, often christened with flashy acronyms, appear in books sold in airport kiosks from O'Hare to Osaka. A recent survey by Bain & Company focused on 25 leading management techniques used by nearly 1,000 companies around the world. They reported that the average big firm used about 12 of those 25 methods in 1993, 13 methods a year later and over 14 in 1995. Interestingly, while managers in the United States (12.8) are often seen as the biggest consumers of modern management fads, they were only slightly higher than their counterparts in France (11.4) and Japan (11.5), all of whom were less voracious consumers than the British (13.7). What's even worse about these fads is that by the time a conscientious manager gets one up and running, it is outdated and *passé*. Some experts believe the 'product' life cycle has condensed from around a decade to about a year.[15] Apparently, what's here today in management practice will be 'reengineered' by tomorrow.

The marketing and selling of management theory is certainly big business, and the ever-growing number of fads can account for the rising revenues. In fact, in the US alone nearly $1 billion is spent on business books, not including money generated by seminars, speeches, tapes and videos. Tired and overwhelmed by this mountain of management 'technology', executives have turned in large numbers to outside experts for help. This advice industry now employs some

100,000 people worldwide. Billings in the US alone in 1996 exceeded 15 billion! The names of these firms are familiar to most businesspeople, including Andersen Consulting, McKinsey, and the Boston Consulting Group. Many of their employees are generated by the over 700 business schools in the US, which produce some 75,000 MBAs a year – 15 times their 'production' three decades earlier.

And plenty of egos are fed in the process. Consulting firms aren't likely to snare a lot of repeat business by telling executives that their approach is wrongheaded or that they are flawed, self-absorbed narcissists who need to get their heads on straight. The bottom line is that management 'knowledge', especially that peddled by the management consultancies, is paid for by executives and the leadership of corporations. If that leadership has narcissistic tendencies, then the possibilities are troubling. Just being able to hire consultants in the first place serves as a testimonial for the executive's power and importance. For more on this point, take a look at the accompanying 'Me, Myself and I' box.

ME, MYSELF AND I

Confessions of a consultant: Beware of FON (friends of the narcissist)

Top management has looked around and they don't like what they see. Other companies seem to be reengineering, outsourcing, 'managing innovation' and more. Worse yet, numbers for this quarter aren't too encouraging and people are getting edgy. Narcissist or not, what's the instinctive response by many US executives? Hire consultants. That's right, bringing on a hired gun is now *de rigueur*. Take a look at your local phone listings under 'management consulting' if you think we're exaggerating, or consider the number of consultants who write books that are little more than 250-page marketing brochures. You'll be simply amazed at the number of providers there are. In fact, hiring consultants can be considered a fad in itself among US companies, some of whom have become 'consultant junkies'.

For some firms, much of their business planning and operational decision-making has been turned over to consultants. Why do they do it? The party-line answer is that firms want to bring the latest and best knowledge into their businesses. And they need some additional 'arms and legs' to roll out new strategies and initiatives. Of course, some of what's offered isn't new. One flashy entrepreneur we know spoke to us about shifting his attention away from his successful business. He wanted to get into the consulting game in a big way. He started out by giving evangelical speeches to managers from companies in his industry and was well received. His 'strategic message' was as basic as you could get: that good customer service is the most important thing. With a confidential tone that betrayed a hint of incredulity, he confided to us, 'It amazes me that when I say, "Customer service is important", people in the audience actually feel that they have to write it down!' It was like hearing a magician explain his most basic parlour trick.

Critics of this advice movement point to other motives as well. One expert, an ex-partner at a major consulting firm and now a corporate executive himself, has this to say: 'These companies get hooked because it's easy, it's safe, or their management doesn't have confidence in their own troops.' He says companies have gone too far: they've in effect outsourced the job of managing and thinking, the very thing top leadership is paid to do.

This doesn't mean you should never hire a consultant. For example, when AT&T first toyed with the idea of going into the credit card business, they were clearly outside their element. They called in the cavalry to help in this unfamiliar territory. But such cases aren't necessarily multi-year or long-term consulting gigs. Instead, they are discrete and well-defined reasons for bringing in help. Seeking help with a new cafeteria benefits plan or a networking system is one thing, but with corporate strategy and organization? As the ex-consultant put it, 'If there's a guy at a consulting firm that can build a better strategy for Company X than the CEO, then that guy should be hired as CEO!' If you have informed management who are up to speed on the relevant issues and you seem to have the right business strategy, what's the point of turning to consultants? As a managing partner at one consulting firm said, 'If you already know what to do, you should just do it.'

Critics also say that another bad reason to hire consultants – but one that is also all too common – is to use them to referee internal disputes. If you have two powerful but competing narcissists who are fighting to determine overall vision or strategy, bringing in an umpire could also cause trouble. You might be better off making the decision inside – after all, eventually top management will have to make a decision anyway. Holding a consultant's report in your hand while pronouncing the decision probably won't convince the losing side, even if the report is accurate. Again, as a worldwide managing director at one consulting firm said: 'Consultants may figure out who's right, which only makes the losing side more angry and resentful. But, they may get it wrong, which is also a waste of your money.' It might be money well spent, however, by a narcissist, since he or she can use the entire consultation process to lead to a predetermined outcome – a consolidation of the narcissist's power.

We know that using consultants to sell the executive's agenda fits well with the special skills of the narcissistic leader. How does this happen? In its mildest form, consultants may be brought in to second-guess people in the firm. At best, this is an indirect way to deal with problems – and it signals that you don't trust the skills of your people. If this is the case, an obvious thing to do is to select better people or better train the ones you have. But as we've shown earlier in this book, narcissistic leaders have often eliminated the most competent people in the organization and replaced them with weak and subservient lieutenants.

Even more problematic, however, is the use of consultants effectively to rubber-stamp a pet project of the narcissist. Unfortunately, the dynamics of the business arrangement may act to make consultants FON – friends of the narcissist. As one 20-year veteran put it: 'When I was a consultant, I spent more time thinking about what I was going to sell the client next than the problem I was supposed to be fixing. My goal was to stay inside forever.' He advised prospective clients to keep in mind that consulting firms are partnerships, not public companies. The only way for partners in the firm to make money is by generating billable hours. In a sense, consulting is a contrived-demand business. The idea is to convince companies that they are sick and that the consulting firm can make them well. Yet the truly sick companies are the ones least able to afford big consulting fees. The real challenge is 'to make a relatively healthy company think they're sick or that they could be a lot healthier'.

Often this sales job includes an explicit or implied statement about how 'we' (the consulting firm) have helped companies like yours in the past. But buyer beware! As one ex-consultant said: 'My old firm is selling my experience, even though I'm not there anymore.' So one question is: who are the 'we'? Consider again the ex-consultant's experience. At any one time, his firm makes pitches to many different companies. Often the firm will win several different contracts with various firms all around the same time. How will they complete the jobs? The first (deep-pocket) company to sign will get the best team they have, the second company will get the 'B' team and so on. Of course, the client who gets the 'D' team has no idea this is the case. Often, the person doing the pitch will not be with the consulting team that comes to your company. Instead, the company with deeper pockets or that gets there first will get the 'A' team, and a bus-load of newly minted Harvard MBAs will pull up at your door.

The veteran consultant also brought to light another possible consulting gambit. His advice? Make sure you're getting a customized product that fits the specific problems of your company. For example, one consulting firm analysed the cost structure of every European steel company, and then sold the same set of information to those Europeans firms. Another recent scenario involved a well-known firm that allegedly sold a large number of clients the same boilerplate report on diversity issues (eg how to create a more diverse workplace etc).

Much of this is of little concern to narcissistic leaders who control the chequebook. Their only interest is that their agenda and image receive strong support. If they see teams as a way to make their particular splash, then the consultants damn well better come to that conclusion. And they had better do so in a way that involves no criticism of the narcissist's regime. For example, during an initial presentation, consultants told one executive about a mild level of employee scepticism uncovered regarding a team-based initiative that was being considered. The executive nearly jumped out of his seat and violently protested. The consultants at the meeting watched as the executive pounded the table and lambasted their report – and knew that they were gone. Next day, a new consulting firm was invited in.

Once a firm is hired and knows the narcissist's desired message and agenda, it can look forward to having to work with the narcissist's lap-dogs and sycophants, subordinates whose positions are based on loyalty, not competence. We suspect few narcissists would want to do things the way one company VP does: 'The way we look at it, we always put some of our best people on these projects, because we know they'll learn and grow.' Even though his 'A' team is naturally spread thin, he says, 'If I put the "A" team on it, they learn it and then we can throw the consultants out.'[16]

COMBATING NARCISSISTIC CHANGE AND FADDISM

As we've shown above, many companies are more than willing to jump at the latest management fads. So it's not surprising that employee cynicism about change efforts is rampant.[17] If you're not sure exactly how cynical you or your fellow employees are, take a look at the Appendix at the end of the book: there you'll find a brief survey that might help shed some light on the subject. In any case, when change efforts are spearheaded by a narcissistic leader, companies and employees are stung even harder. And even if a narcissistic leader moves on quickly, his or her negative legacy remains.

But the biggest challenge is trying to deal with the 'change' plans of a sitting narcissist. We've already shown that there is often a strong corporate bias towards change, at least superficially. Narcissists are also likely to use all their powers and skills to sell their change plan (ie their career advancement plan), including the use of highly paid allies (consultants). If the narcissistic leader is new to the firm, he or she will also receive the benefit of the doubt from virtually every stakeholder.

You're more likely to have success coping with a change effort if the narcissist has been around for a while. There are several reasons for this. Over time, narcissists usually make enemies who are often looking for opportunities to strike back. Eventually, people run afoul of the narcissist's arrogance, misplaced hostility, credit-stealing nonsense and so on – take your pick. Whatever the source, you can bet that the narcissist has created intense resentment in some quarters and that it's still happening. So what are some options for dealing with change efforts led by a narcissist?

Stay Involved in the Change Effort

Research shows that most employees would like to be involved in change efforts.[18] Of course, cynicism – as well as having to deal with a narcissistic leader – will put a damper on that. When dealing with a narcissistic regime, direct attempts at input or at sharing information with others can be met with swift and serious retribution, hence the need to be more subtle and clever, especially if you aren't in a position to influence corporate policies and procedures directly.

For instance, you can try to convince the narcissistic leader that it's in his or her self-interest to get the input of others. Or you could point out that other companies are adopting this participative approach and that 'we're falling behind'. Finally, perhaps some subtle work behind the scenes can help you identify a consulting group that has a participation bias. Of course, if the narcissist is on the way out, then any number of traditional involvement procedures that might otherwise be blocked can be used directly (eg idea reward programmes, quality initiatives, upward feedback methods, etc). The idea is to stay involved and at least try to contribute. It will provide some cover against being labelled a naysayer, a critic, or an outlaw opposed to change, labels that can isolate you from friends and foes alike.

Improve Communication

The involvement we discussed above usually goes hand in hand with better communication. Nevertheless, we mention better communication as a factor that can be improved independently of involvement. Almost certainly this means keeping people informed about what's coming or what's being considered early on. This often has to be done in subtle and indirect ways to avoid confrontations with the narcissist, whose tendency will be to hoard information if not manipulate it outright. Even then, the narcissist could become aware of information leaks because of his or her sensitivities to possible challenges. But using the grapevine to provide advance notice of impending changes is still better than being blindsided.

Of course, having policies that reward supervisors for efforts to communicate would be a more systematic way to encourage information sharing and help minimize employee scepticism.[19] Data also show that the use of multiple 'channels' of communication – in addition to the face-to-face variety from supervisors – can marshal support for organizational change. These may include newsletters, memos, e-mails and informal gatherings (probably not including the narcissist!). Interestingly, some experts even suggest that part of all this communication should directly deal with past failures to bring about change. Needless to say, if the narcissist leading the change effort is at the top of the organization, there's little chance that such policies will be implemented, much less encouraged. Our point, however, is that companies can institute procedures that make it more difficult for narcissistic leaders in the ranks to use change for their own purposes.

Evaluating Change Efforts

Finally, companies should evaluate their efforts systematically, especially if they plan to brag about 'successful' change. While we have criticized many change efforts, there have been some clear successes.[20] Most of these are the result of elaborate and time-consuming efforts. That underscores something that's always been disturbing to us: the lack of evaluation. Why aren't companies more interested in evaluating whether a particular change effort works? One thing's for sure – whether they succeed or fail, change efforts are extraordinarily expensive. Yet few organizations systematically evaluate such efforts. One company we're aware of spent over $1 million on a team-building project targeted at a few hundred employees. But not a cent was devoted to evaluating whether those efforts resulted in any tangible value. Of course, narcissistic leaders aren't likely to be interested in systematic evaluation, but you can be sure all of their programmes will be positioned as 'successful'.

So why does evaluation get short shrift? For one thing, it's hard to get a budget line essentially for doing research, something seen as secondary if not irrelevant by definition. Then there are the political reasons, which brings us right back to narcissism. Your career may take a hit if someone finds out that lots of money was spent on a change effort (yours!) that went nowhere. And research shows that success is far from automatic regardless of how much money you spend. Interestingly, one of the most important predictors of success is the consistent and sustained support of top management (in terms of resources, management visibility and a 'match' between words and deeds). If change is treated as just another programme of the month, real success is unlikely.[21]

Unfortunately, this hits the nail on the head when narcissistic leaders are involved. Narcissists are unlikely to give a change programme real support (recall that their attention spans are short and interest in details minimal). Instead, narcissists view change efforts as mere vehicles for advancing their own selfish agendas. If the change programme does actually succeed, that's fine for narcissists – they'll be happy to take credit and trumpet 'their' success. If not, however, they'll still sell it as a success (eg as 'progress' over what was happening before).

Blunting such nonsense means identifying desired outcomes ahead of time and putting mechanisms in place to measure them. If these outcomes can be quantified and are listed as 'deliverables' on some piece of paper somewhere, then at least the change effort can be evaluated fairly, if not succeed. Most experts suggest building in an evaluation component from the start. If the goal of a change programme is to increase customer satisfaction, how will you index this? What is the current level of satisfaction? How can you measure this, and what improvements do you hope to make?

CHAPTER TAKE-AWAYS

▨ Organizational change is all the rage, and perhaps it should be. But beware of narcissists who carry the change flag. They may have it right, but if they're unwilling to tolerate input or improvement, then who's really against change?

▨ Worse yet, many companies around the world are happy to jump headfirst into the latest management fad. Both these trends make it much easier for narcissistic leaders to get a foothold in corporations and vigorously pursue their visions of grandeur.

▨ Narcissistic leaders can cleverly use the latest management buzzwords and the hottest consulting firms to convince the necessary parties that the environment they create is 'necessary' to 'fulfil the vision'.

▨ We suggest that anyone who faces this combination of forces (a narcissist, normal and contrived pressures for change, and consultants) has a very difficult task indeed. You may be better off lying low or leaving for better opportunities. Nevertheless, we do provide some suggestions for trying to bring about successful change.

Chapter 10

Corporate cultures that invite and sustain the narcissist

ME, MYSELF AND I

An education in deceit. . . and how not to stop it

An engineer from a manufacturing firm learned a valuable lesson about the depths to which a narcissistic boss might be willing to stoop. Unfortunately, he also learned that companies sometimes fail to do the right thing when narcissistic behaviour is observed. And that, in effect, is rewarding the behaviour. Doing nothing, as it turns out, sends a strong message too. Ultimately, the company lost two good employees and ended up with an out-of-control narcissist in its midst. That's the price the firm paid for not learning the same lesson.

Here's the scenario. The engineer worked for a particular department manager, handling the scheduling of shift foremen as well as a variety of records and paperwork. One of the foremen was particularly disliked by the department manager because he was extremely conscientious and an outstanding performer. The department manager was very threatened and was worried that the foreman, who was very popular with employees, was gunning for his job.

Soon the engineer started seeing some very odd behaviour. Near the end of the shift, the manager would suddenly vanish from his office without warning, only to reappear some time later wearing a grin 'like the cat who ate the canary'. Then bizarre problems started occurring during the foreman's shift. He was held responsible and took the blame. The engineer was suspicious and decided to check things out for himself: 'I discovered this guy pouring solvent on uniball joints that required much lubricant to keep them in operation, putting metal shavings into gearboxes, changing the settings on heat exhaust doors to change temperatures in the melters, and so on. The manager did this and much more to create problems for the foreman he disliked until he finally got the guy fired for low production and poor job performance.'

The engineer shared his observations with the company's industrial relations department, but was flabbergasted to hear that if the firm pushed the matter with the manager, he could turn around and challenge any disciplinary action. . . and might possibly win. If that happened, the engineer, as well as the foreman, could lose his job. So, a deal was cut. The foreman took a layoff notice instead of being fired and was given some assistance in finding another job. And the narcissistic manager who started it all? The engineer, who subsequently joined another company, said that not only is the manager still with the company today, but that he's 'just as arrogant and underhanded as ever'.[1]

THE CORPORATE CULTURE AS BREEDING GROUND

In the last several chapters, we've talked a lot about the damaging effects of the narcissistic leader and how to cope with them. But some might criticize our approach so far as dealing with the symptoms but not the cause. In particular, we've said very little about how a narcissist might rise to a position of leadership in a company. What sort of corporate environment encourages and invites the abuse of a narcissistic leader? As our opening 'Me, Myself and I' example suggests, the company can play an important role, in this case effectively aiding and abetting narcissistic behaviour. So what do narcissists need to succeed? What can a firm do to protect itself against this type of self-interested leadership? We'll turn our attention to these topics now, and along the way we'll talk about why some organizations may foster and actually nurture the narcissist, even if unwittingly.[2]

While all of us have some narcissistic tendencies, those people with unhealthy doses of the six key characteristics are likely to show their true colours when interacting with others in organizational settings. But not always. In some organizations, those destructive tendencies are not tolerated and remain suppressed. In other firms, however, narcissists seem to 'flower' and their power and influence grows. What accounts for this important difference? Why do some companies seem to be inoculated against narcissism, while others seem to foster it?

Ambiguous Goals and Organizational Uncertainty

There are a variety of conditions that form an environment conducive to narcissists.[3] One condition that can act as a trigger for a narcissist's rise to power is uncertainty. While companies vary widely in their control over uncertainty and ambiguity, there are some common ways to index this vagueness. For example, if the overall corporate mission is imprecise, then you have one major source of uncertainty. Of course, just having an explicit mission is no panacea. A clear mission that no one really pays attention to, much less follows, might be just as bad as not having one at all. Either way, it might be indicative of organizational ambiguity. Likewise, if jobs are unclear more uncertainty exists. And if performance appraisals are based on shifting and nebulous criteria, you have still more uncertainty.

It's also important to note that there are many causes of ambiguity over which the organization has little control. In fact, the biggest source of uncertainty might the firm's environment. Here, we're referring to changing governmental regulations, economic downturns, the unexpected moves of competitors and rising costs of critical supplies or equipment, all of which can dramatically affect your business.

Narcissists take advantage of ambiguity

How can narcissistic leaders capitalize on ambiguity or uncertainty? In a nutshell, uncertainty provides opportunities. Those opportunities, combined with a little power and some influence skills, are a winning combination; that is, if you define 'winning' as getting all the personal advancement and benefits you can.

One key to understanding the ability of narcissists to take advantage of ambiguity is provided by looking a little more closely at what 'ambiguity' means. To elaborate further, consider this scene from *Alice in Wonderland*: Alice came to a fork in the road and spotted the Cheshire

Cat in a tree. 'Which road do I take?' she asked. His response was a question: 'Where do you want to go?' 'I don't know,' Alice answered. 'Then,' said the cat, 'it doesn't matter.'

So, ambiguity promotes confusion and this permits opportunities for someone to swoop in, provide clarity and in so doing assume power.[4] Consider this quote from a prominent management writer:

> The most power goes to those people in those functions that provide greater control over what the organization finds currently problematic: sales and marketing people when markets are competitive; production experts when materials are scarce; personnel specialists when governmental regulations impinge; finance and accounting types when business is bad and money tight. There is a turning to those elements of the system that seem to have the power to create more certainty. . . to generate a more advantageous position for the organization.[5]

With their combination of traits, narcissistic leaders are often in a good position to impose structure on an otherwise ambiguous situation. If you combine this with a situation where there are few limits as to what is correct and appropriate behaviour, then you've got some fertile ground for narcissists.

Actually, lack of clarity can give **everyone** – good leaders included – opportunities. If a good leader can come in, impose some structure and nurture some good ideas, then you can have some very positive outcomes for the firm. The same could be true for the narcissist; some good outcomes could also result for the firm. While this is a question mark for either type of leader, one thing is rarely in question: you can be pretty sure that narcissistic leaders will personally benefit regardless of whether or not the company does. All of their energy and powers will be put into trying to redefine organizational goals to their advantage.

Ambiguity in human resource practices

Most human resource professionals will tell you that there is often a lot of ambiguity surrounding key organizational processes such as promotion decisions, compensation methods and performance appraisals. This allows for some dubious practices to take root. In fact, take a look at Table 10.1 where we present a list of questionable HR practices. There you'll see the results of a survey of nearly 1,000 HR managers who were asked to list management routines they considered unethical. We note several things about these findings. First, the list is formidable: there seem to be plenty of 'opportunities' for narcissists. Second, there seems to be considerable agreement among the HR professionals as to what constitutes a very questionable practice. Third, many of the practices listed were used as examples of narcissistic behaviour in our earlier chapters.

A lot of progress has been made over the last 20 years to develop procedures that reduce the subjectivity associated with HR functions. For instance, we have a growing set of tools in performance evaluation that can help a manager impose structure and clarity on assessments like these. Yet, as shown in Table 10.1, there are many questionable practices that still exist. Partly, this is because many organizations have been slow to adopt proven methods such as objective observation scales and multiple outcome measures. It's also due to the resources their adoption might require; bigger firms with bigger pockets are better able to integrate these methods into their appraisal systems. But, even among those companies that do use the more objective techniques, there's still ample opportunity for subjectivity to play a role. The large number of firms using the more traditional (and subjective) methods provides an even greater setting for ambiguity to be used for personal gain.

Table 10.1 Ratings of various unethical HR practices

Unethical Practice	Percentage Viewing the Practice as Very Serious
Hiring, training, or promoting based on favouritism	31
Allowing differences in pay due to friendship	31
Sexual harassment	28
Gender discrimination in promotion	27
Using discipline inconsistently	27
Not maintaining confidentiality	26
Gender discrimination in compensation	26
Use of non-performance factors in appraisals	24
Arrangements with vendors resulting in personal gain	23

Adapted from Greenberg and Baron[6]

In short, subjective performance and evaluation criteria are a big source of ambiguity, which narcissistic managers can capitalize on. Research has shown that in making personnel decisions, average managers are at least as concerned about the implications of their promotion and pay-rise decisions for their own careers (eg will this person support me and make me look good?) as they are about doing what is best for their company.[7] If this is the orientation of the average manager, imagine the perspective taken by the narcissist! Research is also consistent with these findings. For example, one in-depth study of executives revealed some very interesting observations:[8]

- By their own admission, 'politics' was nearly always part of their performance evaluation process.
- Interpersonal relations and dynamics with their subordinates were among the driving forces in performance evaluations.
- Most of the managers believed there was usually a justifiable reason for providing appraisals that were less than accurate: they felt it was part of the managerial discretion at their disposal.
- Finally, by their own admission, accuracy of appraisal was not the main concern of these managers; they were more concerned with motivation of subordinates. They made it clear they would use the evaluation process to their own advantage and they wouldn't let an 'obsession' with accuracy cause problems for themselves.

Consider the following quote by one manager, which illustrates what we're referring to:

> There is really no getting around the fact that whenever I evaluate one of my people, I stop and think about the impact, the ramifications of my decisions on my relationship with the guy and his future here. I'd be stupid not to. Call it being politically minded, or using managerial discretion, or fine-tuning the guy's ratings, but in the end I've got to live with him, and I'm not going to rate a guy without thinking about the fallout. There are a lot of games played in the rating process and whether we [managers] admit it or not we are all guilty of playing them at our discretion.[9]

In summary, this discussion suggests that there is still a lot of ambiguity in human resources activities. In the hands of a benevolent or even benign manager, this might not be bad, as shown in the quote above. At the same time, however, this makes HR operations a prime candidate for exploitation by the narcissistic manager. And – consonant with the theme of this chapter – if you permit or encourage ambiguity in organizational practices, you invite the unwanted influence of self-interested leaders to a similar extent!

Change or External Threats

Periods of organizational change present opportunities for the narcissistic brand of politics to emerge. We touched on this theme in Chapter 9, that change can be an excellent smokescreen for the narcissistic leader. Even if there are bona fide external threats, the restructuring of areas, the elimination of product lines, the downsizing and the mergers that are designed to meet them often provide open invitations for the narcissist. In fact, all this activity suggests – among other things – a good deal of ambiguity and probably not much accurate information, further allowing the narcissist to solidify his or her hold on power.

In these circumstances there is clearly a lot a stake. Specific people or whole units might also lose their jobs. Indeed, research also shows that 'reorganization changes' prompted more political activity on the part of managers than any other type of change.[9] This situation might also characterize firms in an industry with rapidly changing environments or technology. In this kind of industry, change is much more prominent by definition, and coincidentally the uncertainty of a rapidly changing present and future also play a role. This is the fertilizer that can grow a narcissistic leader.

A Hierarchical Culture

Another plus for the narcissist is to operate in a traditionally hierarchical culture. If employees are used to 'going through channels' and blindly obeying supervisors and upper management, then the characteristics of the narcissist would not be that out of line. This is especially interesting in the light of our discussion of ambiguity. One of the usual advantages of a strict hierarchy is that it provides a lot of clarity. Employees typically know what procedures they should follow, whom they should answer to, and the form and speed of that answer. Accordingly, you might think that hierarchies are not good places to spawn a narcissist. Yet, other features of hierarchies do seem to be well suited for this type of leadership. For example, decision-making control is held closely in tall organizations. Likewise, communication patterns can be better controlled and monitored, another plus for the narcissist's need to control the outflow of information (or disinformation). In other words, a narcissist would fit in nicely – and probably function much better and longer – in a historically hierarchical culture.

Overt Signs of a Culture Conducive to Narcissists

Overall, what should you look for that might be indicative of a good situation for narcissistic leadership to emerge? Here are a few things to look for in your own organization:

■ Does your firm have a strong need to put a positive spin on everything? While this may be a tendency for many of us, if it happens all the time and about nearly everything, there could be a problem, one that would invite the solutions posed by a narcissist.

■ As a corollary to the above, how does the company handle critics, especially internal ones? If there is an almost natural tendency to blame or even kill the messenger, this is suggestive of problems in receiving and integrating feedback.

■ Are leaders given significant status symbols? Do they have a dramatically different set of perquisites from the average employee? Are there a lot of stories about 'hero' leaders of the past or present? Does the firm go to great lengths to justify dramatically higher compensation packages for leaders? Such attributes would suggest an overemphasis of the impact of the leader on the organization – just the kind of opening a narcissist is seeking.

■ Has a major organizational change taken place recently, especially one that has involved buyouts or other large-scale movements of managers? The ambiguity created by the change, in combination with a possible power vacuum, could spell trouble.

■ Is information scarce? Do people get key information from media stories or when it's trickled out via internal company newsletters? Is there an evaluation procedure in place, one that is well explained and communicated? The presence or absence of these things is relatively easy to observe. The narcissist could always abolish or nullify them once in power, but their existence discourages the acquisition of power in the first place.

WHAT THE NARCISSIST NEEDS TO SUCCEED

Just because the corporate culture is right for narcissists doesn't necessarily mean that they'll get to feast on the firm. Instead, they generally need to have a few things in place to ensure their success.

Accomplices

In many cases, narcissistic leaders need a base of support. They need somebody they can count on to sell their self-interested agenda in a non-threatening way. Or even better, they need someone to sell it as exactly what the organization needs here and now. In Chapter 9, we talked about the role of consultants in pitching this story. While they may represent a very good first step, especially in fleshing out the general direction of the narcissistic agenda in acceptable ways, their sales role is a bit circumscribed. Everybody knows the advocacy role that most consultants play. As a result, their credibility in selling and carrying forward the agenda is limited. Insiders are much better at carrying the torch. The motivation of these 'accomplices' is varied. Some well-intentioned people may truly and genuinely believe in the new agenda being brought forward by the narcissistic leader. They may strongly believe in the need for sweeping, positive change for the organization, a story often spun by the narcissist. Accordingly, they will be among the narcissist's most credible advocates and may take positive steps to enact the agenda.

Go along to get along

Others, however, have much seamier motives in mind when they agree to be accomplices. Some may have done a frank assessment of their skills and what they have to offer, and end up concluding that they had better play along. Such people are relatively easy to spot by real organizational contributors. The 'Me, Myself and I' box below says it all.

So, in some cases you have people who've sat down with themselves, read the writing on the wall and made the calculated decision to be accomplices to the narcissist. While these people are unlikely to carry the day with their credibility, in certain numbers, and in combination with other accomplices, they provide the narcissist with a comfortable and formidable base from which to draw support.

Silent support

Another group that adds to this effect is the 'silent set'. These are people who hold some sort of power position in the organization, although subsidiary to the narcissist. They might be a set of senior managers, an executive committee, or an advisory panel. If this group itself consists of poor leaders, or worse yet, a set of people fearful of losing their positions of influence or the little empires they've acquired over the years,

ME, MYSELF AND I

So which way is the wind blowing?

Jim threw in the towel some time ago. While he can work hard if he wanted to, for some reason he just doesn't. He's been skating by now for several years and the previous VP just didn't call him on it. The weird thing is most of us at Jim's level know he's a loser and so do many of the employees. Of course, you don't have much clout or moral authority when employees have to call you on your cell phone out at the country club.

Lately, since Bill has come on board as the new VP, Jim's done a psychological 180 degrees. Jim knows that Bill is trying to move up fast and only wants ass-kissers hanging around. So now the same guy who never met a change he liked is now this passionate champion for corporate renewal. Now he's mouthing support for every new programme that Bill wants to trot out, like that goofy operation proposed in the Middle East. Where's the market in Yemen? And you know what the funny thing is? Jim still doesn't do a lick of work. As long as he nods his head every time Bill opens his mouth, he can keep putting out 10%. Jim's just the worst kind of snake.

Department manager, environmental services firm

then the organization's in even more trouble. The acquiescence of this group to the narcissist's power plays provides a mixed signal to many organizational members. If you assume the group is composed of at least some people who have earned widespread respect in the firm, then their silence can speak loudly.

Let's assume that the narcissists have revealed their true selves to a few people who've had the unfortunate experience of getting in their way. If these people speak up either publicly or in private, they could risk their positions. If they have enough power or respect, and the narcissists are still new or on shaky ground, what impact will speaking up have? Probably little. Employees and other managers might logically analyse a situation this way. How could this one person be right with these hardball and nutty things he or she is saying about the new VP? If they were true, wouldn't other executives also have had the same experiences? In short, the 'silent set' provides a valuable buffer for narcissists while they consolidate their power even further. When they do, there won't be any further public or semi-private complaints aired, you can bet on that.

Counting on the 'support' of opposition

Finally, the narcissist might benefit from the 'services' of a set of unwitting accomplices as well. A group of people can provide a certain level of support for the self-interested leader if they are at odds with other groups opposed to the narcissist. In normal circumstances these groups could band together in their opposition, but because they are now in different camps their differences and vulnerabilities can be exploited by the narcissist. In fact, not only can't they put up a united front, but the narcissist can point to these conflicts as a justification for his or her strong leadership style, essentially saying, 'You need me to take care of the serious divisions that exist here.'

Support of a Second Constituency

While not a strict necessity, it's often valuable for the narcissist to have the support of a second constituency, usually outside the firm. So, if the narcissistic CEO can make direct and credible appeals to shareholders, the financial community, or the press, then he or she has another weapon in a self-imposed war.

Scarce Resources

Political behaviour of all sorts is likely to increase when resources become scarce).[11] And, as we've documented, politicking is one of the narcissist's special skills. So a situation of scarce resources is one that the narcissist is perfectly suited to exploit. One way to do this is to scatter 'IOUs' around judiciously. Granting favours both with internal groups of accomplices and among the external bases of support is probably always useful, but especially valuable in hard times when resources are scarce.

The Right Climatic Conditions

Sometimes narcissists can just get lucky in their choice of an industry or organization. For example, new division heads could capitalize on the spotty reputation of their managers. They could gather support by bad-mouthing that group, and be listened to. Or new CEOs of an airline might pick up credits toward enacting their self-serving agendas because of the reputation of their workforce. You know what we mean – pilots are people who really don't work very long or hard, and are prima donnas who won't play team ball in the business world. Instead, they and their accomplices (flight attendants, maintenance staff, etc) often create positive damage to the company for no good reason. The same is true for those damn university professors – they only teach a few days a week, have lifetime employment and can't be motivated. Speaking as professors, we can tell you that there are in fact lazy professors who don't add too much to the organization. But, let's face it, many firms and industries have similar baggage to carry and problems with deadwood of one kind or another. Nevertheless, sometimes narcissists can just get lucky by exploiting some long-standing animosity or underlying tension.

The Availability of a Group to Blame

Another function provided by standing animosity is that narcissists have a built-in group to blame when and if things go wrong. The 'Me, Myself and I' box below illustrates what we mean.

ME, MYSELF AND I

Road trip gone awry

I remember early on when Mindy was trying to get us involved in that ridiculous venture in the Dominican Republic. Already there were lots of questions about the outlandish things she was saying and her credit grabs. Anyway, she was on her way there to resurrect a venture we nixed long ago – after much more analysis than she's put in now. She first flew to Miami to pick up a connecting flight. Somehow she got on the wrong plane and didn't realize it until the pilot came on the intercom to announce that 'we're beginning our final descent to Port-au-Prince' (Haiti). The idiot just got in line, boarded the wrong flight and then didn't listen when the obligatory announcements were made – including the one that said the flight was going to Haiti! She had to stay overnight because there were no other flights and missed the meeting altogether in the Dominican Republic. That was bad enough, but of course she couldn't take the blame herself. She bitched out the office staff publicly the first thing on her return. Right then we all should have realized what we had on our hands.

Unit manager, financial services firm

Wrapping Things Up

In this section we've shown that there seems to be a set of 'climatic' conditions that is ideal for the formation of a narcissistic regime. Such conditions can promote and accelerate narcissists' rise and consolidation of power. When these cultural conditions interact with some other favourable conditions, as outlined above, a 'supercell' of narcissists can form faster than you can say 'Dilbert'. When it does you had better find some shelter, and we don't mean retreating to your cubicle. You'd better get to the organizational equivalent of your basement, and fast. Throughout the book we have talked about steps that individuals or sets of people can take to prevent the roof blowing off their careers. But we've said little about what the **organization** can (or should) do to change the conditions that promote self-interested leadership to start with. We'll finish this chapter with such a discussion.

WHAT COMPANIES CAN DO TO LIMIT NARCISSISTIC INFLUENCES

What can an organization do to prevent self-interested leadership from taking hold? We feel we should be candid with you before you read our suggestions. Frankly, our opinion is that it is often damn near impossible to prevent a narcissist from rising to power. Many of the above organizational conditions we've outlined above are common in US firms. Indeed, some of those conditions are directly fostered by upper management. For example, a time-honoured technique is to pit different groups within the firm against one another in an ostensibly healthy competition. And in theory there's nothing wrong with this – it's as American as apple pie, downsizing and overpaid executives. Seriously though, internal competition is often a very good thing, providing a number of tangible pluses for the firm. But part of the baggage carried with those pluses is the negative that results from providing an opening for a narcissistic manager.

Likewise, a hierarchical culture is common. While tall organizations have been criticized by popular business writers and academics alike, they seem to stick around. One reason is that they make it easy for managers to get things done. And also, people in the United States like 'doers', people who can cut through stuff and get something done. While we've argued that upon close inspection narcissists often get a house of cards built, they at least have the initial reputation of getting things done.

So it's no surprise that US firms like definitive and decisive leaders who can think on their feet. Plus, as we said back in Chapter 1, nowhere is individualism worshipped more strongly than in the US.[12] Interestingly, Japan and some other Asian countries are at the opposite end of the spectrum, holding among the most collective attitudes. Collectivism refers to a concern for the outcomes of the work group and company as opposed to those of specific individuals. This may explain why currently popular techniques such as teams and total quality programmes seem to be more successful in Asian (collective) countries. The individual-collective dimension may also explain why narcissistic, self-interested leadership is more common in the US.

Regardless, there seem to be a number of overarching reasons why it might be extremely difficult for an organization to eliminate the conditions that give rise to narcissistic leadership patterns. So, while we think it is very difficult to prevent narcissists from gaining power, it is still useful to consider some longer-range things a firm can do to minimize their impact.

Get Rid of Uncertainty

If you've just endured a very bad experience with a narcissist maybe you've given them what they need – lots of organizational ambiguity. We've argued that this is exactly what narcissists covet. In fact, once they do take the reins of power, they often act to increase any uncertainty that already exists. What should you do?[13]

- **Make it clear to people what the processes for evaluation are.** In addition to adding clarity, this can reduce the dependency of employees on particular managers, which reduces the ability of narcissists to cultivate followers.
- **Be sure the system differentiates between good and bad performers.** This limits narcissists' ability to create sycophants and foster bootlicking.
- **Reward as quickly and directly as you can and communicate the basis for rewards.**

Of course, some organizations just won't insist on any of these steps. In fact, some firms claim that ambiguity in performance standards is a good thing. A senior partner at one consulting firm recently said that management feels that it can get a lot more productivity from new accountants if the standards for promotion are unclear. What's the average work week? 'I really can't say – but a lot of people work really hard. . . 60, 70 hours per week is not uncommon.' What is a typical path to partnership? 'That's not exactly clear. . . the only commonality is extremely hard work and dedication.' And the partner revealed that this ambiguity is deliberate and strategic: the firm believes it leads to more work and higher performance. Whether it does or not is not our concern here – it very well might. But our point is that this 'deliberate' ambiguity is a big opening for narcissists.

Open the Flow of Information

The influence of narcissists is greatly enhanced when they can control the flow of information. For example, narcissists can increase ambiguity by releasing slanted information. And, of course, they can let out only the details that support their self-interested agendas. So, what specifically can be done here?

- **Consider the use of bottom-up methods of communication, with the appropriate protections of anonymity if necessary, as opposed to top-down methods.** Consider personal meetings, open door policies and other ways to encourage relevant feedback.
- **Take advantage of the firm's intranet, if one exists.** This is a useful and widespread way to communicate. Management can respond rapidly to issues that arise, fending off the ambiguity and rumours that might result from slower forms of communication. Computer communication can be more 'democratic' and representative of opinions – certainly more so than relying on the narcissist's set of groupies.
- **Use an open-book management style.** This entails sharing a lot of information throughout the organization, and is certainly an enemy of narcissistic leadership. (We'll have more to say about open-book management in Chapter 11.)

Don't Turn a Blind Eye to Warning Signs

It's amazing how quickly a signal can be sent that politicking – the special skills that are the purview of narcissists – is in season. Sometimes you may need just one critical event. This may involve some sort of corruption, like a promotion that was given for political support instead of performance. Then it becomes a division of the spoils and sides are taken (as we described in earlier chapters). Accordingly, failure to take action in the face of corruption can be a strong signal to members of the organization. What should you do?

- **Lead by example: don't do these things.** Or if you do, you had better fully and clearly explain why it was necessary.
- **Discourage personal attacks and backbiting.** If an employee comes in to complain about someone and in so doing delivers what amounts to an unjustified and personalized assault, stop him or her – in mid-sentence if you have to. Explain that complaints should focus on issues and behaviours without resorting to verbal abuse and personal attacks. Such a message sends a strong signal that will help discourage this kind of personal destruction.
- **Monitor intra-company competition so it doesn't get out of hand.** And, in the future, consider some co-operative scheme to counter-balance any negative effects of competition.
- **Consider the practice of job rotation.** This would encourage broader thinking and could actually promote a better understanding across groups, thereby obviating the ability of the narcissist to play camps against one another. Likewise, if job rotation won't work, try breaking up the fiefdoms that a narcissist can exploit.

CHAPTER TAKE-AWAYS

- Although narcissism is a personality trait that is built up and encouraged by years of experience, this doesn't mean you have to attack it at the personal level. There seem to be some organizational cultures and conditions that encourage this type of self-interested leadership.
- Forewarned is forearmed. If you're aware of these conditions you can do a couple of things. First, you can analyse the culture and decide if it's place you want to stay at. Second, if you do want to stay, you can work to change those conditions that make it ripe for the taking by a narcissist.
- Be especially sensitive to the cultural characteristics of the firm that seem to encourage ambiguity. These might include a lack of clarity in performance evaluations, uncertain promotion criteria, and poor or restrictive communication patterns. Collectively, these and other conditions make a favourable culture for a narcissist.

▓ Just because the culture recipe is right for narcissists doesn't necessarily mean that they'll get to feast on the firm. A few other things generally have to be in place to ensure their success. It's here that management might have the best chance of blocking a narcissist's rise and consolidation of power. Be aware of things like accomplices, narcissistic appeals to a sympathetic audience, and scapegoats.

Chapter 11

Picking up the pieces: Life after the narcissist

ME, MYSELF AND I

Down the road to cynicism and anger

We intensely disliked him. No one respected or trusted him. This significantly hurt morale and created cynicism. When the boss was transferred, it was to be announced at a section meeting attended by several hundred people. When the announcement came, the crowd actually clapped and cheered in front of him and the rest of the top executives!

Manager, electric utility

My reactions to my narcissistic boss were ones of irritation and frustration. We would also make fun of her and ridicule her. I was embarrassed to even work for her. There were many times when I would walk away from her swearing under my breath at what a self-absorbed idiot she was.

Accounting manager, power transmission equipment firm

We all hated his guts and constantly talked about him behind his back. Our favourite names for him were 'psycho', 'Mr Evil' and 'that little fuck!' We had an 'alumni club' of ex-subordinates that we called 'The Post-Traumatic Stress Society'. Whenever people quit, the 'Society' threw them a congratulatory party. Some of us who were left used to have an office pool about who would be the next to leave. We also had this fake chessboard. We moved around the little paper 'pawns' that represented each of us.

Manager, software and database marketing firm

We hated him and went around saying mean and cruel things about him. Some of us had violent thoughts about what we would like to do to him, like hitting him or worse. What was really hard to understand was how the other two business partners (he was one of three owners) could stand him.

Line supervisor, automotive component manufacturer

LOST LIVES

These comments from employees underscore how hard it is to rebuild true commitment and loyalty given what the victims of narcissistic leaders feel and experience. This should give companies real reason to worry. Part of the problem is that many corporations simply haven't grasped one basic reality: that all employees work under a contract. And we're not talking about unions. What we're saying is that employees work according to the psychological contract that they believe exists between themselves and their firms. Of course, not all contracts are good. 'You pretend to pay me, and I'll pretend to work' captures the essence of one such contract! But a quality employment relationship is based on mutual obligation, respect and concern. If the company – or its representatives – violates that contract, employees often react with intense anger and a sense of betrayal.[1] Left to fester, that can produce an unhealthy level of cynicism that lasts for years.

While a narcissistic leader is in place, there's often a sense of raw incredulity about how the company can let the narcissist continue to destroy the place from within. That's one of the reasons why bitterness and cynicism linger even after the narcissist is gone. In other words, narcissistic leadership destroys employees' belief that the company will act fairly and do the right thing over the long haul. That's especially the case because the narcissistic leader is someone who, as a representative of the company, couldn't care less about subordinates. So when it comes to the perceived contract between employee and company, a narcissist is the psychological equivalent of a paper shredder!

Up to this point in the book, we've spent a lot of time considering organizational life under the narcissist. We've tried to give you a picture of what everyday work life might be like in a narcissistic organization. And it's not a pretty picture. What's more, we have just completed a chapter showing that there may be all sorts of organizational inertia, norms and structures that encourage and even foster self-serving leaders. If you survive this (and many do not) because the narcissist finally leaves or is forced out, don't necessarily count yourself among the lucky. In fact, many people think that the hard work has really only just begun. A few years after the narcissist's accession, he or she may be on the road to a new gig. You should certainly take a little time and thank your lucky stars that you were able to dump the narcissist because the poor saps at some other company didn't do their homework either. Or you can temporarily pat the board or higher management on the back for finally pulling the trigger, if that's the way the narcissist left. But don't take a long vacation, because now it's time to pick up the pieces and the psychological debris left behind by this narcissistic tornado.

What happens after the narcissist is gone? As we've said, many at first give thanks. But they should recognize that another narcissist might see the opening and move in. In other words, it is quite possible that after suffering one self-interested regime, along comes another person with equally blind ambition. This is a familiar pattern since it's unlikely that any of the cultural characteristics that invited narcissism in the first place have been dealt with (as we showed in the previous chapter).

Another common pattern after the departure of a narcissist is for his or her replacement to come from the ranks. This can often mean that the replacement is an ex-accomplice of the narcissist, someone who was in the right place because of a close association with the former boss. In this situation, you obviously still have a load of trouble. While you may not see abusive behaviour rise to the previously high levels, it could still rise high enough to sting. Plus, you may also see a 'circling of the wagons' among the accomplices. There may be great efforts made by accomplices to rehabilitate their reputations and to distance themselves from the deposed narcissist.

At a minimum, this kind of strategy is extremely annoying to any subordinates who resisted the narcissist's siren calls. Outrage is also a likely reaction (eg 'Who do these people think they're kidding, saying that they were fighting back all along!'). But there are also deeper worries here for the company as a whole. The reality is that the ex-accomplices – their public spin notwithstanding – are essentially power-holders trying to retain the status quo. After all, they benefit if the current system continues and they certainly wouldn't want to blow the whistle on the edifice created by the narcissist, from which they gained. In this case, you would be less likely to see the toxic effects we've described in earlier chapters, but you're not likely to see a lot of real improvement either.

Hopefully, however, your organization will find someone who wants to try to tackle the cultural features that promote narcissistic behavioural styles. Clearly, this offers the most hope for 'survivors' of the 'ego warrior' who has departed for more bountiful conquests. But even if you're lucky enough to get a good replacement for the self-interested leader, what is he or she likely to face and how might the issues be dealt with? The challenges are many. Key people have probably left because they were fed up. Many of their replacements, especially those hired by narcissists, are likely to be less skilled and generally weak-kneed (see earlier chapters). So cleaning out the place may still be necessary, prompting a high level of turnover that will make the new leader's job difficult and unsettled for some time. Certainly, there is likely to be a lack of co-ordination and teamwork among units or subgroups of subordinates who have been played off against one another (again, please see earlier chapters). But the biggest challenge faced by the new leadership will be to overcome the incredible amount of **cynicism** that clings to the firm.

Understanding Cynicism

Cynicism is many things, but one of its general characteristics is a lack of trust. Cynics question the motives of others; they doubt that people have the best of intentions and they are pessimistic and bleak about the future. They distrust other people and their take on events. Ironically, that's an important thing when it comes to narcissism – that the cynical perspective is also accurate! Cynics' perceptions and feelings, dismal and sceptical as they may be, are borne out by their experience with narcissism. In fact, the transformation from a positive, forward-thinking employee to a cynical one is a complex process. Cynicism is something that sneaks up on employees slowly and may even be resisted by them. In fact, earlier we highlighted how difficult it is for some people to adopt a cynical view, even after very bad experiences with narcissists. But in the end, many employees find themselves second-guessing every move the company makes as being driven by some unholy mix of hubris and ineptitude. What's even worse is that employees know they're the ones who pay the price for executive miscues.

The decline of trust

There's also a wider phenomenon at work here that isn't limited to the US. Trust has taken it on the chin in many organizations around the globe. Years of shenanigans by self-interested leadership – double-speaking, downsizing, rightsizing, layoffs and involvement – have left far too many employees with a jaundiced view of their companies. The popularity of the Dilbert character – the 'everyman' employee whose basic thesis is that all leaders are self-absorbed, stupid, or both – speaks to that view. In fact, it's hard not to run into Dilbert paraphernalia (there are best-selling books, calendars, comic strips, videos and even a cartoon show on TV).

Likewise, quasi-documentary films such as *Roger and Me* are another case in point).[2] One study, for example, showed that a viewing of *Roger and Me* – a highly critical look at General Motors and its former CEO Roger Smith – was enough to push already cynical workers toward embracing even more negative attitudes about corporations. By the way, the man responsible for all this – Michael Moore – also has made it on to TV with his own show, which among other things continues to target corporate big shots. For instance, in a recent episode, Moore showed up at Bill Gates's home outside Seattle to give the Microsoft chairman a few birthday presents, among them a toaster and a weed-whacker, useful items for 'the billionaire who has everything'.

It wasn't always this way. Back in 1966, most people probably wouldn't have given someone like Michael Moore the time of day. In fact, that year a study done found that over 75 per cent of people in the United States trusted statements made by corporate officials. By the mid-1990s, however, only about 15 per cent were willing to say the same.[3] We are not going to say that this entire precipitous plunge is due to narcissism. But we believe a decent chunk of it is!

The growth of cynicism

Let's be more specific about what we mean. For example, consider a situation in which virtually everybody agrees that the company already has serious problems or is about to be overtaken by competitive threats. Even the supporters and accomplices of the narcissistic leader acknowledge the gravity of the situation. What's also commonly known is that the narcissist has a well-deserved reputation for a variety of extreme and excessive behaviours (eg self-interested bullying). In fact, not only do top executives recognize these behaviours, they may also feel that the behaviours are actually positives given the situation facing the company. Put another way, they may effectively be saying, 'Yes, this guy's a self-interested bastard, but he's our self-interested bastard. Let's turn him loose. This is the guy who will get in there and finally kick some ass to get things moving!'

Of course, if everybody knows about the behavioural quirks of the narcissist, 'everybody' includes employees. That knowledge plus awareness that senior management is effectively condoning narcis-sistic abuses is bound to give cynical attitudes a major boost! For instance, in one organization that we're familiar with, one particular narcissistic leader was so well known that his behaviour was the subject of several newspaper articles within a matter of months. Later, after a group of several mid-level managers resigned, another set of managers anonymously took their juicy titbits and stories about the narcissist to the press after failing to get upper management to act on their complaints. The resulting level of cynicism within the organization basically rotted out its ability to perform well. Eventually, senior management in the firm realized that they had made a mistake and that the price for turning unbridled narcissism loose was too high. But when – **or if** – the narcissist is replaced under these circumstances, that's hardly the end of the story. Indeed, it's arguably when a pattern of even bigger trouble begins.

For example, let's say that to fix their mistake, senior leaders have the narcissist in question quickly and quietly moved out. But if the narcissist has been playing true to form all along (eg manipulating information, publicly bullying subordinates, etc), then senior management has a huge job ahead. On the one hand, they have to explain why the narcissist left to his or her supporters. On the other, they have to continue to prop up the explanations that caused them to bring the narcissistic leader in to begin with (eg a poorly performing unit, or great resistance to change), especially those that were constantly mouthed by the narcissist. After all, the company may have publicly bragged about and rewarded the narcissist for his or her 'successes' in changing the direction of the unit or organization. And, as we've documented, if the narcissist is anywhere near the point of controlling information sources, then there will have been successes – lots of them – and no real failures. And now is no time to admit that those successes were largely a house of cards if not complete fictions.

In other words, those executives who removed the narcissist – often the same people who supported his or her behaviour earlier – are now in a tough position. They often have to simultaneously protect their reputation and the firm's while at the same time explaining why the narcissist had to go. Of course, managing such contradictions is damn near impossible in the best of circumstances, much less when cynical employees are wearing their 'BS detectors' like badges of honour. From their perspective, the machinations of upper management only deepen and cement their cynicism. Employees will argue that top executives are hypocrites – that they knowingly let the narcissist rampage on, and only put a stop to things when the situation got completely out of control.

One response to the deepening employee cynicism that we sometimes see is for the firm's top management essentially to plead *nolo contendere*. They'll claim that they didn't have knowledge of the narcissist's self-absorbed excesses until it was brought to their attention. Alternatively, they may employ a 'duck and cover' manoeuvre. In other words, company management will claim that:

- the narcissistic leader actually did a lot of good work;
- the narcissistic leader got the company or unit moving in the right direction;
- the 'bad behaviour' of the narcissistic leader was wildly exaggerated by naysayers and political opponents;
- the narcissistic leader left the company of his or her own volition to 'pursue a better opportunity'.

In short, they do a little information manipulation of their own. Now, we can all see 'good' reasons why the company may not want to admit publicly its role in promoting and encouraging the narcissist. But all of us should also recognize that a toll will be exacted for: a) letting the narcissist run wild; and b) not acknowledging that this is in fact what has occurred. The cost: cynicism – in spades.

RECOGNIZING SIGNS OF MISTRUST AND CYNICISM

Short of living through this experience, how might you recognize the signs of cynicism? There are often some conspicuous symptoms of the more latent disease of organizational cynicism. Of course, while it's difficult directly to observe this particular state of mind in employees, nevertheless there are some overt signs.

Communication problems

As we've documented earlier, narcissists are expert at crafting and presenting information to support their agendas. Often this comes in the form of visions wrapped around selfish fantasies, excessive impression management, and the manipulation and exploitation of subordinates. So if you want to make a dent in that enormous level of cynicism, be on the lookout for poor communication, especially of the deliberate variety.

In general, corporations are not very good at communicating with either their employees or the general public about their actions. As we noted above, in many firms employee cynicism may be at an all-time high. Undoubtedly, part of this is due to poor communication patterns. Above, we've implied that there are situational pressures on management to 'miscommunicate' about departing narcissists and surviving employees. This accounts for some communication problems. But when a set of poor skills meets the need to mislead, bad communication can have even more insidious effects. There's even a term for this – 'corporate doublespeak'. It refers to the skill and ability – often possessed by narcissists, but certainly not their exclusive province – to mislead deliberately. There is a variety of euphemisms for this, including 'corporate-babble' and 'business-speak'. Of course, at the individual level we have a much more familiar term for this behaviour: we call it just plain lying. As we mentioned in Chapter 3, there are varying attitudes toward candour at work. Even though most people think that lying is wrong, many of those same individuals will think lying is justified to protect a company secret or even to avoid bad publicity.[4]

But one thing is clear: misleading communication is an art that is cultivated by narcissists. They know the scam well – 'doublespeak' is their way of pretending to communicate, but is in reality designed to turn bad into good, while shifting blame at the same time. Doublespeak has always been popular among government leaders, where we are told that taxes are 'revenue enhancements', invasions are 'pre-dawn vertical insertions' and accidental deaths are 'incidental effects of friendly fire'. Fortunately, most corporate doublespeak, while annoying, doesn't deal with matters of life and death. Instead, it's laughably used to hawk 'real counterfeit diamonds', 'previously owned cars' and 'imported polyester and vegetarian leather' (aka vinyl).

Especially troublesome is language used not only to deliberately confuse, but also to hide important facts. Consider these examples:

- Some years ago, an airline had the unenviable task of telling shareholders that the firm earned $1.7 million (from insurance payments) after one of its Boeing 727 jets crashed, killing three people. The airline's annual report said the income resulted from 'involuntary conversion of a 727 aircraft'.
- A car company had to recall two of its models to fix a mechanical deficiency. In a letter to owners, the firm admitted that the rear axle bearings 'can deteriorate'. They also said that 'continued driving could result in disengagement of the axle shaft and adversely affect vehicle control'. The letter seemed to obfuscate both responsibility

and potential bad outcomes. The 'continued driving' part of the sentence subtly shifts responsibility from the company to a persistent driver, and we all know what 'adversely affect control' really means. The company allegedly sold cars with serious defects that could throw them out of control, causing a crash.

Unfortunately, these aren't the only disturbing examples. Consider the annual reports of many US firms. Some companies spend tens of millions of dollars on these documents. One study looked at chairman's letters in the annual reports of companies that made Workplace America's list of the 50 biggest job-reduction announcements. Ironically, many of these letters made specific reference to their employees, using words such as 'motivated', 'committed' and 'the best' (10 firms), 'skilled' or 'talented' (nine firms) and 'dedicated' (eight). Here are some quotes taken from those reports, with the number of layoffs for each firm in parentheses:

- 'Outstanding people. . . if we have a secret weapon, this is it.' *Cummings Engine* (2,000)
- 'Our skilled, dedicated, and hard-working employees remain our most important asset.' *American Home Products* (6,500)
- 'Satisfied employees are a necessary precondition for satisfied customers. We deeply appreciate the accomplishments of thousands of dedicated employees.' *Bank of Boston* (2,000)
- 'We are fortunate in having bright, highly motivated men and women. . . Our employees' interests have never been more in line with our shareholders' interests.' *Chemical Bank* (12,000)

A few of the CEOs in this study truly sounded sorrowful and direct. Northrup's CEO called their 5,400 job cuts as 'being our toughest decision'. Other CEOs even took the blame for company failures. GE's industrial electronic division didn't translate record sales into better earnings, which was explained as 'a management execution miss'. B.F. Goodrich lost millions when their prediction of a polyvinyl chloride shortage went sour. The company admitted that it fell short, saying simply that 'many of our forecasts were wrong'. But, for the most part, CEOs talked about job cuts in **positive** ways. Times Mirror (3,000 jobs lost) cited layoffs as among its 'several operating improvements'. This may explain why some critics claim that top executives are 'the world's worst communicators'.[5] As we have shown, however, deliberate miscommunication is one of the narcissist's special skills. In these cases, the company grapevine is probably operating at full bandwidth.

Turnover problems

Ultimately, people with options may respond to narcissism with their feet, not their mouths. In our own surveys of employees, turnover issues were spontaneously mentioned by many as one of the consequences of narcissistic leaders. Some employees put a number on the problem: our observed range was from 40 per cent to 400 per cent annual turnover! Further, this turnover typically occurs disproportionately among the best performers. High performers tend to be the least tolerant of narcissism and are often the biggest targets of narcissists. Not surprisingly, many high performers are active resisters of narcissists. If you can remember a lot of good stories about these people, but you don't see their faces any more, that's a strong symptom of the problem. Losing good people is doubly bad: they often go to the competition and while there attack your company, sharing lots of tales about narcissistic excesses.

Rising complaints

One relatively objective thing you can examine is the number of formal complaints made against the company. In the US, these could include EEOC (Equal Employment Opportunity Commission) filings, formal grievances, appeals of decisions, lawsuits and workplace compensation requests. If some or all of these have been on the rise or are at an all-time high, it might reflect the rippling effects of self-interested narcissists. Unfortunately, many firms learn too late that employees can pull out technicalities just as easily as the firm can. The departing narcissist often leaves a firm facing a wealth of circumstantial and direct evidence for employee claims.

Other assorted signals

Sometimes the final 'days' of narcissists are characterized by a strict adherence to the formal, published rules of the organization. Following rules, of course, is the one thing narcissists think other people should do, not they. Toward the end of their tenure, they may have pulled out rules that no one ever knew existed in order to protect their fiefdoms. People who are not playing ball with them might for example find travel vouchers and expenses rejected because they failed to file them within three days – an obscure rule that had never been enforced. As a result of this kind of enforcement effort, an organization often becomes much more rigid under a narcissist. Of course, two can play that game. Employees, for example, often insist on this as a way to cover themselves in the event of a narcissist turning his or her wrath their way. So a rigid, formal culture with lots of rules and procedures, while not definitive, can sometimes be observed after a narcissist leaves.

Finally, if you're new to the organization, don't expect to hear a lot of this information from the existing workforce. Managers as well as employees, whether or not they have joined the ranks of accomplices, are often overly quiet even when prompted about the presence of problems.[6] There will still be considerable fear among employees; and there will be cynicism about those who come along and say they want to change things for the better.

RE-ESTABLISHING TRUST

Throughout the book, we've been focusing essentially on those things narcissists do that destroy trust. If your company has been smart enough to depose a powerful narcissistic leader quickly, it probably knows better than us how to work on re-establishing lost trust. On the other hand, if this process took a very long time or other reasons explain the departure of the narcissist (eg some other company was foolish enough to make a better offer), then we may have some useful advice.

You'll Need Some Luck

We must offer a caveat, however, before we get started. It is very likely that you will be unsuccessful, even if you perfectly apply all of these ideas. We've said earlier that cynicism is likely to be at a generally high level already; combined with what probably happened under a narcissistic leader, this is a formidable obstacle. Consider the case of a narcissist who was CEO of a software development company. His style included yelling and swearing, the public dressing-down of employees, and pitting various VPs against one another. In general, he created a high level of fear and cynicism. Many people were working on an elaborate software system that was seen as the new jewel of their product line. A bright young woman on the project team had the temerity to mildly criticize the process used to develop the program in a meeting.

The CEO stopped the meeting after she expressed her reservations. She was escorted from the room and fired within the hour by a 'VP who was tight with the CEO'. Eventually, the CEO was removed when the company lost over $6 million in the first year after the software release. The program was a disaster and didn't work well. In the view of the new CEO, 'more energy and time was spent covering your butt than on the quality of the program', as illustrated by the firing story. The new CEO gave his overall assessment in this way: 'People were scared here. They were like starved children. Their security was threatened. Their self-esteem was damaged. They had lost their belief in themselves and their ability to do quality work. Some people will never really get over that kind of experience no matter how different I am'.[7]

What a Task!

So how do you rebuild trust? Like the new CEO in the above story, people brought in to clean up after narcissists have their work cut out for them. Often they are not told of the enormity of the task they face: in fact, they may often get exactly the opposite picture. We can see why this should be the case. Those instrumental in acclimatizing the new leader are often the same people who were left holding the reins of power after the old leader left – the accomplices, the yes-men and the hangers-on. They provide the initial story to the new, incoming leader about the 'state of the firm'.

Depending on the severity of the post-narcissist problems, this story could be pitched in one of a number of ways. New leaders may be told that everything has been blown completely out of proportion. Or the new person may get an acknowledgement of the fact that damage has been done. But there's a twist. To protect the company reputation ('How could you hire such an SOB?' or 'Why would you keep such a person on the staff?'), the source of the problem is shifted. Perhaps the blame is laid on problem employees, middle managers trying to retain their newly earned perks, or jealous upper management. So in addition to all the problems detailed above, another one may intensify the whole situation: the failure to come to grips with what has really happened. And, as we've just mentioned, there will be plenty of efforts made to rewrite history. The immensity of the task aside, what sort of things should be done to re-energize the demoralized and cynical employees, at least those who are left?

Reach Out to the Survivors

First, sit down with the cynics and hear them out. After all, these 'survivors' are the repository of lots of information and history about the organization and its support of narcissism. Like a traditional 'exit' interview, these discussions can be the source of some valuable – but uncomfortable – information about the culture that might have spawned and fostered a narcissist. This information can be collected by an outside consultant or by the new leadership team; either mode can be fruitful.

This process can be time-consuming and gut-wrenching. In fact, some critics suggest that such discussion amounts to dwelling on the negative past rather than looking forward to a brighter future. While there is something to be said for this view, it's important to note that it's often espoused by the surviving accomplices of the narcissist. In many cases, it is to their advantage to drop any analysis of the past and 'move on' to the brighter future. But doing just that may create even more cynicism. For example, several of the participants in our research pointed out that accomplices of the departed narcissist often said things like 'We need to move on and do some healing around here rather than focus on the negative.' Likewise, our participants reported even more anger in response to statements such as 'You need to get over it.' It might be just as bad to ignore the past bad feelings as simply to belittle or dismiss them. Some managers and consultants alike approach their work with an organization as if it were a blank screen. Employees, of course, know better, and this can be seen in many other management initiatives. For example, just because a consultant or company leader is serious about an intention to explore the use of teams, this doesn't mean that sceptical employees won't see it as a 'this week we want to do teams' approach, a perception based on their history with the organization.

If you want to tackle the cynicism created by an experience with a narcissistic leader, you've got to recognize that just because you're new or you've got a fresh idea doesn't mean that the past should be ignored. In many cases, it is useful to recognize explicitly the havoc that's been created by a narcissistic administration, and even to recognize publicly the accuracy of the cynics' observations. On rare occasions, the poor souls that fought the narcissist are even held up as the heroes they actually are. But, as noted, firms more commonly act as if nothing has happened or take a 'that was before, this is now' approach. So the survivors are often left to fend for themselves as far as recovering and coming to grips with what has happened is concerned. That's why it's not uncommon to see them huddling in halls discussing what has happened, why it happened, and why it will probably continue to happen.

But personally recognizing that the cynicism was created by a narcissistic leader is at best a Pyrrhic victory. In fact, we have time and time again seen employees go to great lengths and expend enormous energies trying to convince people that they were right! But repeatedly arguing that the ex-leader was a self-interested bastard is, in the end, counter-productive. For one thing, the accomplices will never publicly come around to this view: it would be tantamount to admitting that they are hypocrites.

Second, the whole picture is just too unbelievable for an outsider or a new member of the company to fathom. Third, explaining what happened can often be seen by disinterested outsiders as complaining after the horse has left the barn. And, in effect it is – whether it's accurate or not! But regardless, all this explains why the clean-up process after a narcissist is complex. Some want the truth to come out, some wish to rehabilitate their reputations, others simply wish to retain their influence and many just want to forget. Nevertheless, it's useful to conduct a serious examination of what happened, learn some lessons and then move on. Again we would suggest that you:

- seek out people who are known to be cynics, especially recent converts with regard to the narcissist;
- use an anonymous survey or consultants to collect valuable information from cynics if fear is still rampant in the company;
- share and acknowledge the negative history that you learn;
- take steps to enact suggestions for preventing a repeat of narcissistic episodes.

Improve Communication

Earlier we said that one of the hallmarks of a narcissistic regime is the control over information sources. People may feel uninformed, or worse yet misinformed, about what's going on in the organization. How can a narcissist's successor improve communication and thereby recover lost trust, if only little by little?

- **Keep people informed with detailed, accurate feedback.** Taking a little time to explain your decisions can go a very long way. Do not use information as a tool, or dole it out as a reward. People will eventually find this out.

■ **Consider a variety of communication channels.** Newsletters are fine, but meetings, video conferences and especially face-to-face communication are valued sources of transmitting important information. Employees from all walks regularly rate the face-to-face mode at the top of the list of effective techniques. While some managers are happy to deliver good news this way, they are loath to convey bad news in so personal a way. Yet, it is preferred and effective.

■ **Tell the truth.** People will probably understand if you don't, since many people think it's OK to lie or mislead in the course of protecting business interests. But this doesn't extend to your employees. People would much rather hear some bad news than be lied to.

So communicate the truth; it will increase your credibility and it might be the antidote to the Dilbert effect in your organization.[8] As noted just above, there are various ways and methods to do this. One extreme version is to employ open-book management – an approach we mentioned briefly back in Chapter 10. This approach involves sharing what most executives would consider sensitive and proprietary information with employees. Examples of how some leaders do this are given in the accompanying 'Me, Myself and I' box.

ME, MYSELF AND I

Open-book management: A story with a happy ending

One of the well-understood principles of narcissistic management is to keep employees in the dark. In fact, it's probably fair to say that many managers believe that their employees neither need nor want, and should not have access to, the information that is the essence of any business. Hold the financial information near and dear. Don't tell employees your strategy or upcoming moves until it's over.

If you recognize this attitude, we're not surprised. Even with all the new 'empowerment' techniques that have been ushered in during the last few years, the 'closed-book' attitude of management still predominates. Most business meetings are still like a school assembly where the principal or headmaster gets up and tells employees some pedestrian things that they already know ('We're getting new photocopy machines', 'Our new product has just been launched' or 'We're considering a new health care provider').

Some companies, though, have a different mind-set. They point out that if you want your employees to be more committed and act like 'owners', then you have to give them all the information that any owner might want. Speaking of open books, if we're now in a brain-based economy with employee knowledge being the major asset, why are so many using the 'high school' model? Springfield Remanufacturing Corp. graduated beyond this approach. At SRC, managers prepare annotated financial statements for all employees that detail and define all the particulars. Line workers are taught to digest everything their president knows about costs and revenues, productivity and strategic interests. In fact, SRC spent $300,000 on financial training, six times what they spent on improving production skills. Every week, the machines are shut down for about an hour while the nearly 1,000 employees huddle in small groups to study and discuss the latest financial statements.

The idea of letting information flow easily within a company – open-book management – is hardly a brand new idea. In fact, at least as far back as 1954, Peter Drucker claimed that the employee 'should be enabled to control, measure, and guide his own performance. [He] should know how he is doing without being told'. Nevertheless, these ideas are seeing a revival, as illustrated at SRC. SRC, located in the middle of nowhere (in the Ozarks of southern Missouri), has become a Mecca for companies looking to open their own books. In fact, experts feel that trends such as the computerization of work, and the expansion of duties and responsibility (eg teams) may increase the number of firms using 'open-book' techniques.

Consider YSI Inc., an instrument-maker in Ohio. They recently organized into work teams that are responsible for their own hiring, firing and problem-solving. The teams have explicitly been given access to all the information they need to get their jobs done – customer files, inventories, budgets and more. The company has bought and written routines that the teams determined they needed. As a result, this small company saved nearly $1 million in manufacturing costs alone in one year.

San Diego-based COMPS, an information services firm, also experimented with the open-book approach. Things were bad for the company; it hadn't been profitable for the previous three years, competition was fierce and morale was bad. 'People were walking on eggshells. Are we making money or not? Will we even have jobs tomorrow? No one knew if the axe was going to fall,' said one long-time employee. They began to have regular monthly meetings that focused on financial performance and budgets. Gradually, COMPS developed a system for tracking performance – employee by employee, department by department. Charts began to appear that tracked the daily cash situation, timeliness of billings and the age of receivables. Clarity started to emerge, and people began to know the relation of their performance to company profits.

The COMPS experiment was not perfect. But when problems came up, managers walked employees through what was being done to correct them. By most accounts, this got the employees over the hump. As one employee said, it was simple: 'We believed that management wasn't lying.'

If COMPS, eschewed the 'high school' approach for a more 'collegial' one, then the Oticon company must be working on a PhD. This company, based in Copenhagen, is a trendsetter in the hearing-aid business. Instead of focusing on low-margin mass production, Oticon concentrates on cutting-edge products that use the latest technology. With this strategy, the sharing of knowledge and information is crucial. To encourage openness, Oticon has constructed an egalitarian, 'spaghetti' structure that seemed to do the job.

What's their secret? Well, for one, barriers to communication don't exist – at least physical ones. People can't close their office doors because there are no offices. In fact, they have no desks either, at least not personally assigned ones. Each desk is commandeered by whoever needs it. All you have to do is wheel your personal filing cabinet (it's literally on wheels) to where you need it and set up shop. No space is sacred. One day when the CEO returned from a two-week trip, he was told by a secretary that her team had moved his cart to another floor because they needed his desk. Another open feature of Oticon is that all incoming mail (including the CEO's) is scanned and placed into a database that anyone can access. Indeed, project teams are encouraged to grab and use these and any other files if they will help get the job done better.

Certainly most leaders will continue to keep their 'secrets', releasing information only when they think it's right. But, if the companies profiled here are any gauge, the walls may not come tumbling down if you share numbers or your goals with employees. If history is any judge, you probably won't be able to keep many secrets anyway; maybe more companies need to 'go to school' on open-book management.[9]

Use Turnover to Your Advantage

If you've experienced a narcissist in your organization, you will have employee turnover. Of course, sometimes a retirement or a job switch by an employee is a good thing not only for the employee, but also for the organization. If the firm is in a cost-cutting mode, turnovers like these make it easier to reduce costs. Further, some of these people might not be the best producers in the company. Worse yet, they could create problems of all sorts if they were to remain. So, all in all, this type of turnover is good. During and after the reign of a narcissist, however, you will usually see substantial levels of bad turnover. This means that the firm has lost good performers and organizational citizens.

There will also be a variety of indirect, but equally damaging effects. For example, no one will miss the fact that a) lots of people are leaving; and b) they are among the best and brightest. There are any number of reasons why restaffing the organization should be done carefully. Be specific in regard to what you're looking for in a new employee, and carefully screen for these characteristics.

Consider using what experts call a 'realistic job preview'. Unlike a traditional job preview, which has a tendency to highlight only the cheery or fun parts of a job, a realistic one provides a more accurate picture. One researcher observed that a telephone company's recruiting video showed operators handling emergency calls, chatting away with interesting and sultry-sounding callers and using the latest technology. In reality, however, operators had to turn over emergencies to supervisors, their calls were monitored and timed, and their equipment was outdated and low-tech.[10] Existing employees prepared a new video that showed some of the tedium and other downsides to the job, while at the same time illustrating its pluses. Data show that more realistic job previews like this help prevent expectations from being dashed on the job. This is especially important in the aftermath of a narcissistic leader since new employees are likely to be exposed to high levels of cynicism. Dealing with the poor expectations of veteran employees is quite another matter.

Look at Your Pay System

A major source of organizational difficulties, cynicism looming large among them, are problems with the pay system. Take a close look at your system and consider changes. If you think it's fine, look again. We say this because surveys show that nearly 75 per cent of the workforce believe that pay level has little to do with the quality and quantity of work they produce.[11] If you still think the system is OK, then at least consider a better communication plan for the system. Emphasize what makes the system fair. This may involve any number of information sources. Provide salary survey data and show your employees where they stand. Consider the use of an outside auditor to examine fairness; there are many such firms who will study whether pay and promotion decisions actually are reflective of performance. Finally, there are firms who use groups of employees and managers to study, design and set pay levels. Steps such as these may help remove some of the vestiges of cynicism.

Improve Opportunities for Participation in Decision-making

Remember that cynicism is a reflection of significant distrust in the motives and actions of others. One way to combat this disease is to include employees in the decision-making process. Harley-Davidson is one company that has experimented with employee participation in decision-making, partly out of desperation. The motorcycle company was in very bad straits some years ago, so bad that it requested special tariff protection from foreign competition. The protection was granted by the US government, and this gave Harley-Davidson some breathing room to get its act together. And, get it together it did; a new open-management style with a greater emphasis on quality permitted Harley-Davidson to request early removal of that special tariff.

One major tool in this movement was an increased emphasis on employee involvement and input into decisions. Harley-Davidson finally realized that management was the cause of all of its earlier problems. So it asked workers how to redesign its manufacturing process. Gone now is the cynicism among workers about the poor quality they were producing, and it's been replaced by a general sense of pride and 'ownership' in the company. Top Harley-Davidson executives routinely visit groups of workers on the plant floors – across all three shifts – to tell them about where things stand and solicit advice and ideas. Today, Harley-Davidson's biggest struggles involve how to turn out enough quality bikes fast enough to keep up with demand. Just in the past few years Harley-Davidson has spent some $250 million to bring a new engine plant, assembly facility, product development centre and distribution warehouse on line. Those are the kinds of growth 'problems' many firms would kill to have!

And Be Patient

It's going to take time; post-narcissistic patience is definitely a virtue. As we've stated above, the process of bringing people around will be slow, hard work. Trust is something that is earned over a relatively long period of time. Earning it back may take just as long.

CHAPTER TAKE-AWAYS

- Getting a good person to replace a narcissist, while tough, is the least of a company's worries.
- The biggest challenge for the new leader, and for the survivors of a narcissistic leader, is to pick up the pieces that are left of employee morale. Chief among these problems is a whopping amount of cynicism.
- Cynicism is a general lack of trust in the motives and actions of others. Clearly, this is going to be an impediment for any new leader who tries to institute real and comprehensive change in the organization – often exactly what it really needs.
- One step for the new leader is to recognize the signs of this morale problem. Occasionally, cynicism will be obvious, but many other times it will be important to look at communication patterns, the rigidity of the structure, and whether there is a rising number of formal complaints, actions, or appeals against the organization.
- Recognizing cynicism is one important step, but attacking it is quite another. Trust is often built up over years, yet dashed by a few critical incidents. Among other things, time and patience are necessary. A new leader can inject new and varied forms of communication, involve workers in decisions and do other things to break the cynicism cycle.

Part 4

Conclusion

Chapter 12

Cain and Abel: Rediscovering both sides of narcissistic leadership

---

ME, MYSELF AND I

Narcissistic shades of grey

I have seen managers who aren't 'fully' narcissistic but have some of their tendencies some of the time. My boss is a brilliant and talented person who has lots of good ideas. Sometime he pushes too hard or gets caught up in trying to achieve what he honestly believes is the best for the company. When that happens, when the 'game face' comes out, then look out.

Marketing manager, electrical equipment supplier

TURNING THE TABLES

Our opening box underscores where we're going in this final chapter. Now that we've spent 11 chapters dissecting narcissistic leaders we want to step back and say it: narcissism isn't always bad. This may strike you as inconsistent with the theme of this book, if not downright crazy. But it really isn't. Narcissism is not a dichotomy (ie either you're a narcissistic lunatic or you're not). That's far too simple. Rather, narcissism should be viewed on a continuum or as a set of categories. As we said at the beginning of this book, people possess varying levels and combinations of narcissistic tendencies. Once they reach a certain point, they cross over into the realm of pathology, manifesting the six basic characteristics we've described.

Unfortunately, it's hard to detect where that fuzzy line is – where the grey areas fade into black. You've probably wondered how many narcissistic leaders manage to get so far. Part of the answer has to do with the fuzziness of the line – in short, some narcissistic leaders skate up to the line, but don't cross it. Their individual cases have not been extreme enough to manifest all of the behavioural tendencies we've discussed. Alternatively, you may have been exposed to narcissists who fit the pathological profile, but who are better at fooling you and hiding their true motives because they possess good interpersonal skills. Plus, the issue of diagnosis ultimately revolves around your assessment of the leader's true motivation, a psychological phenomenon that's very tough to gauge. In fact, that's why we focused so much throughout this book on assessment – knowing the outward signs, clues and signals associated with pathological narcissism.

But our central thesis in this chapter goes beyond the issue of detecting the 'bad narcissists' that we've focused on in this book. We agree with experts who argue that a moderate level of narcissism can actually be a big plus from a leadership standpoint.[1] Indeed, we feel that some of the most effective business leaders of our day could be considered 'positive narcissists'. As a consequence, the main goal of this chapter is to:

   make the point that narcissism can be a two-edged sword – there's a positive side to it that we don't want to ignore;
   clarify the distinction between 'good' and 'bad' forms of narcissism;
   identify leaders that arguably have positive narcissistic tendencies;
   make suggestions for finding leaders and companies who embrace 'good' narcissism.

Telling Reactive, Self-Deceptive and Constructive Narcissists Apart

Let's briefly revisit some developmental themes we touched on earlier in the book. In Chapter 2, we talked about tracing the roots of patho-logical narcissism back to a variety of childhood hardships, including conflict-ridden and inconsistent parenting. Most children go through periods of narcissism where they are self-focused and self-absorbed. Difficult childhoods, however, can freeze moral development and instil self-doubts that are manifested in narcissistic excesses as adults. Of course, a 'difficult childhood' can mean just about anything.

But without getting into the details of various developmental pathways, we'd like to clarify a couple of points. First, experts believe that inadequate childhood experiences can produce two types of 'bad' narcissistic leaders. The most destructive variety – and the focus of our book – is reactive narcissism. In leadership roles, reactive narcissists are the most likely to display the six characteristics we described back in Chapter 1. Such people are consumed by grandiose fantasies, are extremely Machiavellian in their relations with others, will reject dissent and any responsibility for failure, and basically care nothing for their subordinates' feelings and needs. Decision-making will involve little in the way of analysis or data collection since the reactive narcissist believes that all challenges can be overcome simply by force of will. They will pursue bold visions in a way designed to attract attention to themselves, flashing their stunning brilliance for the world to see. Reactive narcissists may go far, but they leave plenty of interpersonal wreckage along the way. Eventually most reactive narcissists will over-reach and be brought down.

However, there are other forms of pathological narcissism that also produce negative outcomes. For example, children viewed as 'perfect darlings' are often pushed into becoming the mechanisms by which parents can pursue their own unfulfilled dreams. That may lead to a long string of uninterrupted successes, something that eventually collides with unexpected failure. Such experiences can lead to the development of self-deceptive narcissism. In short, unrealistic expectations are built up that later create confusion about the person's abilities when reality intrudes. Self-deceptive narcissists are people who, as a result of having to reconcile their setbacks with the exalted expectations foisted on them, possess a fragile sense of self-worth. When placed in leadership positions, self-deceptive narcissists may display many of the characteristics of their reactive brethren. Usually, however, the symptoms will be milder or take a somewhat different direction.

For example, instead of wanting to cover themselves with glory for the whole world to see, self-deceptive narcissists are content to pursue the affection of those around them. Simply put, they want to be loved by their immediate circle, and their symptoms tend to gyrate according to how much of that love has been achieved. Although insecure and extremely sensitive to criticism, self-deceptive narcissists are more responsive to subordinates than reactive narcissists. They will listen and react positively to subordinate complaints, but more out of a desire to project an aura of sympathy and cultivate devotion rather than out of any real concern. Self-deceptive narcissists will also tend to surround themselves with weak subordinates, especially adoring ones. And if close, adoring subordinates later turn critical, they'll be viewed as traitors. Overall, while they may accept some criticism without flying into blind rages, self-deceptive narcissists will carry grudges. Over time, more independent-minded and vocal subordinates will find themselves isolated from a self-deceptive narcissist.

Interestingly, self-deceptive narcissists tend to project a palpable insecurity in their decision-making. Unlike reactive narcissists – who usually can't be bothered with doing their homework – self-deceptive narcissists tend to be exceptionally afraid of failure and, as a result, will spend enormous amounts of time analysing opportunities and threats. And that can produce plenty of perfectionist wheel-spinning if not outright paralysis. The self-deceptive leader will procrastinate on making the big calls, moving slowly and deliberately to avoid mistakes.[2]

General George B McClellan, who commanded the Union Army of the Potomac in the American Civil War, exemplified many characteristics of self-deceptive narcissism. As a leader, McClellan's legacy was undercut by his extreme caution and conservatism. A perfectionist, McClellan would obsessively train and drill his troops, stockpile supplies and plan logistics. Despite his incessant over-preparation, McClellan was hesitant and never really felt ready to do battle. McClellan was probably more concerned about the admiration of his men than anything else. He was popular with his own troops and loved it. McClellan played to soldiers' expectations of what a general should be. All spit and polish, McClellan was a striking figure who enjoyed strutting before his troops with all of the military pomp he could muster. As a strategist, however, he consistently exaggerated the strength of the Confederate forces aligned against him, sometimes by a factor of two or three. Naturally, McClellan often felt that he needed more resources before he could commit to combat, and spent a good deal of his time pestering his superiors to get them. As a result, getting McClellan to engage the enemy in a sustained fashion was next to impossible. Finally, a frustrated and exasperated President Abraham Lincoln replaced McClellan with Ulysses S Grant, a tenacious battlefield commander known for hounding the enemy. Lincoln's succinct reaction to rumours about Grant's drinking habits spoke volumes about why he eventually turned to him to lead all Union forces: 'I cannot spare this man. He fights'[3].

But what about the other side of the coin? What about 'positive' narcissism? Consider this. Let's say that parents – or whoever – have done a good job with the junior executive-to-be. They manage to temper and channel the child's narcissistic fantasies and exhibitionism into something more constructive. Instead of being a psychological albatross, the child's narcissism is harnessed, providing the basis for challenging ambitions, a clear sense of self-worth and a stable outlook on the world. Those characteristics – whether acquired in childhood or later in life – may provide the best foundation for vital, confident and successful leadership.

In essence, this describes constructive narcissism. That isn't to say, however, that constructive narcissists are perfect. They still want to be admired and don't always take kindly to criticism. On occasion, they may also be manipulative, insensitive, opportunistic or overly demanding, especially when focusing on achieving their goals. But generally, constructive narcissists are grounded in reality. For example, while they enjoy the limelight and are comfortable being the centre of attention, constructive narcissists 'showboat' in ways that entice others to embrace a broader vision, something more important and bigger than themselves. In other words, they understand that their public performances and impression management efforts have value and meaning besides self-aggrandizement. Likewise, while they have tremendous determination and enormous confidence in their skills and ideas, constructive narcissists also grasp their own limitations. They know that they lack certain abilities or that some things are simply beyond them.[4] For example, Jack Welch, after nearly 20 years as General Electric's CEO, knows he can't really get his arms around the world's ninth-biggest company. And it scares him: 'Don't talk to me about how big this place is. I hate it.' Welch constantly urges GE employees to help 'tear this place apart' and make the firm more manageable.[5]

Constructive narcissists also want to surround themselves with competent subordinates, and are willing to listen to them. Why? Because they recognize that they need others, to achieve great things. In fact, being able to delegate to competent subordinates allows them to focus on bigger issues.[6] Once again, Jack Welch is a good example of this principle in action. Under Welch's leadership, GE institutionalized – in fact, trademarked – the term 'Work Out'. Started back in 1989, a 'Work Out' is a no-holds-barred meeting that can be called to deal with any issue or problem, by anyone in the firm, and without a boss being present. Once an action plan is cooked up to solve the problem, the boss is called in and must either agree or disagree with the group there and then, and be prepared to take any heat that follows. Welch argues that 'Work Outs' help bypass the chain of command and undercut executive power, so that the firm can focus on just doing what needs to be done. According to Welch, 'Getting a company to be informal is a huge deal, and no one ever talks about it.' And it seems to work, even in GE subsidiaries located in countries where hierarchy has traditionally been important. As one European employee put it, 'Respect for titles isn't what GE is about, and it's a little strange in the beginning. Once people understand it's safe to think, they love it'.[7]

But constructive narcissists are also decisive and willing to stand by difficult decisions. Plus, delegating certain tasks and giving subordinates a voice doesn't necessarily mean giving up all control. Corporations aren't conflict-free places, especially when change is involved. Effective leaders have to encourage input and debate, but at the end of the day they must have the strength to take stands and make decisions that will upset people. In most cases, someone will be mad at a leader about something. The big question is, who would you rather have mad at you? Your best and most productive people? Those who are more flexible and open to change? Or your mediocre underperformers? For the most part, constructive narcissists are able to zero in on the contributors and take the heat from everyone else. In fact, thanks in large part to Jack Welch, General Electric actually tries to instil this understanding and the conflict management skills necessary to execute it in its leaders. Listen to what GE's chief learning officer, Steven Kerr, had to say on the subject: 'Our executives learn the saying, 'if you're not taking flak, you're not over the target.' Do you know any revolution where nobody got upset? If everybody's on board, you're having a bad revolution. You have to teach that. You don't want total buy-in. The only way you'll ever get total buy-in is if nobody thinks he is going to have to change his behaviour'.[8]

Constructive narcissists will be more concerned about what's right for the company than about what's right for them personally. That approach also means they tend to be flexible and to look for good information before making important decisions. When combined with their confidence, constructive narcissists often have the wherewithal to sketch out challenging visions that rally, inspire and energize employees. And usually their pitch is that the best way to accomplish a common goal is through collective and co-operative action.[9] As Jack Welch once put it: 'I don't want you to fight your neighbor at the next desk. If you are in plastics, I want you to fight DuPont; if in electronics, I want you to fight Westinghouse'.[10] Take a look at Table 12.1:

it summarizes the distinctions we've made between reactive, self-deceptive and constructive narcissists. Then see the accompanying 'Me, myself and I' box. There you'll read about an employee who dealt with two narcissists, one self-deceptive and one constructive. Which would you rather work for?

Table 12.1 From bad to good: comparing types of narcissistic leader

	Reactive Narcissists	Self-deceptive Narcissists	Constructive Narcissists
Most Driven By	need for glory	need for love	need for accomplishment
Manipulation	just another tool	used against 'traitors'	occasional weapon
Concern For Others	nonexistent, Machiavellian	weak, but displaying concern is important	genuine, but subservient to task/goal accomplishment
Temperament	prone to blind fits of towering rage when challenged	hold grudges when 'betrayed', strong fear of failure	usually open and solicitous, but occasionally insensitive and intolerant of criticism
Impression Management	critical – want hero worship by all	wants to be thought of with affection by inner circle	important for rallying employees, attaining goals
Management Tendencies	detail-averse, vacillation between loose delegation and micro-management	cautious, detail-oriented, perfectionistic, hard time seeing the wood for the trees	excellent delegators, keep eye on the big picture
Visioning	bold if not reckless, personalize the vision (the leader as saviour)	conservative, small-change-oriented, emphasis on analysis and preparation	ambitious, inspire by focusing on collective and co-operative action to achieve a greater good
Succession	a dirty word, subordinates are potential threats	prefer weak but adoring subordinates	interested in developing subordinates to maximize goal attainment

THE INTERSECTION OF CONSTRUCTIVE NARCISSISM AND CHARISMATIC LEADERSHIP

There's no doubt that narcissism is a complex subject. And trying to grasp the concept of constructive narcissism certainly makes the point!

ME, MYSELF AND I

Two faces of narcissism

I used to be in a strange situation. My boss's boss was the division manager. He was in a separate location from us and had his own office staff. This guy loaded his office with spineless cronies and he was very protective of them. It bordered on affection and we heard he was having an affair with one of the women in his group. But he could not make a decision to save his skinny ass. He spent lots of time researching things but could never get over the hump. When it finally came time to execute something, he would get panicky and end up turning to someone on his staff to make the actual decision.

My own boss was the greatest. He wanted us to perform our jobs to the best of our ability and would tell us that we were ultimately responsible for the fate of the company because of the products our unit produced. He was confident and aggressive and told us to be the same way. If I had to make a decision, he was fully supportive, even if I wanted to do it without consulting the division manager. Ultimately, the decisions were made for the good of the business and we knew that involving the division manager would mean they would never get done. The division manager never found out why so many good things happened in our group, but he didn't really care since he could take the credit.

Manufacturing manager, electronic health care equipment manufacturer

---

Nevertheless, research suggests that some dimensions of narcissism are actually associated with healthy – 'constructive' – adjustment. For example, optimism and confidence seem to be important parts of constructive narcissism. But it's important to underscore that it's not unbridled or pathological optimism. As we said earlier, constructive narcissists are grounded in reality. While that's true, they also hold on tightly to 'positive illusions'. In short, constructive narcissists are infused with optimism about their ability to help make great things happen, but recognize practical realities. What this really means is that constructive narcissists do not step beyond what one scholar called the 'optimal margin of illusion'. Excessive optimism leads to a deluded disconnection from reality (ie reactive narcissism). However, if constructive narcissists stay on the 'optimal' side of the line, then their 'positive illusions' – when combined with their showmanship and other abilities – can be synonymous with 'visionary leadership'.[11]

Many 'charismatic' leaders who create and sustain large, positive change in organizations fit the description of constructive narcissism. Creating a willingness among subordinates to embrace change in a committed fashion is no easy matter. But the constructive narcissist somehow manages to:

- connect subordinates' work to some higher purpose or stakes;
- convince subordinates to leave their narrow self-interests aside in the pursuit of that higher purpose;
- challenge subordinates to reach for their highest and best potential.[12]

How Constructive Narcissists Create and Sustain Change

The question is, how do they pull it off? Generally speaking, constructive narcissists achieve that in ways considered in the following five sections.

Developing and Articulating an Appealing Vision for the Future

Such a vision must resonate with the abilities and desires of employees. The vision is theirs, not the leader's, since only the people who do the real work can get the job done. On the other hand, while developing the vision may involve many people, it's the leader's restless energy, impatience with the status quo, ambition, stand-up skills and willingness to reach out and suck people in that drive it. For example, back in the 1980s Percy Barnevik envisioned the value of creating a transnational organization to serve an increasingly borderless economy: essentially it was to be a global network of decentralized relationships. Under Barnevik's leadership, two sleepy firms – Sweden's ASEA and the Swiss firm Brown Boveri – were merged, creating the engineering power-house we now know as ABB.[13]

Modelling Key Behaviours

'Walking the talk' with hard work, openness to input and criticism, information-sharing and self-sacrifice is critical for giving the leader a platform to inspire based on credibility and possession of the moral high ground. A willingness to admit weaknesses and limitations is also a key part of this modelling process. For example, Richard Branson, the Virgin Group's charismatic founder, had this to say when asked to talk about his weaknesses: 'I suspect not being able to say no. . . there are so many wonderful ideas. . . I have spread myself too thin.

If someone has an idea, they can pick up the phone and talk to me. Or better still, they can just go ahead and do it. They know that they are not going to get a mouthful from me if they make a mistake'.[14]

Using Symbolic Communication to Focus Subordinates' Work

For instance, former Harley-Davidson CEO Richard Teerlink tried to persuade all employees that the company's purpose wasn't about making motorcycles, but spreading 'the feelings of freedom and independence that people really want in this stressful world'.[15] Motorcycles were symbolic of a higher calling. Harley-Davidson employees were on a quest to promote the lifestyle its motorcycles represented.

Reaching Out to Develop a Special Relationship With Each Subordinate

Employees respond enthusiastically to genuine warmth and empathy. Open displays of personal attention, recognition and coaching pay big dividends, especially when tied to making progress toward a vision. As Percy Barnevik put it, 'The greatest satisfaction is seeing young people whom I have promoted succeed'.[16] Also important is the leader's willingness to extend confidence to employees, to encourage them to believe in themselves and their ability to reach the vision.[17]

Challenging Employees to 'Throw Out the Rule Book'

Often, achieving a vision requires thinking and acting in totally new ways. Today, change hits firms harder and more quickly than ever. Being pushed to 'think outside the box' makes employees feel energized and empowered because they are an important part of something bigger than themselves. This is Percy Barnevik again: 'I want my people to constantly test their imagination, their ability to move further. To create this change mentality, this creative spirit, you have to show them that the environment, the competitors, the customers are changing. In order to survive, we have to change. You know the expression, "when you are through changing, you are through!"'.[18]

How Constructive Narcissists Motivate

One recurring theme running through these points is that constructive narcissists – ambitious and goal-oriented as they are – understand that they must serve others if those goals are to be achieved. And doing so means raising employees' sense of self-worth. After all, most of us want to feel better about ourselves, a powerful motivation if it can be tapped.[19] Constructive narcissists work with that motivation in two basic ways.

Improving Employee Self-Efficacy

As we suggested above, by expressing confidence in them and insisting on high performance expectations, constructive narcissists improve the odds that employees will feel competent and able to take on extreme challenges. That's the essence of self-efficacy, and it boosts effort, individually and collectively. It's the *modus operandi* of Michael Dell, Dell Computer's founder. He pushes employees to execute the company's demanding distribution and manufacturing strategy obsessively. That execution is what makes Dell arguably the best direct-to-the-customer seller of computers. Collectively, Dell employees improved firm sales 1,900 per cent and net income 10,000 per cent in less than 10 years.[20]

Creating Social Identification

Encouraging employees to identify with a greater good associated with the firm is the basis of social identification. A positive way to increase self-worth, social identification provides meaning by linking employee efforts to a larger entity, something beyond themselves. A variety of tools can be used by the leader to connect employee self-esteem to the vision the company is pursuing. In addition to the symbols discussed above, these tools include ceremonies, stories and rituals. For instance, Herb Kelleher, the effusive CEO of Southwest Airlines, values the time he spends at employee-recognition ceremonies. An emotional Kelleher told employees at one such gathering that it was his wish that they would tell their grandchildren that 'Southwest Airlines ennobled and enriched my life; it made me better, and bigger, and stronger than I ever could have been alone'.[21]

Southwest: How Culture Can Maintain Self-efficacy and Social Identity.

And it's the culture at Southwest that's arguably Kelleher's greatest achievement. As Kelleher puts it, 'Our real accomplishment is that we have inspired our people to buy into a concept, to share a feeling and an attitude, to identify with the company – and then to execute.'

Southwest Airlines began in 1968 as a 'joint venture' between entrepreneur Rollin King and his friend, a chain-smoking, whiskey-drinking

Texas lawyer named Herb Kelleher. And since then it's been, as Kelleher might say, 'a helluva ride'. Southwest's track record as a low-fare airline with excellent service can be described in one word – 'spectacular':

- more than 20 years of uninterrupted profitability;
- peaceful labour relations in an industry historically racked with conflict;
- above average wages and below average turnover;
- higher productivity (Southwest averages around 80 employees per plane versus the industry average of well over 100) and lower costs per seat mile than any other major US airline (Southwest's cost advantage is 60% on 500-mile flights and is still a fat 35% on longer 1,500-mile jaunts);
- the only US airline to win the 'triple crown' in one year, much less three years in a row, with fewest late flights, fewest mishandled bags and fewest passenger complaints.

Today, Southwest Airlines' annual revenues are nearly $5 billion, making it one of the largest carriers in the US. Profits for 1999 were expected to hit $510 million, an increase of 18 per cent over 1998.

Experts marvel at the competitive advantage that is Southwest's culture. According to Kelleher, fancy planes and equipment aren't enough to stand out in the airline business. Instead, Kelleher's vision was for an airline culture that focused on its people. Why? So that they could do what's really important in the airline business: deliver what Southwest calls 'positively outrageous service'. As Kelleher himself noted, 'The intangibles are more important than the tangibles. Someone can go out and buy airplanes from Boeing and ticket counters, but they can't buy our culture, our *esprit de corps*'.

That culture was built by hiring in Kelleher's own enthusiastic, glad-handing image. There is no 'human resources' or 'personnel' department. Instead, hiring is co-ordinated through 'the people department'. And the most important characteristic Southwest looks for in all employees – pilots included – is a sense of humour. 'Professionalism' or technical skills simply won't cut it. So if you're interviewing with Southwest, be prepared for questions like 'What was your most embarrassing moment?' Basically, the idea is to recruit employees who: a) are outgoing; b) love people; and c) really want to have fun – just like the flamboyant Kelleher, a man well known for staging outrageous events, and pulling pranks and practical jokes. When Southwest got into a dispute with another firm about using an advertising slogan, Kelleher challenged the company's CEO to an arm-wrestling contest rather than go to court. He lost, but his chutzpah won him the right to keep using the slogan. Kelleher, whom one scribe referred to as 'the High Priest of Ha Ha', put it this way: 'We look for attitudes, people with a sense of humour who don't take themselves too seriously. We'll train you on whatever it is you have to do, but the one thing Southwest cannot change in people is inherent attitudes. At Southwest, hiring is a religious experience'.

Once employees come on board, they find themselves part of a 'family' where two of the most important stated values are 'luv' and 'fun'. 'Luv' includes respect for individuals and real caring and compassion for others, customers included. That respect and caring are manifested in many ways.

When Southwest acquired Morris Air a few years ago, Morris employees found themselves bombarded by letters, cards, gifts, flowers and the like, all sent spontaneously by Southwest staff to welcome them into the fold. Of course, the 'fun' part of the Southwest equation is the stuff of corporate legend. Informality reigns. Parties are ubiquitous. Flight attendants dress up in bunny outfits at Easter, tell jokes, pop out of airline bins to surprise passengers and hold 'who has the biggest hole in their sock' contests when passengers are delayed.

And this fun, family-oriented spirit has some serious payoffs in terms of organizational citizenship. For example, Southwest employees consistently make spontaneous customer service gestures largely unheard of anywhere else. In fact, Southwest routinely receives nominations from the field for its 'winning spirit awards' and reprints them in *Luvlines*, its company newsletter. Consider this story about a ramp agent named Eric: 'A flight destined for Lubbock was diverted to Amarillo due to fog. On this flight was a Customer with no money and no place to go, who had to be in Lubbock as quickly as possible. Without hesitation, Eric offered to take the Customer to a relative's house in Lubbock, driving all night and returning to work at 5 am.'

Day in and day out, Southwest turns its planes around faster than anyone else. Even pilots will pitch in to load bags. In fact, it's not uncommon for Southwest to turn around a plane at the busiest airports in 15–20 minutes, from gate arrival to gate departure. What Southwest does in that short span has been compared to what a finely honed pit crew does with racing cars. In a blur, nearly 140 people and hundreds of bags will be unloaded and another set of people and their bags loaded on to a Boeing 737, along with 4,500 pounds of jet fuel, freight, drinks and snacks. Kelleher described the essence of how Southwest routinely outproduces the competition, managing to turn planes around in half the industry average, this way: 'We've had people come in to see how we turn around planes. They keep looking for gimmicks, special equipment. It's just a bunch of people knocking themselves out.'

Of course, getting people to 'knock themselves out' consistently is incredibly tough, or every company would already be doing it. And that's the real lesson Herb Kelleher and Southwest Airlines offer: aligning the company's people and culture with its mission and strategy is the key to success. That alignment is what gives a firm the power to execute at the highest levels. Employees with the right values and beliefs also represent a competitive advantage that's tough to match. But creating that culture in the first place – much less putting the resources and processes in place to sustain it – requires extraordinary leadership. And that's where Herb comes in.[22]

GOING YOUR OWN WAY: THE SEARCH FOR CONSTRUCTIVE NARCISSISM

At this point, you're probably wondering what we could possibly suggest to 'encourage' constructive narcissism. But many of the suggestions we've made in earlier chapters for blocking pathological narcissists are also relevant for that purpose: building a more empathetic and open culture, developing visions aimed at creating social identification rather than personal identification with the leader, implementing policies that support empowerment, using hiring procedures to screen out reactive narcissists, deploying various leadership development strategies and so on.

Why Not Just Take Charge?

However, your reaction to all of this might be, 'OK, but pursuing these options really requires organization-wide efforts. They certainly can be suggested from below, but require support from above. So anyone who champions these changes has to be fairly influential and highly placed to begin with, right? And that's like saying encouraging constructive narcissism requires a constructive narcissist!'

Well, you could get out there and find a constructive narcissist to work for, ideally one who has great ideas and is willing to start a company! While we're being a bit flip here, we do endorse an expanded version of this advice. Changing companies – and looking for a constructive narcissist or a culture that supports them in the process – is a viable option that we'll discuss below in some detail.

But first things first. Let's get back to the argument that there's nothing you can do to change the situation in your company from where you sit. Granted, you'll have an uphill slog if pathological narcissism is the reason things aren't so pleasant in your current job. We'll also grant that making things happen is tough if you're 'on the ground' in your company and can barely see your senior leaders up there cruising along at 30,000 feet.

Nevertheless, tough doesn't mean impossible. The best way to nurture constructive narcissists informally, and encourage those down through the ranks to step up and 'fight the good fight', is to set the example yourself. So if you're a professional, a technician, a low- to mid-level manager, what can you do to change the place you're at before it drives you nuts?

First, stop and self-reflect. How comfortable with ambiguity are you? How do you evaluate risk? Are you confident in your skills and abilities? Can you see the wood for the trees? What drives you? Are you motivated to stand up and try to make a real difference somewhere? Or are you just keeping score by how much money you make or how much attention you get? How would you rate your interpersonal skills? Are you able to persuade and influence people around you to change directions? How? What we're driving at here of course is whether you might fit the profile of a constructive narcissist yourself, or might want to work for one.

And if you have tendencies in that direction, then look for situations within your current company where you can just take charge and make a difference. And we're not talking about doing stuff merely to get noticed. What we're referring to are honest efforts to make functional changes in the way the company works, changes that are driven by your insights about how things can be improved. Want examples? Consider these 'just do it' possibilities:

- proposing and implementing 'fixes' to significant problems;
- pushing new and improved procedures and work methods;
- changing or eliminating policies that are useless or counterproductive;
- changing or eliminating flawed practices;
- introducing new technologies or approaches to improve efficiency.

There's plenty of room for improvement in these general areas in most companies, even at the departmental or small unit level. And it's a great way to demonstrate informal leadership in the service of 'constructive change' and position yourself to tackle even bigger and better things down the line. Of course, there's a chicken and egg problem here. In order to take advantage of these opportunities, you don't need to be in a senior position, but you do need a decent context. In other words, the culture, if not your boss, has to be reasonably receptive to such moves in the first place. People have to believe that the culture and at least some senior managers truly support constructive efforts from employees to bring about change. Employee-led change can't occur when management isn't open to initiatives from below. Management needs to embrace critical and unconventional thinking, to encourage if not nurture the mavericks within. In fact, research shows employees are most likely to simply go out and take charge of something on their own when:

▓ they believe that top management is open to and supports employee-led change;
▓ they believe in their own abilities to perform and that their take-charge efforts will be successful;
▓ they believe it is their personal responsibility to try to bring about change as a matter of principle, because it's the right thing to do for the company.[23]

These last two points certainly fit the profile of constructive narcissism. In a nutshell, taking charge yourself requires both constructive narcissism and the right playing-field. So give it a try if you feel up to it. If nothing else, it's a good way to test the water and find out where your boss and your company really stand.

Looking to Take Charge Elsewhere

Then again, you may have concluded that your current situation is too difficult or intractable, and that taking charge would be like putting your head in a guillotine. Or perhaps you work for a pathological narcissist, so leaving is an option in any case. Of course, we've alluded to leaving in just about every chapter up until this point. But what we haven't done yet is to offer some advice about how to look for a good fit in a new job, one where you can stretch your proverbial wings. Ideally, what you'd want is the kind of open environment we've described above. Obviously, this isn't as simple as it appears. You could run into a pathological narcissist in an otherwise decent place, and hate every minute of it. Or you could land in a generally backward, plodding company, but end up working for a constructive narcissist determined to shake things up, which could prove both interesting and frustrating at the same time. Finally, you might also end up in a place where the words in no way match what really goes on.

So this is a good moment to remind yourself once again of the importance of an accurate diagnosis. Do you really have a good handle on yourself? Are your self-insight and self-awareness on target? Do you know what you really want? Plus, remember the external challenge you're facing from a diagnostic standpoint. The line between constructive and pathological narcissism is blurry to say the least. There's also the risk that constructive narcissism will morph into the pathological variety over time. As one expert put it (and please forgive the sexist language):

> If he takes no initiative, he is no leader. If he takes too much, he becomes a dictator, particularly if he tries to curtail the process by which members of the group participate in shaping group goals. There is a particular danger for the man who has demonstrated his competence in shaping group goals and in inspiring group members to pursue them. In time both he and they may assume that he knows best, and he may almost imperceptibly change from a democratic to an authoritarian leader.[24]

Organizing Your Quest: Sources, Signs and Signals

If the diagnostic challenges haven't scared you off yet, that's good. Maybe you're a constructive narcissist after all, taking risks into account without being consumed by them. Yes, the costs of misdiagnosing a company or a pathological narcissist are considerable. But the potential rewards of getting it right are even greater. Here's how we'd proceed if we were in your shoes.

First, plan to suck up data like a sponge. Get information from multiple sources. Trust that information if it converges and points in the same direction. Assume companies and leaders are guilty of not supporting constructive narcissism until you prove otherwise. Research companies and individual managers to find clues about whether the environment they offer might support constructive narcissism. Industry research is trickier: there's the risk of overgeneralizing from industry tendencies to individual firms, wiping out good opportunities in the process.

For example, the printing industry, at least in the US, is hardly known as an empowered paradise. Despite that stereotype, one of the most interesting companies we've ever come across is Quad/Graphics, a privately-held printer that we briefly mentioned back in Chapter 7. Founded in the 1970s, Quad today has over $1.4 billion in sales and continues to grow. Basically, co-founder Harry Quadracci – who runs around the company in the same blue jumpsuit his line-employees wear – has created a culture that paradoxically combines a strong sense of common purpose and rigid requirements for continuous learning with a high degree of personal freedom and empowerment.

On the one hand, new Quad employees go through an intense indoctrination into the firm's culture and the 'Quad way'. All employees must attend training courses and continuously learn as long as they're with the firm. Quadracci's basic philosophy is 'the team that knows most wins'. On the other hand, your personal management style is up to you. The idea is that employees will gravitate on their own to managers who are a good fit for them. That speaks volumes about the extent to which employees can go their own way at Quad. In fact, Quadracci describes his firm as a company where decisions get made on the front lines by the people who do the real work. As Quadracci puts it, 'Once you've learned our way, then you've earned the right to tell us how to improve our way.' And we're not just talking about operational ideas, but about developing new products and services too. Part of the firm's mission statement also emphasizes that 'take charge' quality, saying that the goal of Quad is: 'To provide opportunities for advancement in an atmosphere which encourages initiative and creativity for the personal and professional development of our employees.' In this case, the words and deeds generally match up pretty well. (For more information about the company, check out its Web site – www.qg.com)

The Quad/Graphics example also brings up another pair of stereotypes about entrepreneurs. That highlights the fact that some people believe that private, entrepreneurial firms are the only places where you can really take charge without being hamstrung by stock analysts, board members, investors, and so on. The opposite stereotype is also embraced: you should steer clear of entrepreneurial or family-run firms for the same reasons, that there are no restraints on the behaviour of the people running the show. A more accurate position would be that there are plenty of examples of both extremes.

What this says about entrepreneurial firms is that both the upside potential and the downside risk tend to be higher than in publicly held companies. So in the final analysis, seeking to join an entrepreneurial venture depends on the risk–reward equation you can live with. Entrepreneurial firms can certainly be conflict-ridden, stressful places, especially when family members are brought in to help run things. The potential for parent–child battles as well as the 'spoilt kid syndrome' – where the offspring of the entrepreneur become the real narcissistic nightmares in the company – are often realized.[25] In fact, many of our survey respondents bemoaned their hellish lives in family-run firms. They also tended to think that their options were limited to either confrontation or egging on family members to turn against each other. Hardly risk-free strategies!

But our point here is that you should find out about what's going on inside a company before you join it. Don't underestimate the effort required to research companies thoroughly. Let's consider just a few of the information sources you should tap. Obviously, you can consult friends, family and colleagues, as they often have some of the most reliable information about what a company and its leaders are really like. Unfortunately, that's a pretty thin and unsystematic source of data for most of us. Business publications and management books are much wider and deeper sources, but their information is sometimes suspect or reflects questionable motives (eg public relations campaigns by companies). Lists of 'best companies to work for' and the like are useful starting places, nothing more, as even if their methodology is sound (a big if, since in many cases companies provide the 'data'). Such lists are at best providing you with just a broad-brush snapshot.

For example, a recent survey of nearly 11,000 US employees was used to create a 'reputation quotient' designed to assess perceptions of major companies. 'Vision' and 'leadership' were considered major factors. The resulting list of 30 companies with the 'best reputations' included some of the firms we've mentioned in this chapter, such as General Electric and Southwest Airlines (ranked 12th and 25th respectively). In case you're curious, the top five firms were Johnson & Johnson, Coca-Cola, Hewlett-Packard, Intel and Ben & Jerry's.[26] But if you're in the wrong part of these companies or working for the wrong boss it will still be hell. Or perhaps the company simply doesn't live up to its billing and has wrapped itself in little more than hype. As one of our survey respondents put it:

The external reputation of our company is excellent and built on our old successes. The CEO is a narcissist who plays favourites and abuses people. There's lots of professional turnover, especially in entry-level positions. People are attracted by the company reputation. Then they get in and find out about the bad management, lack of concern, low morale and poor pay. They leave in a couple of years and come away OK because the company name is on their résumé. No one knows on the outside what it's really like on the inside.

Department manager, international services company

But our view is that these situations simply underscore how important doing your research is. Your goal should be to flush this kind of disconnection out. And one of your best weapons these days is the Internet. Here's what we suggest. Collect data from both company and non-company sources. The idea is to look for inconsistencies between what the company says it's about and what management actually does. First, peruse corporate Web sites – typically they contain mission statements, annual reports, press releases, hiring criteria and so on. There may be some important clues staring you in the face. For example, has the company been acquiring businesses or dumping them without good competitive reason? Does it mention the impact of these and other major changes on employees? If so, is any mention made of what's being done to help them adjust or survive, especially in the face of stated values like 'people are our most important asset'? Is a lot of attention paid to senior executives? Are they given star treatment, with flashy write-ups and pictures that take up most of your 17-inch monitor? Or are employees and their contributions the focus? And which do you think signals more openness to a take-charge employee like you?

Next, tie in to 'objective' information from non-company sources. The Internet can help you pull years' worth of media stories, government reports, investor assessments and management analyses together about the companies you've targeted. For example, publicly traded US companies have voluminous filing requirements with the government's Securities and Exchange Commission. These reports can be downloaded easily and are often a treasure trove of insights about management pay, strategy and competitive activities. While privately held firms have no such requirements, they are nonetheless the target of industry analysts, news reports and so on that can be pulled off the Internet and zapped into your printer tray.

One of the complaints we hear about what we're suggesting is that the sheer volume of information available makes organizing a Web attack difficult. We beg to differ. You can target 'metasites' that offer career advice, industry and company analyses, skill development help, job postings, links to press stories, and information about professional organizations. In essence, such sites are one-stop-shopping gateways to the information you want. The sites we're familiar with vary somewhat in their approaches. For example, Hoover's Online is an outstanding source of information about companies, some of it free (www.hoovers.com). It provides both basic and detailed reports about firms, along with industry reports and some career development advice. Especially useful are its easy links to press articles, financial reports, other search engines, and company Web sites. But Hoover's strength is really as a business information service. Other sites are perhaps a bit more oriented toward the job seeker. For instance, WetFeet sells itself as a 'leading career research site' that provides 'rigorously researched insider information on companies, industries, and broader career issues' (www.wetfeet.com). It includes career assessment services, connections to head-hunters, job searching advice, as well as company and industry information. Then there's vault.com like WetFeet, it has a career advancement focus, but tends to emphasize industry and company research and job postings first and foremost.

Of course, we're not saying that personal connections and contacts aren't important information sources. Professional organizations – which you can often tap into on the Internet – can help you get started if you don't know anyone. Usually, these organizations will be helpful in providing local chapter contacts – where you can start your networking – and information about conferences and events where you can meet and schmooze with colleagues. In any case, some things to ask about or look for, either in person or on the Internet, include:

- turnover rates (low or high?), especially in particular units or under particular managers;
- levels of politicking and infighting;
- profiles of the leaders, including which type of narcissism they appear to fit;
- whether take-charge behaviours by employees are supported.

Up Close and Personal: Getting Inside and Gathering Intelligence

Now you've done your homework and have targeted some companies that seem to embrace constructive narcissism and have appropriate openings. It certainly would be worth your while to identify people who work – or used to work – at these places, especially if you could quiz them 'offline' about things. Also useful would be to talk with vendors, clients and customers of the target company: they're often a source of excellent insights. If word about your intelligence-gathering gets back to the people who'll be interviewing you, that's good. It will show that you're proceeding with due diligence or, if they're miffed, it will tell you something important – that you don't want to work there. Someone who's put off by your questions about initiative and empowerment isn't likely to be supportive of you acting that way on the job. In fact, we'd advocate that when you send your CV to a company, you should include a 'personal attributes statement' – or whatever you want to call it – something that describes your personality. Put simply, tell the company up front that you are the type of person who likes to take initiative on your own, that you have high standards and that you will 'speak up' to authority when you believe it's warranted. If that screens you out, good. Why waste time interviewing at a place that isn't a good fit?

But when you reach the interview stage, don't lose sight of the fact that this is perhaps your last, best reality check. View the interview as a two-way street: you need to interview them as much as they need to interview you! Plus, don't overlook the importance of all the clues you can pick up just by walking through the offices – they're often excellent signals about the real culture and workplace atmosphere:

- **Are there lots of status markers?** Do executives have reserved parking places, fancy company cars, opulent offices and separate dining rooms? Does everyone else sit in a plastic cubicle with no windows? Are the executives isolated on separate floors away from the 'little people?' These are signals of a winner-take-all culture, which, whether based on performance or not, is hardly conducive for rallying the troops. At Hewlett-Packard, however, egalitarianism rules. Everyone sits in cubicles and, at least in the US, the only company car is a Ford Taurus – even for the CEO.
- **What are the atmospherics like?** What's the tone and demeanour of people as you walk through? Are they happy, chatty and friendly? Or are they head-down doing their work? That could mean lots of things, mostly bad. People might mind their own business because they only care about themselves, or because they don't want to step on anyone else's toes. In any case, it's not likely to help promote a vision that everyone can rally behind!

Are there signs that people are trusted and treated like grown-ups? What's the dress like? Stiff and formal? Informal? A mix? An informal hotchpotch implies that the firm cares more about the workpeople than about a dress code. Likewise, do you see pictures of family members and friends hanging on people's walls? How much evidence is there that people can personalize their own work-spaces? If a company doesn't allow or trust people enough to do that, they're not likely to empower you on the bigger issues either. We know of companies that either do not allow 'personal' pictures to be displayed or have extensive rules and regulations about office décor. In fact, one survey found that while 85% of employees felt that workspace personalization was important, over 40% felt that their firms didn't want them to personalize their offices. But when the company loosens up – one place we know allows employees to bring in furniture from home – the mishmash of office décor becomes a living expression of the firm's willingness to accept individual creativity.[27]

Once you reach that office at the end of the hallway, it's time to shift gears and become the bright-eyed interrogator of whoever's on the other side of the desk. And of course, you've come prepared: you know all about narcissism and have done your homework on the company. So when the opportunity presents itself, ask questions. Lots of them. But avoid broad or vague enquiries: they're likely to elicit platitudes and autopilot recitations of the company mission statement. Instead, rely on behaviourally oriented questions and ask for specific examples – they're much harder to fake. Watch for the non-verbal cues too: lots of fidgeting and fumbling around are signs of discomfort. Likewise, you want to ask the same questions over and over again. In fact, you should talk to as many people as you can – peers, subordinates, your boss and your boss's boss – so you can check for consistency across answers. If you're not allowed to talk with the people you need to, ask why. And don't take the job until you do. It could be a sign of real trouble. In any event, here are some question suggestions:

Set up scenarios about taking charge and ask how they would play out. For instance, ask what would happen if you had an idea about how to change a work procedure or for developing a new product. Is there an officially sanctioned process that you'd have to go through? What if you just went out and did it? What would the reaction be? Has that happened before? What was the result?

■ **Ask about specific types of behavioural issues and how they were handled.** For example, ask for specific examples of recent conflicts, decision problems, or delegation issues. Then follow up by asking what was done to resolve the concern and how frequently that outcome occurs.

■ **Ask about how specific types of decisions are routinely made.** Budget allocations, resource decisions and new product or procedural initiatives are often good choices here because they're likely to reveal how things actually happen.

■ **Ask about the firm's vision and how it relates to the unit you'd be in.** There should be some alignment between the overall vision and the unit's contribution. Good follow-up questions would be to ask how the vision – at both firm and unit level – will be achieved. What procedures and resources are already in place to provide the needed support? Is there a specific battle plan in place for action or is the vision just a bunch of words?

■ **What are the cultural values and how seriously are they taken?** Ask about efforts that managers make to change or sustain those values. How do the company's history, rites and ceremonies fit in? Is the culture critical to the firm's business success? How, and what exemplifies it in this unit? How much time does management spend developing and maintaining the culture? Can people dislike each other but still work together because they believe in the greater goals of the firm? Are there any examples to support that?

■ **Ask about systems, policies and procedures that support the stated values.** Of course, these can always be subverted, but generally, it's better to have them than nothing at all, especially if they're set up properly. For instance, ask about whether 360-degree feedback systems, pay-for-performance plans, structured development opportunities, and career-planning procedures are in place. Then ask how the success or failure of these systems and procedures is assessed and whether managers are held accountable. Are managers, for example, measured on how well they develop subordinates? Another angle on this is to ask what might seem like an innocuous question – how seriously the human resources department is taken. Is HR involved before major changes take place or just after the fact? Is it involved in the development of the business strategy and viewed as part of a core business process or simply seen as 'support'? Are the top managers in HR some of the best and brightest or is it a repository for weak executives, a place to dump losers where they can't do much real damage?

■ **Ask about your potential boss's style and personality.** A good approach is to start with a general question about style, not because you really care about the answer *per se*, but because it will create openings for specific follow-up questions that will be hard to duck. For example:
- What are 'your biggest interpersonal challenges' with peers, superiors and subordinates?
- How are 'difficult' subordinates handled?
- What are your personal goals? What are the unit's goals? How do you plan to achieve them?
- How are you and the unit viewed by various constituencies? Why?
- Can you give specific examples of how you instilled commitment and enthusiasm in subordinates, supported someone who took the initiative on his or her own, or allowed input into your decision-making?

■ **Ask about what distinguishes successful and unsuccessful people.** What personality traits and behaviours characterize those who have done well in the firm? How have they reached the top? What about people who have derailed? What were their mistakes or their 'incorrect' behaviours? Of course, people who 'fit' the cultural values – good or bad – skyrocket upward fastest. What you want to find out is who these people are and what they're like. That's another way of getting at the underlying values of the company.[28]

The Bottom Line

Our goal in this section has been to help you find an environment that encourages constructive narcissism. But there's a broader message here, too. First, know yourself and what you really want. Next, be prepared to do what is necessary to find a company that represents a good fit for your own needs and values. Or perhaps start a company of your own! Ultimately, people who find a good fit stay longer, perform better and are happier. And that's an important thing to remember – whether you're searching for constructive narcissism or for whatever it is that drives you.

CHAPTER TAKE-AWAYS

Reactive narcissists represent the most destructive form of narcissism and are the primary focus of our book. **Self-deceptive narcissists** are more interested in affection than glory. However, **constructive narcissists** are the most grounded in reality: they have a grasp of the big picture, know their own limitations and are able to reach out to others in ways that don't step over the 'optimal margin of illusion'. They recognize that they need others in order to achieve great things.

Constructive narcissists encourage subordinates' self-efficacy and social identification. They are often able to: a) develop and articulate appealing visions; b) model key behaviours and use symbolic communication to hit on key themes; and c) challenge and develop special relationships with each employee.

You can develop your own tendencies toward constructive narcissism by finding – and taking – opportunities to take charge on your own. That might include fixing significant problems, developing new procedures, or changing flawed practices. Alternatively, you might have to seek a job elsewhere to find an environment that will help you grow.

If you choose to go elsewhere, a careful diagnosis is required – of yourself and of other companies. Plan to collect a lot of information from multiple sources. The Internet is an excellent source of diagnostic information, as are colleagues and professional organizations. The key is to look for inconsistencies between what management says the company is about and what actually happens. If the values are right and the words match the deeds, you may have found your fit!

During the interview stage, pay attention to things like status markers, office atmosphere and personal freedom (eg in dress and office décor). These are often important clues to underlying values and culture. Likewise, use the interview to pose diagnostic questions that focus on examples. For instance: a) set up scenarios and ask how they would play out; b) ask about how specific behaviours and decisions are handled; c) ask about the firm's vision and culture, and how they're executed and supported; d) ask about what distinguishes successful and unsuccessful people; and e) try to pin down your potential boss's style and personality. Look for consistency – across answers and across people. Good luck!

Appendix

A SCALE FOR ASSESSING SCEPTICISM ABOUT ORGANIZATIONAL CHANGE

The following is a scale that measures degree of scepticism about organizational change efforts. This might be especially helpful for those well-intentioned leaders who wish to get a sense of the effect of the history of change efforts in the organization. After all, since there are probably few true change programmes that can be undertaken without real employee co-operation, it might be useful to get a sense of the scope of feeling about these efforts. Accordingly, you may wish to have various subgroups, or even all employees, complete the following scale in order to get a sense of the effect of your change history:

1	2	3	4	5	6	7
Disagree strongly			Not sure		Agree strongly	

_____ 1. Most of the programmes that are supposed to solve problems around here won't do much good.

_____ 2. The people who are responsible for solving problems around here don't try hard enough to solve them.

_____ 3. Attempts to make things better around here won't produce good results.

_____ 4. The people who are responsible for making improvements around here don't know enough about what they are doing.

_____ 5. Suggestions on how to solve problems won't produce much real change.

_____ 6. The people who are responsible for making things better around here don't care enough about their jobs.

_____ 7. Plans for future improvement won't amount to much.

_____ 8. The people who are responsible for solving problems around here don't have the skills that are needed to do their jobs.

Note: If the average score is 40 or more (respondents average a '5' on each item), then you have a potentially serious barrier to change. Scores of 24 or less indicate an organizational environment/history that is relatively conducive to change.

Adapted from Reichers, A E, Wanous, J P and Austin, J T (1997) Understanding and managing cynicism about organizational change, *Academy of Management Executive*, **11**, pp 48–59

References

1 Sweeney, P D and McFarlin, D B (forthcoming) *Organizational Behavior: Solutions for management*, Irwin/McGraw-Hill, Burr Ridge, IL
2 *Business Week* (1998a), The top 25 managers of the year, 12 January, pp 54–68
3 Huey, J (1994) The leadership industry, *Fortune*, 21 February, p 54
4 Lancaster, H (1998) How to make sure that you get noticed but not seem pushy, *Wall Street Journal*, 24 February, B1
5 Reinhold, J and Grover, R (1999) Executive pay, *Business Week*, 19 April, pp 73–90
6 Reinhold and Grover
7 Ewing, J, Baker, S and Echikson, W (1999) Eager Europeans press their noses to the glass, *Business Week*, 19 April, p 89
8 Barlett, C A and Ghoshal, S (1997) The myth of the generic manager: new personal competencies for new management roles, *California Management Review*, **40**, pp 92–116
9 Daily, C M and Johnson, J L (1997) Sources of CEO power and firm financial performance: a longitudinal assessment, *Journal of Management*, **23**, pp 97–117
10 Yukl, G (1998) *Leadership in Organizations*, 4th edn, Prentice Hall, Englewood Cliffs, NJ
11 Zachary, G P (1997) CEOs are stars now, but why? And would Alfred Sloan approve? *Wall Street Journal*, 3 September, A1, A8

CHAPTER 2

1 Buss, D M and Chiodo, L M (1991) Narcissistic acts in everyday life, *Journal of Personality*, **59**, pp 179–215
2 Kets de Vries, M F R and Miller, D (1985) Narcissism and leadership: an object relations perspective, *Human Relations*, **38**, pp 583–601
3 Kets de Vries, M F R (1995) *Life and Death in the Executive Fast Lane*, Jossey-Bass, San Francisco; Raskin, R, Novacek, J and Hogan, R (1991) *Journal of Personality and Social Psychology*, **60**, pp 911–18
4 Buss and Chiodo
5 Carvell, T (1998) By the way. . . your staff hate you, *Fortune*, 28 September, pp 200–12; Kets de Vries and Miller
6 Conger, J A (1990) The dark side of leadership, *Organizational Dynamics*, Winter, pp 44–55
7 Sankowsky, D (1995) The charismatic leader as narcissist: understanding the abuse of power, *Organizational Dynamics*, **23**, pp 57–71
8 Waldman, D A and Yammarino, F J (1999) CEO charismatic leadership: levels of management and levels of analysis effects, *Academy of Management Review*, **24**, pp 266–85

9 Adapted from Carvell
10 Horowitz, M J and Arthur, R J (1988) Narcissistic rage in leaders: the intersection of individual dynamics and group process, *International Journal of Social Psychiatry*, **34**, pp 133–41
11 Adapted from Carvell
12 Bolino, M C (1999) Citizenship and impression management: good soldiers or good actors? *Academy of Management Review*, **24**, pp 82–98
13 Conger
14 Conger; Kets de Vries and Miller
15 Kets de Vries (1995); Raskin, Novacek and Hogan

CHAPTER 3

1 House, R J and Howell, J M (1992) Personality and charismatic leadership, *Leadership Quarterly*, **3**, p 98
2 Sankowsky, D (1995) The charismatic leader as narcissist: understanding the abuse of power, *Organizational Dynamics*, **23**, pp 57–71; Wilson, D S, Near, D and Miller, R R (1996) Machiavellianism: a synthesis of the evolutionary and revolutionary literatures, *Psychological Bulletin*, **119**, pp 285–99; Sitkin, S B and Pablo, A L (1992) Reconceptualizing the determinants of risk behavior, *Academy of Management Review*, **17**, pp 9–38
3 Boeker, W (1992) Power and managerial dismissal: scapegoating at the top, *Administrative Science Quarterly*, **37**, pp 400–21
4 Salancik, G R and Pfeffer, J (1977) Who gets power and how they hold on to it: a strategic contingency model of power, *Organizational Dynamics*, **5**, pp 3–21
5 Rose, F (1998) Leaving the wonderful world of Disney: the Eisner school of business, *Fortune*, 6 July, pp 29–30
6 Berglas, S (1997) Liar, liar, pants on fire, *Inc.*, August, p 33; Fisher, A (1997) Why are you so paranoid? *Fortune*, 8 September, pp 171–72
7 Sussman, L (1991) Managers on the defensive, *Business Horizons*, **34**, pp 81–87
8 Kagan, D (1990) Unmasking incompetent managers, *Insight*, **6**, pp 42–44
9 Yukl, G and Falbe, C M (1990) Influence tactics in upward, downward, and lateral influence attempts, *Journal of Applied Psychology*, **76**, pp 416–23
10 Dessler, G (1997) *Human Resource Management*, 7th edn, Prentice Hall, Englewood Cliffs, NJ
11 Ryan, K D and Oestreich, D K (1991) *Driving Fear out of the Workplace: How to overcome the invisible barriers to quality, productivity, and innovation*, Jossey-Bass, San Francisco
12 Bramson, R (1994) *Coping with Difficult Bosses*, Pireside, New York; Mullins, R (1998) E-mail could be managers' worst enemy, *Business Courier*, 24 July, p 2
13 Becker, T E and Martin, S L (1995) Trying to look bad at work: methods and motives for managing poor impressions in organizations, *Academy of Management Journal*, **36**, pp 174–99; Shepperd, J A and Socherman, R E (1997) On the manipulative behavior of low machiavellians: feigning incompetence to 'sandbag' an opponent, *Journal of Personality and Social Psychology*, **72**, pp 1148–59
14 Lancaster, H (1997) Pick fights before going over your boss's head, *Wall Street Journal*, 17 June, B2
15 Lublin, J S (1997b) Dear boss: I'd rather not tell you my name, but. . ., *Wall Street Journal*, 18 June, B1

16 McFarlin, D B and Sweeney, P D (1996) Does having a say only matter if you get your way? Instrumental and value – expressive effects of employee voice, *Basic and Applied Social Psychology*, **18**, pp 289–304

CHAPTER 4

1 O'Connor, J *et al* (1995) Charismatic leaders and destructiveness: an historiometric study, *Leadership Quarterly*, **6**, pp 529–55
2 Horowitz, M J and Arthur, R J (1988) Narcissistic rage in leaders: the intersection of individual dynamics and group process, *International Journal of Social Psychiatry*, **34**, pp 133–41
3 *Industry Week* (1995) The boss from hell, 4 September, pp 12–18
4 *Business Week* (1998b) Maybe Al Dunlap had the right idea, (27 July), p 6
5 Horowitz and Arthur
6 Yukl, G (1998) *Leadership in Organizations*, 4th edn, Prentice Hall, Englewood Cliffs, NJ
7 Horowitz and Arthur
8 Yukl (1998); Yukl, G and Tracey, J B (1992) Consequences of influence tactics used with subordinates, peers, and the boss, *Journal of Applied Psychology*, **77**, pp 525–35
9 Bramson, R (1994) *Coping with Difficult Bosses*, Fireside, New York; Ryan, K D and Oestreich, D K (1991) *Driving Fear out of the Workplace: How to overcome the invisible barriers to quality, productivity, and innovation*, Jossey-Bass, San Francisco
10 Gabriel, Y (1997) Meeting God: when organizational members come face to face with the supreme leader, *Human Relations*, **50**, pp 315–486; Kets de Vries, M F R (1995) *Life and Death in the Executive Fast Lane*, Jossey-Bass, San Francisco; Sankowsky, D (1995) The charismatic leader as narcissist: understanding the abuse of power, *Organizational Dynamics*, **23**, pp 57–71

CHAPTER 5

1 Nakache, N (1997) Is it time to start bragging about yourself? *Fortune*, 27 October, pp 287–88
2 Colvin, G (1998) Revealed: boardroom secrets, *Fortune*, 25 May, pp 199–201
3 *Fortune* (1997) Starbucks: making values pay, 29 September, pp 261–72
4 Meindl, J R (1995) The romance of leadership as a follower-centric theory: a social constructionist approach, *Leadership Quarterly*, **6**, pp 329–41
5 Engle, E M and Lord, R G (1997) Implicit theories, self-schemas and leader-member exchange, *Academy of Management Journal*, **40**, pp 988–1010; Yukl, G (1998) *Leadership in Organizations*, 4th edn, Prentice Hall, Englewood Cliffs, NJ
6 Graen, G B and Cashman, J F (1975) A role-making model of leadership in formal organizations: a developmental approach, in *Leadership Frontiers*, ed J G Hunt and L L Larson, Kent State University Press, Kent, OH
7 Gardner, W L (1992) Lessons in organizational dramaturgy: the art of impression management, *Organizational Dynamics*, **21**, pp 33–46
8 Greenberg, J (1990) Looking fair vs. being fair: managing impressions of organizational justice, in *Research in Organizational Behavior*, ed B M Staw and L L Cummings, **12**, pp 111–57

9 Bolino, M C (1999) Citizenship and impression management: good soldiers or good actors? *Academy of Management Review*, **24**, pp 82–98
10 Rosenfeld, F, Giacalone, R A and Riordan, C A (1995) *Impression Management in Organizations: Theory, measurement, practice*, Routledge, London; Wayne, S J and Liden, R C (1995) Effects of impression management on performance ratings: a longitudinal study, *Academy of Management Journal*, **38**, pp 232–60
11 Bolino; Liden, R C and Mitchell, T R (1988) Ingratiatory behavior in organizational settings, *Academy of Management Review*, **13**, pp 572–87
12 Wayne and Liden
13 Gardner
14 Shepperd, J A and Socherman, R E (1997) On the manipulative behavior of low machiavellians: feigning incompetence to 'sandbag' an opponent, *Journal of Personality and Social Psychology*, **72**, pp 1148–59
15 Becker, T E and Martin, S L (1995) Trying to look bad at work: methods and motives for managing poor impressions in organizations, *Academy of Management Journal*, **36**, pp 174–99
16 Gardner
17 Bolino
18 Gardner, W L and Cleavenger, D J (1996) Impression management behaviors of transformational leaders at the world-class level: a psychohistorical assessment, *Proceedings of the Southern Management Association*
19 Kagan, D (1990) Unmasking incompetent managers, *Insight*, **6**, pp 42–44
20 Kelly, P (1997) Lose the boss, *Inc.*, **19**, pp 45–46

CHAPTER 6

1 Ryan, K D and Oestreich, D K (1991) *Driving Fear Out of the Workplace: How to overcome the invisible barriers to quality, productivity, and innovation*, Jossey-Bass, San Francisco
2 Ryan and Oestreich
3 Bramson, R (1994) *Coping with Difficult Bosses*, Pireside, New York; Mullins, R (1998) E-mail could be managers' worst enemy, *Business Courier*, 24 July, p 2
4 Bramson, p 60
5 Bramson, p 39
6 Byrne, J A, Symmonds, W C and Siler, J F (1991) CEO disease: egotism can breed corporate disaster – and the malady is spreading, *Business Week*, 1 April, pp 52–60
7 Schrage, M (1999) The tangled web of e-deception, *Fortune*, 27 September, p 296
8 Bartolome, F (1989) Nobody trusts the boss completely – now what? *Harvard Business Review*, March-April, pp 135–42

CHAPTER 7

1 Northcroft, G B and Neale, M A (1990) *Organizational Behavior: A management challenge*, Dryden, Chicago
2 Hambrick, D C and Finkelstein, S (1987) Managerial discretion: a bridge between polar views of organizational outcomes, in *Research in Organizational Behavior*, ed L L Cummings and B M Staw, vol 9, pp 369–406, JAI Press, Greenwich, CN
3 John, O P and Robins, R W (1994) Accuracy and bias in self-perception: individual differences in self-enhancement and the role of narcissism, *Journal of Personality and Social Psychology*, **66**, pp 206–19

4 Reed, S *et al* (1999) Deal mania, *Business Week*, 5 April, pp 50–54

5 Hayward, M L A and Hambrick, D C (1997) Explaining the premiums paid for large acquisitions: evidence of CEO hubris, *Administrative Science Quarterly*, **42**, pp 103–27

6 Salancik, G R and Meindll, J R (1984) Corporate attributions as strategic illusions of management control, *Administrative Science Quarterly*, **29**, pp 238–54

7 Hayward and Hambrick

8 Walsh, J P and Kosnick, R D (1993) Corporate raiders and their disciplinary role in the market for corporate control, *Academy of Management Journal*, **36**, pp 671–700

9 Byrne, J A (1998) How to reward failure: reprice stock options, *Business Week*, 12 October, p 50

10 Lublin, J S (1997a) Ageing CEOs stage big deals as career finales, *Wall Street Journal*, 4 June, B1, B3

11 Deogun, N and Raghavan, A (1999) Popularity of the triple play increases in the game of mergers and acquisitions, *Wall Street Journal*, 25 August, C1, C2; Lublin, (1997a)

12 Yukl, G (1998) *Leadership in Organizations*, 4th edn, Prentice Hall, Englewood Cliffs, NJ

13 Gardner, W L and Avolio, D J (1996) The charismatic relationship: a dramaturgical perspective, *Academy of Management Review*, **23**, pp 32–58

14 Yukl

15 Conger, J A and Kanungo, R N (1987) Toward a behavioral theory of charismatic leadership in organizational settings, *Academy of Management Review*, **12**, pp 637–74

16 Shamir, B, House, R J and Arthur, M B (1993) The motivational effects of charismatic leadership: a self-concept based theory, *Organizational Science*, **4**, pp 1–17

17 Stewart, T A (1998) America's most admired companies, *Fortune*, 2 March, pp 70–82

18 Trice, H M and Beyer, J M (1993) *The Cultures of Work Organizations*, Prentice Hall, Englewood Cliffs, NJ

19 Bennis, W G and Nannus, B (1985) *Leaders: The strategies for taking charge*, Harper & Row, New York

20 Elstrom, P, Edmondson, G and Schine, E (1997) Does this Galvin have the right stuff? *Business Week*, 17 March, pp 101–05; Kelly, K and Burrows, P (1994) Motorola: training for the millennium, *Business Week*, 28 March, pp 158–63

21 Bergquist, L (1996) Contrarian tips of a 74-year-old rebel, *Milwaukee Journal Sentinel*, 9 June, D1, D4

22 Conger, J A (1990) The dark side of leadership, *Organizational Dynamics*, Winter, pp 44–55; Gabriel, Y (1997) Meeting God: when organizational members come face to face with the supreme leader, *Human Relations*, **50**, pp 315–486; Kets de Vries, M F R (1995) *Life and Death in the Executive Fast Lane*, Jossey-Bass, San Francisco; Sankowsky, D (1995) The charismatic leader as narcissist: understanding the abuse of power, *Organizational Dynamics*, **23**, pp 57–71

23 Hackman, J R (1999) Why teams don't work, in *Leader to Leader*, ed F Hesselbein and P M Cohen, pp 335–48, Jossey-Bass, San Francisco; Hambrick, D C (1997) Corporate coherence and the top management team, *Strategy & Leadership*, September, pp 21–26; Katzenach, J R (1999) Making teams work at the top, in *Leader to Leader*, ed F Hesselbein and P M Cohen, pp 323–34, Jossey-Bass, San Francisco; Yukl

24 Moskal, B S (1997) From 'no' to 'yo': how CEO Katherine Hudson turned sleepy W H Brady into a growth and innovation powerhouse, *Industry Week*, 1 September, pp 1–4

CHAPTER 8

1 Baum, H S (1992) Mentoring: narcissistic fantasies and Oedipal realities, *Human Relations*, **45**, pp 223–45; Ragins, B R and McFarlin, D B (1990) Perceptions of mentor roles, in Narcissistic self-esteem management in cross-gender mentoring relationships, *Journal of Vocational Behaviour*, **37**, pp 321–39
2 Byrne, J A, Reingold, J and Melcher, R A (1997) Wanted a few good CEOs, *Business Week*, 11 August, pp 64–70
3 Cannella, A A and Lubatkin, M (1993) Succession as a socio-political process: internal impediments to outsider selection, *Academy of Management Journal*, **36**, pp 763–93
4 Byrne, Reingold, and Melcher
5 Hambrick, D C and Cannella, A A (1993) Relative standing: a framework for understanding departures of acquired executives, *Academy of Management Journal*, **36**, pp 733–62
6 Economist (1997) *The secrets of succession*, 25 October, p 73
7 *Managing Office Technology* (1997) Top gunning: qualified CEOs are hard to find, **42**, p 33
8 Zellner, W (1999a) Earth to Herb: pick a co-pilot, *Business Week*, 8 February, pp 58–59
9 Byrne, Reingold and Melcher
10 Stewart, T A (1999) See Jack. See Jack run Europe, *Fortune*, 27 September, pp 124–36
11 Byrne, J A (1999) Memo to the ex-CEO: just let go, *Business Week*, 30 August, p 180; Byrne, Reingold and Melcher
12 Yukl, G (1998) *Leadership in Organizations*, 4th edn, Prentice Hall, Englewood Cliffs, NJ

CHAPTER 9

1 Birkinshaw, J, Morrison, A and Hulland, J (1995) Structural and competitive determinants of a global integration strategy, *Strategic Management Journal*, **16**, pp 637–55; Krugman, P (1997) *Pop Internationalism*, MIT Press, Cambridge, MA
2 *Business Week* (1999) Ideas for the 21st Century, pp 23–30
3 Trice, H M and Beyer, J M (1993) *The Cultures of Work Organizations*, Prentice Hall, Englewood Cliffs, NJ; Yukl, G (1998) *Leadership in Organizations*, 4th edn, Prentice Hall, Englewood Cliffs, NJ
4 Barnes, A E (1987) How to keep rising stars from straying, *Business Week*, 7 June, p 80
5 *Economist* (1992) Food for thought, 29 August, pp 62–63
6 McCartney, S and Friedland, J (1995) Computer sales sizzle as developing nations try to shrink PC gap, *Wall Street Journal*, 29 June, A1, A4
7 Juran, J M (1995) Made in the USA: a renaissance in quality, *Harvard Business Review*, July/August, pp 42–50
8 Peters, T (1994) Crazy times call for crazy organizations, *Success*, July/August, pp 24A–56B
9 Zellner, W (1999b) Southwest's new direction, *Business Week*, 8 February, pp 58–59
10 Atkinson, T (1995) Embracing stability, *Training*, **32**, pp 103–06
11 Bryne, J A (1996) Business fads: what's in – and out: executives latch on to any management idea that looks a quick fix, *Business Week*, 20 January, pp 52–61
12 Micklethwait, J and Wooldridge, A (1996) *The Witch Doctors*, Time Business Publishers, New York
13 Bryne

14 Waldman, D A, Atwater, L E and Antonioni, D (1998) Has 360 degree feedback gone amok? *Academy of Management Executive*, **12**, pp 86–94
15 Micklethwait and Wooldridge
16 Lieber, R B (1996) Controlling your consultants: the pros tell how to get the most out of your hired help – without getting ripped off, *Fortune*, 14 October, pp 114–15; Stewart, T A (1995) Think for yourself, boss, *Fortune*, 2 October, p 162
17 Reichers, A E, Wanous, J P and Austin, J T (1997) Understanding and managing cynicism about organizational change, *Academy of Management Executive*, **11**, pp 48–59
18 Reichers, Wanous and Austin
19 Reichers, Wanous and Austin
20 Porras, J I and Robertson, P J (1992) Organizational development: theory, practice, and research, in *Handbook of Industrial and Organizational Psychology*, 2nd edn, vol 3, ed M D Dunnette and L M Hough, Consulting Psychologists Press, Palo Alto, CA; Robertson, P J, Roberts, D R and Porras, J I (1993) Dynamics of planned organizational change: assessing empirical support for a theoretical model, *Academy of Management Journal*, **36**, pp 619–34
21 Nicholas, J M (1982) The comparative impact of organization development intervention on hard criteria measures, *Academy of Management Review*, October, pp 530–39

CHAPTER 10

1 Braham, J (1996) Bosses from hell, *Machine Design*, **68**, pp 48–50
2 Beeman, D R and Sharkey, T W (1987) The use and abuse of corporate politics, *Business Horizons*, March-April, pp 36–30
3 Beeman and Sharkey
4 Johns, G (1996) *Organizational Behavior: Understanding and managing life at work*, HarperCollins, New York
5 Kanter, R M (1977) *Men and Women of the Corporation*, Basic Books, New York
6 Greenberg, J and Baron, R A (1997) *Behavior in organizations*, Prentice Hall, Upper Saddle River, NJ, p 425
7 Ferris, G R and King (1991) T R Politics in human resources decisions: a walk on the dark side, *Organizational Dynamics*, **20**, pp 59–71
8 Longnecker, C, Sims, H and Gioia, D (1987) Behind the mask: the politics of employee appraisal, *Academy of Management Executive*, **1**, pp 183–93
9 Steers, R M and Black, J S (1994) *Organizational Behavior*, HarperCollins, New York, p 358
10 Madison, D L *et al* (1980) Organizational politics: an exploration of managers' perceptions, *Human Relations*, **33**, pp 79–100; DuBrin, A J (1988) Career maturity, organizational rank, and political behavioural tendencies: a correlational analysis of organizational politics and career experience, *Psychological Reports*, **63**, pp 531–37
11 Farrell, D and Petersen, J C (1982) Patterns of political behavior in organizations, *Academy of Management Review*, July, pp 400–12; Drory, A and Romm, T (1990) The definition of organizational politics: a review, *Human Relations*, November, pp 1133–54
12 Hofstede, G (1980) *Culture's Consequences: International differences in work-related values*, Sage, Beverley Hills, CA; Hofstede, G (1993) Cultural constraints in management theories, *Academy of Management Executive*, **7**, pp 81–94
13 Beeman and Sharkey

CHAPTER 11

1 Morrison, E W and Robinson, S L (1997) When employees feel betrayed: a model of how psychological contact violation develops, *Academy of Management Review*, **22**, pp 226–56

2 Bateman, T S, Sakano, T and Fujita, M (1992) Roger, me, and my attitude: propaganda and cynicism toward corporate leadership, *Journal of Applied Psychology*, **77**, pp 768–71; Greilsamer, M (1995) The Dilbert barometer, *Across the Board*, **32**, March, pp 39–41

3 Kanter, D L and Mirvis, P H (1989) *The Cynical Americans: Living and working in an age of discontent and disillusion*, Jossey-Bass, San Francisco; Samuelson, R J (1996) Great expectations, *Newsweek*, 8 January, pp 24–33

4 Lutz, W D (1983) Corporate doublespeak: making bad news look good, *Business and Society Review*, **44** p 19; Cantoni, C J (1993) *Corporate Dandelions: How the weed of bureaucracy is choking American companies*, AMACOM, New York; Gaunt, J (1998) Why corporations use doublespeak in troubled times – it's better to 'derecruit' workers than to just plain fire them!, *San Francisco Chronicle*, I November, C3

5 Levinson, R L (1986) How's that again? Execs: the world's worst communicators, *Management World*, **6**, pp 40–41

6 Ryan, K D and Oestreich, D K (1991) *Driving Fear out of the Workplace: How to overcome the invisible barriers to quality, productivity, and innovation*, Jossey-Bass, San Francisco

7 Ryan and Oestreich

8 Champy, J (1999) The Dilbert antidote, *Computerworld*, 22 March, pp 46–47

9 Byrne, J A (1995) Management meccas, *Business Week*, 18 September, pp 122–32; Case, J (1996) The open-book managers, *Inc.*, **12**, pp 104–13; Eisenberg, E M and Witten, M G (1987) Reconsidering openness in organizational communication, *Academy of Management Review*, **12**, pp 418–26; Fierman, J (1995) Winning ideas from maverick managers, *Fortune*, 6 February, pp 70–80; Harari, O (1995) Open doors, tell the truth, *Management Review*, **84**, pp 33–35

10 Mirvis, P H and Kanter, D L (1989) Combating cynicism in the workplace, *National Productivity Review*, **8**, pp 377–94

11 Mirvis, P H and Kanter, D L

CHAPTER 12

1 Kets de Vries, M F R (1994) The leadership mystique, *Academy of Management Executive*, **8**, pp 73–89

2 Kets de Vries, M F R and Miller, D (1985) Narcissism and leadership: an object relations perspective, *Human Relations*, **38**, pp 583–601

3 Glatthaar, J T (1994) *Partners in Command: The relationship between leaders in the civil war*, The Free Press, New York

4 Kets de Vries and Miller

5 Stewart, T A (1999) See Jack. See Jack run Europe, *Fortune*, 2 March, pp 70–82

6 Kets de Vries and Miller

7 Stewart

8 Kerr, S (1999) GE's collective genius, in *Leader to Leader*, ed F Hesselbein and P M Cohen, pp 227–36, Jossey-Bass, San Francisco

9 Bass, B M (1998) *Transformational Leadership: Industrial, military, and educational impact*, Lawrence Erlbaum, Mahwah, NJ; Kets de Vries (1994)

10 Kets de Vries (1994)

11 Baumeister, R F (1989) The optimal margin of illusion, *Journal of Social and Clinical Psychology*, **8**, pp 176–89; Hickman, S E, Watson, P J and Morris, R J (1996) Optimism, pessimism, and the complexity of narcissism, *Personality and Individual Differences*, **20**, pp 521–25

12 Bass, B M (1985) *Leadership and Performance Beyond Expectations*, Free Press, New York; Bass, B M and Avolio, B J (1990) Developing transformational leadership: 1992 and beyond, *Journal of European Industrial Training*, **14**, pp 21–27

13 Kets de Vries, M F R (1998) Charisma in action: the transformational abilities of Virgin's Richard Branson and ABB's Percy Barnevik, *Organizational Dynamics*, **26**, pp 7–16

14 Kets de Vries (1998)

15 Lieber, R B (1997) Selling the sizzle, *Fortune*, 23 June, p 80

16 Kets de Vries (1998)

17 Goodwin, D K (1999) Ten lessons from presidents, in *Leader to Leader*, ed F Hesselbein and P M Cohen, pp 25–36, Jossey-Bass, San Francisco; Kotter, J P (1999) Making change happen, in *Leader to Leader*, ed F Hesselbein and P M Cohen, pp 69–80, Jossey-Bass, San Francisco; Tichy, N M (1993) *Control Your Destiny or Someone Else Will*, Doubleday, New York

18 Kets de Vries (1998)

19 Howell, J M and Avolio, B J (1992) The ethics of charismatic leadership: submission or liberation? *Academy of Management Executive*, **6**, pp 43–53; Shamir, B, House, R J and Arthur, M B (1993) The motivational effects of charismatic leadership: a self-concept based theory, *Organizational Science*, **4**, pp 1–17

20 Serwer, A E (1997) Michael Dell turns the PC world inside out, *Fortune*, 8 September, pp 76–93

21 Freiberg, K and Freiberg, J (1996) *Nuts! Southwest Airlines' Crazy Recipe for Business and Personal Success*, Bard Press, Austin, TX

22 Hallowell, R (1996) Southwest Airlines: a case study linking employee needs, satisfaction and organizational capabilities to competitive advantage, *Human Resource Management*, **35**, pp 513–34; Kelleher, H (1999) The best lesson in leadership, in *Leader to Leader*, ed F Hesselbein and P M Cohen, pp 43–50, Jossey-Bass, San Francisco; Zellner, W (1999a) Earth to Herb: pick a co-pilot, *Business Week*, 8 February, pp 58–59; Zellner, W (1999b) Southwest's new direction, *Business Week*, 8 February, pp 58–59

23 Morrison, E W and Phelps, C C (1999) Taking charge at work: extra role efforts to initiate workplace change, *Academy of Management Journal*, **42**, pp 403–419

24 McClelland, D C (1975) *Power: The inner experience*, p 266, Irvington, New York

25 Kets de Vries, M F R (1995) *Life and Death in the Executive Fast Lane*, Jossey-Bass, San Francisco

26 Alsop, R (1999) The best corporate reputations in America, *Wall Street Journal*, 23 September, B1, B20

27 Merisalo, L (1997) The personal touch: trinkets from home can boost morale in the office, *Business Journal*, 4 July, p 10

28 Siegel, M (1998) The perils of culture conflict, *Fortune*, 9 November, pp 257–62

Index